Working with Mystical Experiences in Psychoanalysis

A mystical experience, no matter what else, is a subjective occurrence in psyche. However, when it appears in the psychoanalytic consulting room, its origin, content, and meaning are unknowable. Yet it is there in the room, and it must be addressed. It is not a minor illusion but rather one that requires attention as its occurrence may lead to a profound alteration of consciousness and, as Carl Jung suggests, a cure for neurosis.

Leslie Stein interviewed twenty-nine mystics in order to understand the origin, progression, phasing, emotions, and individual variations of a mystical experience in order to make sense of how it should be addressed, the appropriate analytic attitude in the face of a mystery, the way to work with its content, and its psychological meaning. In doing so, he uncovered that there may be specific development markers that create a proclivity to be receptive to such an experience that has clinical significance for psychoanalysis.

Leslie Stein is a Jungian analyst in private practice in Sydney, Australia. He is a graduate of the C.G. Jung Institute of New York and a member of the New York Association for Analytical Psychology, the Australia and New Zealand Society of Jungian Analysts, and the International Association for Analytical Psychology. His books on mysticism include *Becoming Whole: Jung's Equation for Realizing God* (New York: Helios, 2012, 2018) and *The Journey of Adam Kadmon: A Novel* (New York: Arcade, 2001, 2012).

Working with Mystical Experiences in Psychoanalysis

Opening to the Numinous

Leslie Stein

Routledge
Taylor & Francis Group

LONDON AND NEW YORK

First published 2019
by Routledge
2 Park Square, Milton Park, Abingdon, Oxon OX14 4RN

and by Routledge
52 Vanderbilt Avenue, New York, NY 10017

Routledge is an imprint of the Taylor & Francis Group, an informa business

British Library Cataloguing in Publication Data
A catalogue record for this book is available from the British Library

Library of Congress Cataloging in Publication Data
Names: Stein, Leslie, 1945- author.
Title: Depth psychology of the mystical experience : receptivity to the
numinous / Leslie Stein.
Description: 1 Edition. | New York : Routledge, 2019.
Identifiers: LCCN 2018021799 (print) | LCCN 2018038957 (ebook) |
ISBN 9780429449093 (e-book) | ISBN 9781138327719 (hardback) |
ISBN 9781138327733 (pbk.) | ISBN 9780429449093 (ebk)
Subjects: LCSH: Jungian psychology. | Psychoanalysis.
Classification: LCC BF175 (ebook) | LCC BF175 .S6613 2019 (print) |
DDC 150.19/54--dc23
LC record available at https://lccn.loc.gov/2018021799

ISBN: 978-1-138-32771-9 (hbk)
ISBN: 978-1-138-32773-3 (pbk)
ISBN: 978-0-429-44909-3 (ebk)

Typeset in Garamond
by Taylor & Francis Books

Contents

Figures

Preface

A mystical experience has the unique quality of being an overpowering immersion in an altered state wherein there is a profound revelation of a critical, universal truth of the relationship of the individual to the forces of existence. It enters the gate of psychoanalysis as a subjective event that has a potential effect on consciousness. It is only one of many subjective events of which psychoanalysis is concerned, most of which arrive with greater regularity, but it is elevated in importance because it has the potential to create the most profound change.

The concern of psychoanalysis is focused entirely on the potential of the event to change ego consciousness. It is not directed to where the experience fits within a cultural, spiritual, or religious tradition or how it is categorised or described. The central matter is whether the patient is or will be affected by the experience and, if so, to what extent. Accordingly, the goal of this work is to provide insight into whether a patient is likely to be receptive to the experience so that it will alter consciousness.

The goal is phrased in terms of "receptivity" because, from the point of view of psychoanalysis, there is no mystical experience if it cannot have an effect on consciousness. If there is no possibility of receptivity – of it being accepted and allowed to change the conscious position – there will be no subject matter to be analysed. The same is true of a dream, as an example. If it is not recalled, it will have no effect on the subject and therefore no place in the consulting room. It bites, for the purposes of psychoanalysis, when the conscious position is capable of being altered.

This importance of receptivity as the psychoanalytic basis for examining a mystical experience emerged from my clinical practice as some patients were uninterested, fearful, or even disdainful of these experiences, no matter how profound, yet a few drew a new, healing perspective from them that quickly resolved stubborn neuroses that had been prominent for many years in the work. The issue of receptivity is therefore the critical determinant as to whether the phenomenon will be capable of analysis.

The consideration that naturally follows is whether it is possible to enhance or encourage receptivity. The analyst sits in the presence of a revelation of a universal truth that will have had the initial effect of overwhelming the conscious position of the patient. Where then to start, where to stop, what to discuss, what to ignore, and, most importantly, what is the *primum suspicari* for enhancing the possibility of the experience being received and having an effect on consciousness?

Working with patients who have had these experiences and reading the works of many others, such as Wilfred Bion, James Grotstein, and Daniel Merkur, all of whom struggled with a psychoanalytical approach to mystical experiences, I did not find any therapeutic model for approaching an analytical session to enhance or even understand receptivity. Furthermore, I had only a limited number of patients with these experiences, so it was not possible to draw conclusions as to how to proceed. Hence, I was concerned that it was not enough to rely on the many anecdotal and historical experiences recorded by other authors without access to a wider picture.

I decided to interview a significant number of mystics, who were, by definition, receptive to mystical experiences, in order to observe not only if there was some psychological or developmental pattern that led to their receptivity but also to find an effective means to share in their explanations and connect more deeply with their experiences. I wanted to learn how best to approach a discussion of such an experience and the types of issues that arose in that dialogue.

In early preparation for this work, in 2001, when the ideas were incipient, I attended the Kumbh Mela in Allahabad, India – a gathering of endless multitudes that takes place every twelve years. This particular staging of the event was the Maha ("Great") Kumbh Mela, which is held only every 144 years (12 × 12). It attracted numerous Indian and foreign mystics, including shamans, witch doctors, and healers from all over the world in the daily crowd of thirty million. In that crowd, I found eleven Indian monks (sahdus) from the Himalayas who spoke fluent English as well as two Westerners who had become sadhus and joined an akhara (a traditional monastic community).

They were willing to speak about themselves in detail and, as everything moved at the Kumbh Mela very slowly, I was able to sit with each of them for hours at a time, drinking chai. I asked them about their upbringings, what mystical experiences they had had, what they had felt at each stage of those occurrences, and how they had changed their perspective. I paid particular attention when the conversation drifted into abstraction and where it touched on psychological truths. I was also able to interview four non-sadhu Westerners who attended the event and proclaimed that they had had mystical experiences: two from Germany who lived most of the year in India; one from the United Kingdom, where he practised Buddhism, who had come to see the Dalai Lama; and one from the Ukraine, who claimed to have had profound visions.

In further preparation for this book, as the ideas began to take shape, I interviewed six mystics (three male and three female) in New York in 2015; two male and two female Western mystics in Rajasthan, India, in 2016; and two Western Buddhist monks in Cambodia in 2017. By "interview," I do not mean a formal, sit-down, pencil-and-pad series of questions and answers, but rather a conversation relating to personal background and developmental markers to understand what may have led them to have a passion for the mystical. I also asked them, as I did with those at the Kumbh Mela, to try to break down their mystical experiences in terms of emotions, phases, and idea formation – how they understood what had happened.

The interviews with these twenty-nine self-declared mystics are not offered here as proof of any experience, theory, or concept. True proof is only available to those who have had mystical experiences and it withers when exposed to scientific investigation or the need for a sufficient study sample. Each mystic spoke a similar language of having experienced an overwhelming, profound event that was unexpected and reoriented their viewpoint. The experience, in all cases, was described as answering a pre-existing longing, and each mystic seemed to remain excited by what they had found, even when it had occurred years before. The interviews are used here in aid of psychoanalytic ideas in order to strive for some meaning and insight from what cannot be otherwise described.

Since these interviews, in pursuit of the mystery of receptivity, I sought to understand the backgrounds of historical, iconic mystics and also compared and contrasted the childhood and life experiences of Carl Jung and Sri Aurobindo, both of whom figure prominently in this work. Gradually, in answer to this question of receptivity, developmental patterns emerged of particular parental issues. The patterns I discovered do not suggest a clear, direct concordance between specific developmental milestones and being receptive to the experience, so as to be able to derive a determinative explanation. However, I did find convincing proof that the patterns, where present, pointed to the existence of a *proclivity* to be open to numinosity – to receive and be affected by mystical experiences. I should add that in reaching a conclusion as to the patterns that may developmentally lead to a receptivity to mystical experiences, there is no doubt that other complex interactions in the mind and heart of a child may create patterns that are etched over the years and later integrate inexplicably to manifest such an experience.

In writing this work, I felt at times a sense of dissatisfaction occasioned by the need for the continuous reduction of the mystical experience to a psychological frame, reducing its profundity and the contribution to humanity of mystical and religious insights into the unknowable. I was torn between the attempt to undertake psychological analysis of the subject at arm's length and the compelling sense of magic and awe arising from my own experiences and those whom I interviewed. I often found Freud and others irritating in their dismissal of these experiences, but could see the psychological logic behind their scepticism. The book took me inside, to my own experience, and then outside, to some Archimedean, psychoanalytic point of reference, then back inside again.

I originally thought that the vast subject matter might be contained through organisation by presenting one mystical chapter followed by one psychoanalytic chapter throughout the book, but soon realised that the mystical experience refused to be tethered. Every discussion I had with a psychoanalyst or scholar about these experiences was immediately bogged down in terms of language, definitions, interpretations, and knowledge. The literature is confusing, with each writer, like the blind men and the elephant, describing it from a different perspective, yet all with absolute certainty. The subject matter therefore resisted me – and particularly my capacity to think it all through – and required me, I thought, to choose my orientation either for it, in its mystery, or against it, in its psychological or even neurological logic. In the end, though, I chose no particular approach and simply accepted the paradox of trying to reinterpret a complete mystery, so the different points of view are interlaced and there is thus an element of drift from one to the other. In describing the essence of Zen, Jung (1936b: para. 881, n. 8) made his own apology:

> If in spite of this I attempt "explanation" in what follows, I am never-theless fully aware that in the sense of satori I have said nothing valid. All the same, I had to make an attempt to manoeuvre our Western understanding into at least the proximity of understanding – a task so difficult that in doing so one must take upon oneself certain crimes against the spirit of Zen.

I too must add that where this work falters is in its attempt to explain the unknowable and by suggesting a pattern emerging within the mystery. Sitting at a *dhuni*, an everlasting fire burning deep at a sacred temple in the Himalayas, surrounded by left-handed-path Avidya Tantrics wearing black robes in the dark night, assured me that my attempt to unravel the mystery for psychoanalysis was possibly futile. However, as an analyst, I still felt it important to try to make some sense of it because the mystery is there in us and our patients, as Bion reminds us with his explanation of the "O" – the unknowable substrate of all phenomena and therapeutic work. It cannot be parked as just an inexplicable experience; and it is very much a valid subject for psychoanalysis, as is any psychic occurrence.

My training and practice as a Jungian analyst clearly privileges Jung's analysis of numinous experiences and the importance of underlying arche-types, as will be obvious to the reader. However, I have tried to draw on the writings of others insofar as they assist in opening new lines of thought. I have not followed a breadcrumb trail through the religious and mystical lit-erature, tracing talmudicly what each said about the others to arrive at explanations of mystical experiences. I have attempted not to build too much on the thinking of others but have instead tried to establish a very personal relationship with the subject matter through my own mystical experiences and the revelations of those I interviewed and studied.

Mystical literature across all traditions may constitute one of the largest accumulations of religious and scholarly writing. It is possible to draw endlessly on the ideas of others in the literature in addition to the viewpoints of those who told their stories and shared insights with me. There is very little work, however, that examines the issue of what makes a person receptive to mystical experiences or that concentrates on the experience according to its effect on consciousness. Accordingly, although I have drunk from the deep well of mystical literature, I pick only those references that add a perspective on the subject matter for psychoanalysis as to the effect of the experience.

I would like to thank Dr Miriam Stein for offering different dimensions based on her own experiences and for reading drafts that led to this final attempt. Like-minded people eventually find each other, even for a moment, and understand that we do little else than serve the mystery when looking for patterns and then opening to what can never be described, so this work is but a small bead on a long string.

Chapter 1

The mystical experience

In discussing a mystical experience (hereinafter abbreviated to "ME"), psychoanalysts are sure to cross the threshold of psychoanalytic theory immediately and drift into the mention of God or call upon the statements found in religious and spiritual traditions. Terms have thus emerged in psychoanalysis that lack psychological precision in relation to a ME and are employed to provide labels for the genus of the experience. "Religious" is usually associated with experiences that take place in the context of Western religious practice. "Mystical" is used to describe experiences that have an Eastern connection: a merging with the godhead or other extraordinary occurrences, usually but not always disconnected from liturgical Western religion. "Spiritual" is a generalised term that is used to describe an internalised feeling state associated with religious or mystical sentiments. The word "numinous" is often invoked by psychoanalysts to describe a "spiritual" event or a feeling tone of religiosity or mysticism. For Jungians, the term "numinous" is always chosen as it was used by Jung himself as inclusive of other types.

"Mystical" is chosen here because it is a pointer to all aspects of the mystery of a ME in order to describe a subject matter that is not within expected, conscious parameters. "The intensification of religious life that characterizes most forms of mysticism culminates at times in paranormal experiences" (Idel, 1988, p. 35).

These one-size-fits-all categories of numinous, spiritual, religious, and mystical are understandable because they conveniently offer a shared notion and understood communication of the nature of these events. The categories then become easy repositories for psychoanalysis in which to place and name these occurrences that are not capable of a clear explanation. The reliance on these non-psychological categories is ironic as so much of psychoanalysis – the functioning of the ego, the structure of the unconscious – is just as mysterious yet contained neatly within theoretical structures created by the great exponents Freud and Jung. They both managed to confine it to an outlier experience of advanced souls or poorly defined excess baggage; Freud (1938/1941, p. 300) calls a ME the "obscure self-perception of the realm outside the Ego." This has perhaps been a reason why only relatively few analysts have given it greater relevance, leaving the general categories necessary.

Analysts do not have exposure to highly evolved mystics so as to understand the passage and effect of a ME. If a person has such a life-changing experience, it is not likely that they will be in analysis; none of those who were interviewed entered psychoanalysis after their experience. If psychological issues arose for these mystics, they were understood in the context of a tradition as a necessary working through of blockages or the need to perfect meditation. For many, the idealised psychoanalytic goals were in them as a result of their practices and experiences by a marked sense of a unifying principle, a lessening of neurosis, and a reduction of fear and desire.

Patients do indeed have MEs. Few of those that are reported in the psychological literature appear to be experiences where they have created an indelible reorientation by a merging with the godhead or nothingness. Very many patients, however, participate in spiritual and religious traditions or turn to meditation and prayer and have or hope for experiences. These may be experiences of a different type or intensity than those that declared themselves mystics as they do not appear to have that same profound effect of a complete reorientation. Nevertheless, these MEs, when presented, are just as inexplicable as they occur outside the established course of the analysis and offer the possibility of bringing a new perspective to the patient.

When patients bring a ME into analysis, the experience is then contained within an analytical field where the phenomenon is as strange to them as to the analyst. It then is absolutely in the room and requires a space for it to be observed and somehow integrated. To do so, it is necessary for the analyst to understand what has occurred psychologically in order to ground it in professional theory.

The starting point for integrating a ME into psychoanalytic theory is not to drift into mystical or religious language but to keep it intact as an intrapsychic event that has occurred within the subjective experience of the patient. The psychological focus is that the ME is relevant because it has or could have an effect on consciousness – the subject matter of psychoanalysis. Words of cross-over at this time are confusing for this integration, such as Grotstein's (2000, p. xxx) statement that "The analyst, without realizing it, is a practicing mystic." This form of the analytic position takes it away from its actual effect on consciousness and places it in the abstract region of a mystical quality of analysis, therefore removing it from clear-eyed examination as pertaining to psychoanalytic theory and practice.

What emerges as the critical issue in psychoanalysis, either immediately or eventually, is the effect of the experience on the conscious position measured by the receptivity of the subject. It is this marker alone that will determine if a ME will have an effect on consciousness and is a question that does not need to leave psychoanalytic practice and theory. As this – the character and receptivity of the patient – is the essential question relating to the psychological effect of a ME, it is surprising that there is little, if any, evaluation of what makes a person open to a ME or how it is possible to tell if one person will make a more radical change than another or even how to help a patient make sense of it. Yet, this is the defining issue for practice: is the person with the experience able to receive it so that it has a chance to alter consciousness? Is it therefore worth keeping that experience alive in the analysis and is there anything that can be done as it fades away?

The second question may seem to run counter to the traditional, analytical attitude of the analyst's lack of memory and desire or may appear to hint at too much interpretation or unwanted intervention. However, as with a profound dream or a dominant projection, a ME is a psychological event that is in the consulting room and is sufficiently rare and powerful that it cannot be just ignored on the basis that further dreams or psychoanalytic work will reveal what is unconscious. In fact, it is a seminal event; and, when we witness it, it is a psychological celebration that we must attend.

Psychoanalytic subject matter

It is impossible to deny, as Wilfred Bion reminds us, that there is a mysterious, underlying layer in all psychoanalytic work; there is always something beyond our understanding. We can sense it, feel it, and observe how it touches us and the patient. We completely accept that this mystery is not just an interesting backdrop but essential to the process of analysis; as the Gnostic text *Pistis Sophia* (Mead, 1921, ch. 133) explains, "Without the mysteries no one will enter into the realm of light, whether he be a just man or a sinner."

Of all the mysteries that occur in an analytic session, a ME is the most specific example because, "As an experience, it claims to have encountered mystery" (Fanous and Gillespie, 2011, p. ix). As opposed to just a wide variety of unknowable mysteries that arise in endless and amorphous ways in analysis, a ME is a unique mysterious occurrence that is reported as a wondrous narrative of a singular event.

As the details of this experience may be set out in the narrative, it can appropriately be attributed by psychoanalysis to the indecipherable mission of the unconscious. As it is indeed the stuff of unconscious and a subjective experience, it deserves attention as much as any other specific source of unconscious revelation, such as a dream, a projection, or a waking fantasy. However, the professional tools that we have to work with this – the transference, projective identification, conversational methods, developmental attachment theories, and repressed wish fulfilments – cannot give us even a toehold on something that is so alien to logic and understanding. The consequence is that the experience is not given sufficient attention, or is passed off as the gift of a divine power, both as the reason for its occurrence and to account for the nature of its content.

The tendency of an analyst and patient to place a ME into a religious context rather than an eruption from the unconscious is inevitable and will always occur to some extent as it is more convenient than accepting that an alien force seemingly imposed from outside is a force arising from the inside – the deep unconscious. The mechanisms and content of the vast, deep unconscious is vaguer than the idea of a transcendent God. At least with God we can have an opinion fortified by doctrine and belief. The few psychoanalysts who have ventured into an explanation of the mystical as arising from the unconscious, such as Bion, Eigen, and Grotstein, still eventually cross back into a discussion of divine intervention (Merkur, 2010, chs. 9, 10, 12) as the real basis of the experience, as there is no easy bridge to a ME arising from unconscious forces.

The attribution of a ME to a divine source cannot be criticised but it has the effect of removing it from the probability that there was a breakthrough into consciousness of a profound message from the unconscious that deserves enquiry. Since it is utterly inexplicable, with no means to enter the reason for its breakthrough into consciousness, this helpful vessel of the grace of God is always there and may of course be all that it is, and psychoanalysis should just look on in awe and stay out of it. There are, after all, so many mystical or spiritual traditions where explanations of union with a transcendent, external godhead flow from the experiences of its adherents. These are so well defined and documented that they include a refined psychology of their own for the attainment and experience of the mystical. If the psychology is not explicit, as it is with the systematic refined explanations of the Buddhist *Abhidhamma*, it is at least symbolic as to psychological states, as with Hindu doctrine or Kabbalah.

A ME, no matter what its source, remains a subjective occurrence that may have a profound effect on the conscious position; it is always a psychoanalytic issue for that reason. It does not therefore require an answer as to its source but it does demand an understanding of what it means for the workings of the unconscious. This question is rarely addressed because the day-to-day work of analysis is with a patient's struggles with shadow elements, developmental pitfalls, inter-generational trauma, or the myriad other issues that require attention. However, MEs do indeed occur in some form for some patients and cannot, in a professional sense, just be passed off as either inexplicable or grace. The recognition that a ME is *also* a psychological event and suitable subject matter for psychoanalysis has the effect of requiring that it receive the same attention as other experiences that affect ego consciousness.

Issues for psychoanalysis

A patient (MH) related this experience:

> It was lunchtime and I was in Madison Square Park [mid-town Manhattan] and I sat down to eat my sushi on a bench by the dog run. After I finished, I looked up and there shimmering before me was the Virgin Mary. She must have been about ten feet tall. There was light coming

out of her stomach area. At first, I was panicked and then, for a moment, I felt like I joined with her as if we were one and then I was filled with love and a sense that my life was fine, but, after about thirty seconds, she disappeared. She looked like my ex-girlfriend so that probably was it and I am sure it was the crabstick in the California roll that gave me the hallucination.

At the time of this session, MH was a forty-eight-year-old accountant whose presenting problem was depression that he blamed on being stuck in an office and having a stale relationship. At the time of the experience, he had been in analysis once a week for four years. He had never had such an experience before and did not for the following year. After mentioning the vision, he was adamant that talking about it was a waste of time. If I mentioned the vision, he would shake his head from side to side and say, "Crabstick." If I even wanted to speak of the role of the crabstick, he shut down the discussion.

At the next session, I quoted to him from St Teresa of Avila (1987, p. 247): "I have never regretted having seen these heavenly visions, and I would not exchange even one of them for all the goods and delights of the world." At another, I suggested treating the experience as a dream. He began a discussion of the contents of the experience, only to turn away and dissociate. In respect for this resistance, I did not bring it up again.

The experience itself raises many questions for psychoanalysis and offers no answers. I was drawn instantly to the experience because of my own interest in mysticism and because it reminded me of the vision of Hildegard of Bingen, the twelfth-century mystic who described a vision of the Virgin Mary as "light burst from your untouched womb like a flower on the farther side of death ... Two realms become one" (Furlong, 1996, p. 100). I did my best to hide my enthusiasm. When the session with MH was over, I wrote down the questions that arose from his rejection. Was his experience a sign of him dissociating or the emergence of a psychosis? Why did it occur at this stage of the analysis? Was it a legitimate ME and, if so, what does that mean for him? How can it be brought into the consulting room, given his refusal to talk about it? Did it arise because of my own deep interest in mysticism, my countertransference and its presence in the field or even my analytic attitude? Is it relevant for the analysis at all if he refuses to discuss it or should I just expect that it will carry on to some further effect in his psyche?

The contents of his experience would neatly fit within any definition of a ME: a merging with the divine, the revelation of an absolute truth, and the vision itself. These characteristics constitute what is referred to as a "unitive" experience – a merging and becoming one with the divine – the hallmark of the ultimate ME. In fact, had MH declared that he was now a "mystic," there would be no basis for anyone to dispute his assertion. However, his refusal to discuss it and his attribution of the experience to the crabstick makes it, arguably, *not effective* in the psychoanalytic process.

His rejection squarely raises the psychoanalytic issue of when such an experience is useful and a subject matter for analysis. It is fundamental that, for it to be useful, it needs to have some impact on the conscious mind; for, if the experience is not entertained by him, it ceases to have any relevance and is merely a curious, historical element in the field, more likely to interest the analyst than the patient.

It makes particular sense that for the relational basis of psychoanalysis, a ME loses significance if it cannot be made a subject matter for both the analyst and the patient. Bion (1965/2014a, p. 169), in reference to the mystical, unknowable core of psychoanalysis – which he called "O" – explained: "In psychoanalysis, any O not common to the analyst and analysand alike, and not available therefore for transformation by both, may be ignored as irrelevant to psychoanalysis." This would be true of any experience but for those that are caused by an external occurrence, such as a trauma or a betrayal, there is a factual basis on which to continue to base a discussion. When the experience is sudden, without a known source, and enters the realm of a unitive merging with a divine object, there is no clear entry point to investigate the occurrence. Accordingly, an examination of a ME suggests four end points that are as relevant as the starting point for any psychoanalytic examination of the event – see Figure 1.1.

Between a ME at the apex and the horizontal line, there is a gradation of experience – from a full unitive experience to a lesser experience of a mystical nature. Once it descends below the line, in whatever intensity, it falls into the realm of a disorder and is more an experience that has diagnostic, rather than analytical, relevance. However, no matter where it sits on the vertical axis above that line, a ME is of no effect if it is rejected or not reported and it then crosses the horizontal axis to lose effectiveness on the vertical line. In both cases – below the horizontal line or to the right of the vertical line – it ceases to be a subject of analysis although it may be information retained by the analyst (to what end, though, is unclear). To be a ME that is effective and

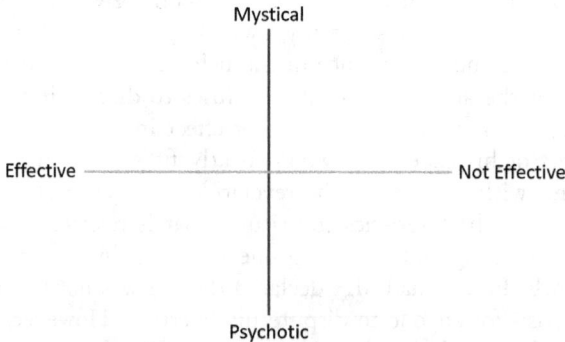

Figure 1.1 Psychoanalytic limits of a mystical experience

relevant for psychoanalysis, it must stay above the horizontal line and remain effective and not cross the vertical line.

In the case of MH, it did not appear from subsequent sessions that the vision was a result of a disorder; it remained above the horizontal line. There was no disturbance to his pattern of thinking, no disquiet, and no negative reaction to his experience. It failed the test of effectiveness along the horizontal line, however, as it crossed the vertical line; and, at most, it confirmed his initial dream. In this dream, he was in an unfamiliar house and afraid to go up to the attic. Instead, he sat comfortably in a chair on the ground floor and did not want to get up. The dream and his reluctance to move could be attributed to many complexes and issues, but the reality was that the possible breakthrough in the experience did not find a place in the consulting room.

It is possible, in this diagrammatic formulation, to assert that there are two meaningful elements for consideration in investigating the depth psychology of the ME. Is the experience to be classified as a ME above the horizontal line and therefore of interest? And, secondly, will it have a possible impact on consciousness by staying in the analysis? Both are necessary for the experience to be considered a ME that is relevant for psychoanalysis.

Characteristics of a mystical experience

A ME has as many variations in content as there are those who have had such an experience. However, the discussions over centuries have strived for a complete, exhaustive, and inclusive explanation having specific characteristics because it is equated with the highest goal of human accomplishment as the realisation of a complete unity or merger with the divine or formlessness and a consequent loss of individuality (Stace, 1960, p. 11). Bharati (197682, p. 63) calls this highest level of ME a "zero experience" – a loss of ego identity in the merger with the cosmic ground. The equivalent Buddhist expression is *sunyata*, meaning "zero-ness." Although the Hindu and Buddhist traditions have different orientations, the description of the experience is essentially the same. It is described (Noh, 1977, p. 17) more graphically as:

> You are immediately non-existent, in the sense that you transcend the realm of objectified experience and enter the Void of the Absolute, Nonexistence. Thus, you transcend all forms of being, you are totally unconditioned. You exist beyond any form of awareness or self-consciousness. There is nothing left which can be identified as "I"; everything that *is* "winks out," ceases to be, radically stops. There is no sensation of time – it is an eternal moment.

This narrative of a unitive ME invokes poetic illusions and references to ideas and concepts that logically make no sense, such as "non-existence." In describing the "Void" in the Tantric tradition, for example, it is said to be "very secret and subtle, being ... like the ten millionth part of the end of a hair" (Woodroffe, 1974, p. 430). In writing his epic *Savitri*, Sri Aurobindo (Ghose, 1951, p. 13), the Indian mystic and philosopher, explains that this is inevitable because:

> The mystic feels real and present, even ever present to his experience, intimate to his being, truths which to the ordinary reader are intellectual abstractions or metaphysical speculations. He is writing of experiences that are foreign to the ordinary mentality ... To the mystic there is no such thing as an abstraction.

This level of abstraction for non-mystics has meant that the grand narratives of mysticism have received little attention from psychoanalysis that seeks, especially in this century, rational explanation. As a consequence, a ME is regarded as in the realm of psychological abstraction and illusion. An analysis (Blass, 2004, p. 616) of the conciliation of psychoanalysis with the question of God's existence (and thereby mystical union) repeats that it is most likely to be regarded as "more of a kind of self- or relational experiencing within a realm of illusion."

This designation of a ME as an illusion arises because what the mystic appears to hold true is not the non-mystic's experience of reality. In psychoanalysis, the irrational or non-logical should have pride of place to accommodate what Bollas (1989) calls "the unthought known," or that which is available but not yet understood. The professional problem is that a ME's characteristics remain an illusion rather than what may be discoverable because it cannot be known by the non-mystic so it is outside the realm of imaging and ideas. This is obviously another historical reason why psychoanalysis has placed these experiences into a fringe category, standing outside developmental, relational, and other schemas. It becomes then impossible to determine the psychological effect of an illusion on the subject. Magid (2002, p. x), a psychoanalyst and Zen teacher, explains that "it is very hard, if not impossible, to explain in words the difference between a life that is fixed and one that is transformed."

Yet, the examination of the non-logical, illusion characteristics of a ME is inevitable as it is always judged in relation to its well-documented highest form. In justification for that examination, Freud's (1927, p. 25) admonition is that there is still an enquiry to be made in the face of religious (or mystical) abstraction on the basis that there must somehow be a logical or explainable answer: "Religious ideas are teachings and assertions about facts and conditions of external (or internal) reality which tells one something one has not discovered for oneself and which lay claims to one's belief." This is made difficult because the historic, classical characteristics of mystical consciousness consists *only* of that higher, unitive goal of a merging but not lesser states because a ME, in the formulation of religious and mystical traditions, is an unfiltered connection with God: "It develops the power of apprehending the Absolute, Pure Being, the utterly Transcendent; or, as its possessor would say, can experience 'passive union with God'" (Underhill, 1990, p. 36).

Descriptions of a unitive ME do make it clear that it is an experience that will cause a profound effect. The nature of that effect is either implied or expressed both as a fact but, more importantly, as an incentive. The "power of apprehending the Absolute" implies that it is an overwhelming experience that carries powerful affect, the details of which must be imagined. In most traditions, the effect is expressed as a series of outcomes, as in various stanzas of the ancient *Katha Upanishad*: "The calm soul having comprehended the great Lord, the omnipresent Self by whom one beholds both to the end of the dream and to the end of waking ceases from grieving." The effect of the ME in the *Upanishad* is that it reorients the subject: "so he that sees separate law and action of the One Spirit, [and] follows in the track of what he sees." In this translation and analysis of the *Upanishad*, Sri Aurobindo (Ghose, 1996, p. 185) explains that a ME confers an "immortality," shifting to "the absolute life of the soul as opposed to the transient and mutable life in the body."

Every ME, however defined or expressed, has three clear aspects: the experience itself, the meaning of the experience, and a change in conscious-ness as a result. Sells (1994, p. 88) explains that the "meaning event" for the experience is based on what is understood in consciousness when the "dual-isms of self–other, time and space are temporarily fused through the collapse of the semantic structures that reflect them." Sells is referring to a unitive experience with the loss of duality as the touchstone for deriving meaning from the contents that will cause the change in consciousness. The dualism of "self–other" is the appearance of some force or object – the other – that is not referable to any prior ego-oriented experience. The fusion Sells refers to is what makes the occurrence significant as a unique event. There is thus a continuum represented by the stages as the ME leads to the meaning event, and it is that which has the effect on consciousness.

It should be mentioned that the alternation of time and space to which Sells refers is a common characteristic of all MEs – at the highest level and even for lesser experiences. An early argument (Noyes and Kletti, 1976) is that time is effectively altered when there is depersonalisation or loss of ego identity, which is consistent with St Augustine's axiom that time does not exist outside thought (Hausheer, 1937). The most enticing explanation of time in respect of all MEs is that of the Dzogchen Tantric Buddhist tradition: that there is a dimension of time called "timeless time," which is the absence of time within an experience of the fundamental ground of being (Yao, 2007). Accordingly, if the connection with the ground of being occurs, time is not present.

Jung (1935/1953, para. 782), in analysing the *Tibetan Book of the Great Lib-eration*, proposed that timelessness was a quality that arises in the experience of the collective unconscious:

Since we cannot attribute any particular form to the unconscious, the Eastern assertion that the Universal Mind is without form ... yet is the source of all forms ... is psychologically justified. In so far as forms or patterns of the unconscious belong to no time in particular, being seemingly eternal, they convey a particular feeling of timelessness when consciously realized.

A ME does not require timelessness but absolutely must have a meaning event – an internal process of recognition – as a precondition of creating a change in consciousness. It is possible that, as with MH, the experience of the event could not be ascribed a meaning as it was so alien to his consciousness and therefore did not have any effect. It could also be given a meaning or explanation that is confusing or insufficient and not alter consciousness. The emphasis in the mystical literature is therefore on a meaning event that is consciously *realised*, thus incorporating the effect as necessary to the meaning event.

The psychological impact of a ME is derived from a realisation arising from the meaning event, not the process during the experience or any other aspect of its content or characteristics, although they are necessary as a prelude to the meaning event. Its quality as a zero or unitive experience is, in fact, ultimately analysed in all explanations in relation to what a realisation accomplishes, such as freedom from suffering, awakening, or enlightenment. This is consistent with the mystical tradition that requires that the mystic must have a "realisation" so that the experience itself is of significance: "Once you *realize* that you are not the body and the mind, you have no needs and demands, then you are one with the manifest consciousness" (Nisargadatta, 2004, p. 93; emphasis added). It is the realisation arising from the meaning event that makes the event important both in its essence and for psychoanalysis.

Realisation is the direct apprehension of the existence of a pre-existing dimension that is the underlying substrate of human existence, characterised by a non-logical but certain knowing. Sri Aurobindo (Ghose, 1970a, p. 87) explains the importance of knowing rather than just the experience or its content: "When you see light, that is a vision. The vision signifies a future realization. When you feel light entering into you, that is experience. When light settles in you and brings illumination and knowledge, that is a realization." In the case of MH, there was a vision as the light was observed, so there was an obvious experience, but that experience did not bring illumination or knowledge and therefore there was no realisation. In psychological terms, realisation of a ME is its reception into consciousness that results in a change caused by the revelation of the truth of the nature of life and being. This is as far as psychoanalysis needs to go, although for the mystic the experience moves beyond the realisation and by its force and effect establishes a path for intensifying the insights. In Tibetan Buddhism (Stearns, 2006, p. 25), it is explained that a realisation opens three new paths – the path of severing attachment, the path of eliminating entry (purifying the mind), and the path of enlightenment (calm, abiding, penetrating insight) – all constituting refinements of the realisation.

Distinctions are made in all traditions as to the degree of intensity of a realisation by comparing the different resultant states of consciousness. Turning again to the Tibetan tradition, one form of realisation is a state of mind that conceptualises the event by images and the other is non-conceptual, which perceives the truth directly without images. (Komarovski, 2015, chs. 2, 9). In the Hindu tradition, the Yoga-Sutras of Patanjali (Hartranft, 2003, p. 15) make a distinction between the initial appearance of profound stillness arising from a conceptual analysis, insight, bliss, and a feeling of self, but then a greater form of "coalescence," a new, transparent way of seeing without labels or associations: "like a jewel, it reflects equally whatever lies before it." If thoughts then arise, it is coalescence with thought; and if no thoughts, formlessness. The Tibetan sage Tilopa describes the formlessness as the highest degree of realisation: "Self awareness ... *fruit* of the real ... what falls within the range of thought ... is not the ultimate" (Komarovski, 2015, chs. 2, 4; emphasis added). Consequently, although there are different forms, it is the experience without cognition that is equated with the highest form of self-awareness and as an indication of the greatest effect on consciousness.

The essence of these distinctions is that a lesser realisation will not have the same effect on the state of consciousness as that resulting from higher, unitive experiences. The higher state is one where the effect is permanent; "coalescence" without thought is the state where there is no *slippage* back to normal, ego-identified consciousness, where the effect can fade. "Slippage" is a useful word that expresses the key differences in the effectiveness of the ME. This is illustrated well in the Gnostic text *Pistis Sophia* (Mead, 1921, ch. 119), where Jesus explains to Mary that a person is endangered if, having received the First Mystery, there are transgressions. Branco (2011) suggests that the First Mystery is a unitive experience of Jesus, but there remains above this an absorption in the "Divine Plane," also called the Mystery of the Ineffable. The suggestion is that the First Mystery is incomplete, even though it is accompanied by absorption and knowledge, and that the sin, according to Jesus, is "that he hath received the gift of the First Mystery and hath not abided in it" (ibid., p. 149).

The concept of "enlightenment" is usually expressed in terms of a lack of slippage, where the subject is vitrified and impervious to being caught in past conditioning or ego states. A modern guru, Sadhguru (2010, pp. 43–44), states: "If you have reached a certain state of awareness where you cannot fall back then maybe you can call that Enlightenment. Many people reach many states of awareness but they can fall back ... I would not call that Enlightenment." It is impossible for a person who is not enlightened in these terms, and therefore is still subject to slippage, to comprehend who is enlightened or what it is like. The trappings of enlightenment – of peace, love, wisdom – are only *symbolic* and point to the possibility of a life that is able to maintain a higher state, unpolluted by neurosis and trauma. However, as unknown as that state may be, its existence as an *archetypal* formulation rather than a readily achievable state is easier to understand and, perhaps for this reason, Jung (1939a, para. 877) was of the opinion that "It should not be too difficult for the Western mind to grasp what a mystic understands by 'enlightenment.'" He is referring to it here as the equivalent of the alchemical idea of "illuminatio" or a "lighting up" of the unconscious that indicates an idealised state of direct connection with a higher power (Jung, 1936, para. 68).

The goal of higher states or enlightenment, the basis of all mystical traditions, arises naturally as our creative capacity is responsible for imagining this future goal that is increased in importance because it is archetypal. It is therefore understandable that a ME, temporary in nature, would set off a quest for a still higher state and more profound experience. This accounts for the endless declarations and elucidations of gradations in experience and therefore an emphasis on the nature of the experience in terms of its content.

The non-mystical literature places all the emphasis on the contents of the experience in order to indicate its nature. Mystical traditions place greater emphasis on the degree of attainment in relation to the goal of a unitive merging as the test of whether there was a step towards full realisation where there is no slippage. The making of these distinctions between enlightenment and lesser gradations suggests that the elevation in consciousness will be gradual over time. It is said (Hellner-Eshed, 2009, p. 325) in Kabbalah that "mystical experience in the Zohar is akin more to flowing honey than to a wild river bursting its banks. It is characterised more by a thread of grace than a torrent of light and fire." This statement implies that the process of attaining full realisation is one that requires preparation, reaffirmation, increasing knowledge, and surrender so that it is measured by experiences along the way and not a sudden bursting through of a revelation that alters consciousness. However, the end experience is explained as a bursting through: full realisation in the Zohar is described as being encompassed by fire and ecstasy, so that the subject does not know "if it was day or night" (ibid., p. 318).

Gradations of experience

Of the three elements – the experience itself, the meaning event, and the effect on consciousness – emphasis in reported MEs in mystical or religious traditions is primarily on the event of realisation, and less on the effect on consciousness. There are, however, few explanations of which states or degrees of realisation will alter consciousness and to what extent. When the effect on consciousness is described, it is in terms of abstractions, reflecting the difficulty in explaining a loss of ego in the absorption with the divine or a state that is a new, permanent point of view. As an example, in the Zohar it is the appearance of light that most illustrates a ME and the effect in turn begins to appear as a spectrum; even the name Zohar is a reference to radiance. In addition, water, delight, fragrance, altered time, and intimacy are just some of the many and overlapping indicia of effect from an experience.

In all of these traditions, the idea that there are steps along the way, *beginning* with a lesser experience and rising to full mystical absorption, is understood in the teachings. As the final goal is so elusive, this leads to the experiences along the path as a series of gradual steps that must be attained, each offering its own realisation. In the teachings of the Sakya School of Tibetan Buddhism, since the seventh century, there is a warning of "Not Taking the Path as the Result" (Stearns, 2006). The reason given is that the realisations along the path create "impure" appearances and suggest only a lesser, incomplete set of understandings rather than what is attained by a unitive state. The mistake of equating the lesser experiences as mystical or religious goals occurs because of the statement: "The mind of divine form and the mind of sacred commitment are identical" (ibid., p. 35); the desire to achieve enlightenment gives the lesser experiences a subjective linking with a final goal. As a result, various lesser experiences are conflated as an aspect of the mystical end point, even though they lack that higher quality.

In this conflation, where there is an emphasis on what experiences occur along the way, little attention is paid to the actual effect on consciousness. In the *Great Treatise on the Stages of the Path to Enlightenment* (Sopa, 2008), the effects are expressed only generally as the development of an undefined peace and happiness as glimpses given to an awakened mind. The path is then given prominence for it allows an attempt at the perfection of certain qualities of generosity, ethical behaviour, patience, perseverance, meditative stabilisation, and wisdom, all seen as derivatives of what will appear on attainment of the final goal.

There is the tendency in the literature pertaining to MEs to rank the lesser experiences, from the beginning stages through to full absorption, rather than propose gradations of the result or the effects on consciousness. William James (1902/2008) created a ladder of MEs as a classification system with those at the bottom having no religious meaning and the upper rungs having more profound religious experiences. The ladder illustrates the inevitable gradations that arise from having classified the unitive absorption experience, as James did, of "religious mysticism pure and simple" (ibid., p. 305), reducing others to lesser experiences, such as his bottom rung of a déjà vu experience ("been here before"). Merkur (2010, pp. 18–28) lists thirteen categories of "unitive" experiences, such as the "self-transcendent mode," where the existence of the not-self (as a transcendent being) looks back at the self as an object. None of the categories that he lists, however, describes a zero experience in the sense of an illumination, as Sri Aurobindo describes it; rather, all are a variation in content of, for instance, feeling one with music or experiencing a heart opening.

The use of definitions that rely only on the description of a merger and loss of ego identity is the contemporary manner in which the existence of a ME is expressed. There is no emphasis in psychological or mystical expositions on the effect of lesser experiences on the psyche; instead, there is only an analysis of whether the elements of the experience elevate it to one that can be called a unitive ME. The reason why it has been operationalised through content definitions rather than by effect is explained well in a study of sleep paralysis as a spiritual experience (Hufford, 2005, p. 18). The cultural and historical fears of engaging with an unknown force has led to suppression of the reporting of its occurrence and therefore results in the projection of it on to the great realised individuals. The consequence is that the final goal is attributed to the experience of sages, gurus, or spiritual teachers who attain a unique state. To separate it from normal ego consciousness and to indicate its uniqueness, the definition points only to the importance of these states as a complete merger, allowing no room for other, lesser experiences or varying effects. This is enhanced by the literature (Clarke, 2010), which reports a fine line between mystical experience and psychosis, making a true ME have a particular, unique, elevated form and content. It makes for a rarefied and singular definition that is cut off from other experiences, no matter how profound.

The wide range of lesser experiences do not share universal characteristics, especially when viewed through different lenses (Brainard, 1996). The American Psychological Association (Hood and Francis, 2013), for instance, has identified four alternative bases that yield different definitions: theological, philosophical, psychological, and that resulting from a measurement scale. From the viewpoint of psychoanalysis, the main gradation is only between a ME, be it unitive or lesser, and a psychotic episode. This has an obvious historical basis resulting from a cultural bias in the West that MEs are not a liturgical characteristic of religious life for Christianity, Islam, and Judaism. The presence of "Eastern" views may therefore carry a hint of a psychic event that it is aberrant. Perhaps, as a consequence, the psychiatric and psychological literature has often suggested that these experiences are to be treated with caution as they have been linked to various risks, including the onset of illness leading to death (Lukoff, 1985, p. 155). The professional need for a specific definition for diagnostic purposes is therefore binary: disorder or not. The diagnosis in DSM-IV of "Religious or Spiritual Problem," which is carried over in later diagnostic manuals (Chandler, 2012), concentrates on the elements of the experience and not its transformational qualities.

The search for a clear definition is critical for psychology because the attributes of psychosis are *always* present in a ME. The psychiatrist Sannella (1992, pp. 98–99) writes about his own MEs having psychotic elements: "Thinking may be speeded up, slowed down, or altogether inhibited. Thoughts may seem off balance, strange, irrational. The person may feel on the brink of insanity." This is in contrast to where MEs are a universal expectation, such as in India. The Indian mystic Meher Baba went in search of mad mystics who had reached the highest level of MEs: God-merged mystics were the lowest form, followed by God-Intoxicated, God-Absorbed,

God-Communed, and God-Mad, the latter having lost sanity in the ultimate unity with the divine (Donkin, 2000).

A definition for the purpose of ruling out psychosis remains useful because, in terms of psychoanalysis, the ME is not effective and crosses below the horizontal line (Figure 1.1) for those who are psychotic. This is because the experience for a psychotic is not modulated through a sound ego that can provide a meaning event and also carries the possibility that it will lead to a megalomania. When discussing Nietzsche's illness, Jung (1988, Vol. 1, p. 30) suggests, "there is no realization: one cannot realize the thing by which one is inflated." Serious psychosis rules out a ME; in discussing schizophrenia, Jung (1958a, para. 568) states, "the associations are unsystematic, abrupt, grotesque, absurd and correspondingly difficult if not impossible to understand."

There are two essential reasons why there is a concentration on a ME at its highest definition rather than lesser, although still profound, experiences. The first is that the highest experience is a matter of myth in every culture where there are those who are sanctified for their spiritual accomplishments. The story of Milarepa from western Tibet is one such example. Before he could even receive the teachings, his teacher demanded that he must build and then demolish three towers and then build a fourth until finally, after the intercession of his wife, he was given the teachings and became enlightened. This myth is an exemplar for the attainment of a ME in Tibet (Schaeffer et al., 2013, p. 416). Lesser experiences would not do in the survival of the myth, so they are confined to preliminary insights or incipient states, no matter how profound.

The second reason is that it is observable that many lesser experiences may arise because of dissociation, making them linked to neurosis. Although not approaching the psychotic and therefore above the horizontal line, a search for MEs and the attainment of lesser states may be employed as a defence against the contents of the unconscious. In clinical practice, it is common for patients to read and study spiritual literature and have lesser experiences as a means to find some relief from the confusion of neurosis. The incessant search may lead to lesser experiences as the ego is reoriented to their possibility but they will remain only lesser experiences as the search is a defence against a working relationship with the unknown. This search for MEs, and the appearance of lesser experiences arising from dissociative states, is therefore a recognised phenomenon in psychoanalysis.

To describe a ME according to its content or status is to create boundaries that are clear at the centre but grow fuzzy at the edges. A patient who has an experience that their essence is also found in nature may not fit into the definition of a ME if they cannot describe a merger. As a consequence, because an experience describes less than a merger, there are endless possible manifestations of these lesser MEs. Every mystic who has recorded experiences and those whom I interviewed had different sensations, images, and objects occurring as they entered a lesser experience and exited. However, they reported just two basic forms of experience. The first was an experience characterised by a sudden, overwhelming onset that gradually ended, or, as one put it, "like a flattening of a bell curve." The other was characterised by the *absence* of a sudden, overwhelming onset. Instead, there was a gentle entry into the experience and a more rapid disengagement.

These two forms are useful because they relate to the possibility of different psychological effects: alterations of different degrees. Multiple regular, lesser experiences can alter consciousness. A realisation upon visiting relatives that one has been under the spell of an inter-generational trauma may bring unconscious patterns to light; a dream figure could begin a revelation of any manner of understanding. Each of these is an experience and each has the capacity to alter consciousness. Some insights may be more profound than others, such as a sense of wholeness arising in nature or a deep emotional feeling when listening to music. Some may provide an "aha" moment and others may yield a layer of peace. As the basis of psychoanalysis is that the unconscious is purposive, each such experience may be considered a harbinger of a unifying principle within the psyche that seeks its own unfurling. The realisation of such a principle, which Jung called "the Self," may introduce the patient to an intra-psychic "other" that becomes a reference point and offers an alternative to the vicissitudes of the ego. This is a process that requires a long journey of discovery as the patient makes progress in dealing with repressed elements, gradually develops insight, may continue to have lesser experiences, and begins to observe the workings of that unifying principle.

The realisation of the "other" as a journey rather than a sudden, overwhelming experience that alters consciousness is well illustrated in the writings of Wilfred Bion. His work *Transformations* (Bion, 1965/2014a) begins as an explanation of how transformations or interpretations occur in the analytic session about the unknowable essence – "O" (ibid., p. 141) – of what is happening in the room. Both the patient and the analyst experience O and both have different means to transform it into the subject matter of the analysis. Bion sets out a grid to indicate different classifications of the resistances to transformation.

The conflation of the O with the mystical comes suddenly in the text of *Transformations* after Bion expresses that he freely borrows from any tradition that helps explain his work. In writing about Plato's Forms, he states that the significance of O "derives from and inheres in the Platonic Form." Therefore, the Form of God is at the core of O, not as the unknowable God but rather the incarnated godhead that "enables the person to achieve union with an incarnation of the Godhead " (ibid., p. 250). He postulates that the union is the essence of psychoanalysis (as it is the O that is ever present in analysis) and can be achieved by a process of subtle insight, analytic attitude, and continued development.

The purpose of this "digression," as he calls it, (ibid., p. 251) is not that the realisation of the existence of God as indwelling or incarnated is relevant; it cannot be known, loved, or hated but rather "The most and the least that the individual person can do is *be it*" (ibid.; emphasis added). "Being it" suggests a subtle process because "Being identified with it is a measure of distance from it" (ibid.). The identification Bion is referring to is relying on statements or ideas of O, or "acting out," rather than just the alignment with the phenomenon of it indwelling.

The difficult process of *being* O is not subject to transformations through the usual ways attributed to psychoanalysis: "the further steps required to bridge the gap must come from the analysand or a particular part of the analysand, namely his 'godhead,' which must consent to the incarnation in the person of the analysand" (ibid., p. 259). He suggests that this involves abandoning false statements, which are directed towards the goal of reducing resistances by attention to the grid categories. The resistances are states of mind that are primitive and "unassociated with mature experience" (ibid., p. 263).

Bion (ibid. 273) explains the end product of this process: "acceptance in O means that acceptance of an interpretation enabling the patient to 'know' that part of himself to which attention has been drawn is felt to involve 'being' or 'becoming' that person." He says nothing of the qualities of a person who is capable of making that transition but leaves it to the process of analysis and therefore lesser experiences, to allow the transformations to take place so that the "being" may be manifested.

The success of the process is best understood as derived from Bion's idea of the analyst reaching a dream-like state without memory, desire, or understanding. The result of that state is a deeper contact with the analyst's inner experience that leads to "being" rather than an intellectual knowing. The process in the analysis then consists of transformation by the analyst of the patient's "pre-conceptions" or innate characteristics that need to be realised. This is a process in the course of analysis where pre-conceptions, represented by what Bion calls "beta elements" or raw sense impressions and emotional data, become "saturated" by the analyst, who remains unsaturated without memory or desire. This leads, by virtue of the unsaturated state of the analyst, to the analysand achieving an unsaturated dream-like state, approximating to being O.

The role of the analyst is defined in relation to the O as transforming beta elements or unmetabolised experience through a process that leads to "alpha elements" that are the processes that underlie memory, thinking, and the processes of consciousness. It is therefore said that "With the patient's projective identification of beta-elements into the analyst for the analyst to convert by means of alpha-function into alpha-elements, the reversion from phenomena to the unknowable godhead has begun" (Merkur, 2010, p. 242). It is not necessary to unravel more of Bion's writings but to highlight that this is a process of *gradual* immersion, in which lesser experiences are useful, which requires much of the analyst: a discipline of avoidance of memory and desire (Bion, 1965/2014, p. 13) as well as a practice that amounts to meditation (Merkur, 2010, p. 245).

Insights that are gained as to the nature of O are not defined as a category of ME. Bion defined the mystic as a "genius" who contains the "messianic idea" (Bion, 1965/2014, pp. 31–32) and amounts to ultimate evolution. This process of insights he describes is a development over time to alter consciousness to become O: it is within the psychoanalytic process where his concept of O is cast. The development is relational and arises in the interchange between patient and analyst as the latter receives a projective identification and, by a lack of memory, desire, and understanding, creates the empty vessel for the reception of undigested fragments of the unconscious. The patient may, by this process, reach a mystical state, but the whole process is not suggesting a unitive ME, even though it may yield profound insights. It is a gradation on the vertical axis above the horizontal line in which lesser experiences have relevance.

Bion (1973/2014, p. 68) admits that his knowledge of mysticism is "through hearsay." This perhaps explains why he appears to suggest that a ME may occur in an analytical session, even though the analyst is not someone who has direct union with God but is rather "a kind of poet, or artist, or scientist, or theologian" (ibid., p. 22). It does not seem likely that a patient's ME can occur in relationship to an analyst. What does occur is the use of insight that, by a process, leads to an awareness of a deeper order. Merkur (2010, p. 262) quotes Grotstein (2000, p. xxvii) to explain the nature of the Bion process and its results:

> The task of psychoanalysis is not the attainment of insight but, rather, the use of insight to attain transcendence over oneself, over one's masks and disguises, to rebecome one's superordinate subject. The task involves a transcendent reunion with one's ineffable subject.

Although not as specific as Bion with respect to the manner in which unconscious contents become metabolised through the transference, Jung explains that the Self – the sense that there is a unifying principle in the psyche that he equated with the incarnated Godhead – can arise from a process. That process, discussed in detail in his work *Aion: Research into the Phenomenology of the Self* (Jung, 1951, ch. 14), consists of meeting repressed elements of the psyche, gaining some appreciation of the operation of the unconscious, beginning to see the existence of a non-ego force in the psyche, and then orienting to that force so that its universality is understood (Stein, 2015).

The Zohar, the central book of Jewish mysticism, explains the steps that are necessary for the attainment of the final level of merger. It does this by speaking of the development of the soul from its first level, *Nefesh* (Ashlag and Cohen, 2012, Lessor 14). At this level, the soul "corresponds to the inanimate modality of the will to receive" (ibid.). This means that it is in effect dormant and without discrimination so that its individual parts are not recognisable.

Enclosed in the *Nefesh* is the *Ruach* – the source of spiritual light that, when the person strengthens himself or herself, increases the motivation to move on. Within the person lies the point of *Neshamah* – a higher light to move through the inanimate aspects of plant and animal natures – and then the holiest point source of *Chayah* – the full realisation of the One.

The analytic steps developed by Bion and the levels expressed in the Zohar are forms of experience not characterised or defined by a sudden, unbidden experience that is of sufficient force that it can create a change of consciousness by its occurrence. They are steps along the way – gradations – and each can provide a level of insight or refinement that may be a preparation for a ME. At the widest of possibilities, a lesser ME may be said to offer preparation for or a prelude to a unitive ME, but it is different in kind to the sudden onset of an overwhelming experience.

An experience that is an overwhelming, sudden occurrence and does not arise from a process or emerges from a gradual revelation is a useful distinction for psychoanalysis as it concentrates on the *likelihood* that it is an overwhelming experience that will have the greatest, immediate effect on the conscious, ego-directed aspect of the psyche. The psychoanalyst Michael Eigen (1998, p. 36) suggests, contrary to this, that "there are all sorts of mixtures" of experiences, and it is impossible to tell what effect each will have on the complex structure of an individual (personal discussion, February 2016). In his interpretation, a lesser experience may indeed create an alteration of consciousness. However, the distinction serves to separate a sudden, overwhelming occurrence, when viewed from the effect on consciousness, because it expresses the greater possibility that there will be an indelible change, not characterised by a return – or slippage – to a pre-experience consciousness.

A ME's relevance for psychoanalysis is not well served by evaluating an experience in terms of the extent of merger and a loss of identity or applying a definition that incorporates lower levels of insight. This is because it is not the experience itself that is critical but rather the effect on consciousness. As the Kabbalistic scholar Idel (1988, p. xviii) explains, the main difference between a religious sentiment and a ME is in terms of its intensity: its "spiritual impact."

The role of the content

From the point of view of psychoanalysis, concentration on the possible effect shifts the emphasis strongly away from the actual content, usually the essence of a ME: from "The fact of revelation is its content" (Voegelin, 1990, p. 185) to the importance of revelation according to its effect. In terms of effect, it is clear that a sudden occurrence that overwhelms an individual has a greater potential psychological impact as it is more likely to overcome defences and create a change in consciousness.

The efficacy of this approach of emphasising effect over content is suggested by the Buddhist scholar Robert Scharf in his discounting of "experience" because there is no verifiable access to the original event but only a subsequent interpretation, to which may be contrasted the actual observation of its effect. Scharf (1998, p. 113) explains that the epistemological approach to the content fails because of the total subjectivity of the actual experience: "The salient characteristic of private experience that distinguishes it from 'objective reality' is thus its unremitting indeterminacy." He labels an approach that looks away from the content to psychological consequences "productive" (personal communication, 24 July 2017). The search in psychoanalysis for any boundaries or distinctions as to content and ranking are therefore fruitless and, although the content may have symbolic interest, the greater phenomenon is that the experience has altered consciousness.

The content of a ME is what is placed before us by a patient as it is made patent by the manner in which it is ultimately expressed. It contains imagery, visualisations, perhaps divine linkings, and exegetic excess. This will occur because it is impossible to explain the phenomenon of a ME by anything other than a logical narrative and symbols arising as content. The expression of the narrative seems to be important as it is always evocative and may evoke ancient symbols that are equated with such content as luminosity, grandeur, connectedness, or, in the case of some traditions, sexuality.

For the analyst, if the experience is viewed as an emanation of the unconscious, it appears appropriate to take each symbol as a psychological object, for the principle is: "Every psychological expression is a symbol if we assume that it states or signifies something more and other than itself which eludes our present knowledge" (Jung, 1921, para. 817). The difficulty, however, with the symbolic content is that it is then used as the means to categorise a ME, shifting the focus away from its effect. It inevitably invokes a checklist of markers against which the experience is weighed; and the more elaborate the symbols, the greater is judged the experience. This feeds into the improper view that a ME is capable of being understood by its content, as in Kataphatic theology, which speculates on the characteristics of God rather than the inability to know. Sells (1994) calls the nature of the content an "unsaying" as it is incapable of being reduced to words. As the German mystic and poet Kalima Vogt pinpoints, the ultimate understanding is "not haveable" (personal communication, 22 December 2017). In analysing this issue, Baird (2009) explains that the only true response to a ME is therefore silence. It is, to use the Jnana Yoga concept, *neti neti* – not this, not that.

When the symbolic content is made important, it creates a dilemma. The report of a ME of a vision of the Virgin Mary could theoretically raise issues for investigation, such as those pertaining to a mother complex, sexuality, guilt, the anima, or the religious instinct. Each of these might appear to be a fruitful sign on the path of psychological development and it would be hard for any psychoanalyst to put them aside, much as it would be to ignore the contents of a dream.

Bion's idea that the analyst creates, by his or her self-awareness, a dream-like state of being O to absorb and transmute the patient's interpretations comes closer in theory to silence in the face of compelling symbols. It is clear, however, that other than silence in the face of a mystical revelation, symbol formation is still the essence of psychoanalytic process itself and therefore hard to ignore.

The answer to the dilemma lies in understanding the ME as not its content or origin but rather its psychological effect. It could be replete with profound symbols, but if it has no effect, it is irrelevant. Symbols arising from a dissolution in the godhead or nature cannot be analysed as they offer no pointers to any known object. All that can be observed is an alteration of consciousness.

If the emphasis is on the manner of its occurrence – gradual in the case of insights or sudden and overwhelming in the case of a ME – relevance is on the question of what experience will likely be effective in changing consciousness – the subject matter of psychoanalysis. It is more likely that an experience that is overwhelming and occurs unbidden will have a greater impact than one that is gradual or a cumulative result. This is the essence of Jung's relationship to the mystical experience.

Chapter 2

The numinous experience

The underlying proposition for Jung is that a ME is relevant only insofar as it has an effect on consciousness. It may indicate, outside the realm of psychoanalysis, a recognised step on a spiritual path, it could fit clearly within a cultural context and have social meaning, or it could open a path for the person to attain higher states, but this is of no significance. The concern of Jung is solely psychoanalytic: the manner in which the ego position changes to relieve suffering by a reduction of neurosis.

The emphasis in ego-psychology on a ME is for the ego consciousness to enter into a relationship with a new element that has been introduced into the psyche by the experience. The construct of an ego or the conscious mind indicates that there is a structure that is relatively cohesive but subject to vicissitudes resulting from unconscious forces. The goal of psychoanalysis, expressed simply, is to bring to light those unconscious forces for them to be integrated and to be in a relationship with the ego. The ME is then *utilitarian* in indicating to the ego that there are non-ego forces in the unconscious that provide a greater integration of the personality than otherwise thought possible. This requires reframing a ME through the lens of the unconscious.

The mystical and the unconscious

The unconscious has no limits and by definition includes all that is not in conscious awareness. It will offer up its contents in myriad ways to provide a revelation of what is previously hidden and inaccessible. The attribution of the revelation to God or to a teacher of a spiritual tradition is natural because consciousness must make sense of what has occurred. However, God or a spiritual tradition is not necessary from the viewpoint of psychoanalysis as a ME is a subjective, unconscious event.

The concentration on a ME as a purely subjective or an intra-psychic occurrence is a matter of fact. Whatever its source, it arises entirely within the subject and does not depend on an interaction with anything outside for it to be experienced. That experience, as it occurs, may or may not be mediated through a tradition or a cultural context, but it remains an occurrence that is purely subjective arising from the unconscious. MEs, as Jung (1942/1954, para 450) states in respect of dreams, "are statements of the unconscious"; these statements are delivered to the conscious mind.

These "statements," in the case of a ME, can be presented in endless forms. As with a dream, the patient focuses on its content to understand what it is trying to say. Those who have had a ME are therefore primarily concerned with what has been revealed by the actual moment-to-moment content that was experienced. How it occurred, why some and not others have had that experience, and the specific purpose of the revelation are not possible to understand, as one would expect from such a non-logical source. Yet, the tendency is to focus on the contents because we work within the rubric of what the unconscious gives us: hints, signs, and symbols. The dilemma Jung addresses is that we cannot say why it occurred according to a stage of analysis, why a patient has been chosen for such an experience, or why something so seemingly profound is presented, as in the case of MH by a vision or a moment of merger with a divine image; the only concern is then the effect.

It is contrary to logic for psychoanalysis to turn away from an explanation of the details of the contents because a ME always contains an object; otherwise, it would not have any concreteness. That object can be the divine, or nothingness, or nature, but nevertheless it arises as an objective aspect of what was encapsulated within the experience. Sells' (1994, p. 10) use of the concept of "meaning event" is meant to displace that grammatical object in favour of a sense of the evocative immediacy that has occurred. It is, however, in the fixation on an object that the speculation begins because the conscious mind proceeds by way of forms and language to solidify what is observed to allow it to be digested. Psychoanalysis, in the fundamental belief that the unconscious is purposive, will seize on the object as an interaction of a facet of the unconscious entering into a relationship with the conscious mind. When it is seized upon, it takes on its own life as a superordinate construct that then orients the rest of the experience and inevitably yields a transcendent connection.

The traps in analysing the object and thus the content of a ME in terms of developmental complexes, archetypal forms, myths, and cultural nuances appear inevitable. However, Jung was obviously keenly aware that psychoanalysis can only speculate, at best, as to the actual message of the unconscious contained within a ME. There are no psychoanalytic theories of why some subjects are chosen to be presented with such an occurrence, why the contents are as they are, and what is the reason it occurred now. It is only the greatest conjecture to assume that it occurred in a particular form because of the material arising in the analysis or by particular stages in the process. An analyst can only, if there is a desire to be very clear, observe two phenomena. The first is that there was indeed a purely subjective, intra-psychic occurrence that overwhelmed the habitual conscious patterns; the second phenomenon is that the experience had or did not have some impact on consciousness.

It is impossible to abandon hypotheses and avoid theories of what brought about a ME. There can be speculation that this is a result of some prior trauma, pre-natal feeling states, a weakening of consciousness, or some movement within the unconscious. These speculations at least give us a chance to plant a stake in the ground to explain a completely unknowable occurrence. In the end, the two phenomena that there was an event and it had an effect on consciousness are *all* that can definitely be known about a pure subjective state.

There is much to be said for creating a stake in the ground in terms of psychoanalytic practice to try to make statements as to the intra-psychic operation of MEs. The experience is a subjective unfolding that contains strong affect and it is of no consequence for the psychoanalytic enterprise if it cannot be discussed. You have to say something about a subjective occurrence for it to become a subject matter for the therapeutic relationship. At the very least, it opens a discussion on the existence of an unknown aspect of the unconscious, of the existence of an object in the psyche that is alien to the ego consciousness, and that there may be more to our being than we think.

However, it bears repeating that there are only two non-speculative aspects of a mystical experience, as Jung recognised: the fact that it occurred; and the fact that it may alter consciousness. The speculative aspects are the nature of the actual contents, the attribution to a transcendent\divine, and the theory of why it might have occurred. These speculative aspects are part of the conversation arising from the narrative and may open up some fruitful lines of childhood development or complexes, or become a reference point for the concept of the Self.

For Jung, the existence of such an experience arises from the force of an encounter with the archetypes underlying all phenomena. As one illustrative example of this approach, in referring to statements he made about the interpretation of "privatio boni" – that evil is only an absence of good – he adds (Jung, 1952a, para. 459):

> it is possible here, as in the case of other metaphysical statements, especially dogmas, there are archetypal forces in the background, which have existed for an indefinitely long time as preformative psychic forces and therefore would be amendable to empirical research.

The actual underlying archetypes that form the infrastructure and contents of the psyche – all that is conscious and unconscious – are not directly accessible but may break through by unconscious processes, yielded up in a dream, a fantasy, or a projection. The role of the archetype in the production of a ME is Jung's contribution alongside the reality of the subjective experience. If the theory is put aside, however, it remains that there are two phenomena that become the bases of the psychoanalytic interface with a ME: is this an experience that overwhelmed the habitual thoughts and explanations of the conscious mind, and did this event have an impact on the conscious position? The theory is unnecessary but inevitable and provides at least a framework to listen to the narrative and respond.

The numinous concept

For Jung, a ME is subsumed in a larger category of what he calls "numinous experience." The teleology of a numinous experience is that it introduces to the conscious mind the existence of a non-ego force lying in the unconscious. His definition is therefore wide and purposive, bringing all such experiences into psychology as an intra-psychic process that is revelatory rather than allowing them to stand outside as aberrant, related to religious, devotional practice, requiring some form of divine presence, or reflecting a metaphysical explanation.

The essential matters that underlie Jung's numinous experience are indeed the same two non-speculative phenomena: the experience has managed to overwhelm the repetitive, habitual pattern of conscious thought; and it will change the conscious position. It is interesting that Jung does not write a separate opus or even a section on the nature of a numinous experience, and it is raised only tangentially in several places, most prominently in a discussion of the 'psychological approach to the Trinity' (Jung, 1942/1948). In this context, however, he reminds us (ibid., para. 173, n. 4) that when we speak of recognition of and submission to metaphysical forces, he is primarily speaking about the unconscious:

> Submission to any metaphysical authority is, from the psychological standpoint, submission to the unconscious. There are no scientific criteria for distinguishing so-called metaphysical forces from psychic ones. But this does not mean that psychology denies the existence of metaphysical factors.

The idea of submission to the unconscious is embraced in the two phenomena of a change being caused in the conscious mind because the experience has sufficient force to have an impact. The source is a mystery, as Jung acknowledges, but that mystery arises from the depths of the unconscious for psychological purposes, even though it may be attributed to metaphysical factors that are not psychological.

The emphasis in the two phenomena is on the encounter with something novel to the conscious mind that will accordingly have that impact because it is an overwhelming, unmediated experience. It is unmediated in the sense that it does not arise from or within a pattern of thought as it is previously unknown. If it were known, it would not be overwhelming. As it has the quality of a direct, unmediated experience, it has the potential to introduce a new element or aspect of the unconscious of which the subject becomes aware.

It does this by overwhelming the ego and creating an "object" to consider as this is necessary because there are no objects at all in normal self-awareness; all experience is cocooned within existing cognitive parameters:

> The reason one is not presented to oneself "as an object" in self-awareness is that self-awareness is not perceptual awareness, i.e. is not a sort of awareness in which objects are presented. It is awareness of facts unmediated by awareness of objects.
>
> (Shoemaker, 2003, p. 104)

The existence of an unknown aspect of the unconscious makes the unconscious itself an object in consciousness, and that comes as a revelation that there is a new element that can be considered by the conscious mind. This is instrumental in Jung's thought. The German Romanticist Fichte and his student Schelling were part of the historical chain of philosophy that informed Jung's structural theories in this regard (Shamdasani, 2003, pp. 171–173). Fichte insisted that there was a complete non-differentiability of subject and object in self-consciousness (normal waking consciousness), and Schelling emphasised the existence of the unconscious as an object. The only manner in which the unconscious can become conscious in this formulation is by revelation of its contents as an object to the conscious mind. The need for revelation of the unconscious means that those experiences that expose the "other" and arise in an overwhelming and sudden manner become the prime candidates for objectification and revelation.

The numinous experience, as Jung approaches it, is necessarily distinguished as one appearing without any *preconditions* and that which is not previously understood by consciousness. Therefore, it must come upon the subject suddenly – as a surprise – and escape all prior knowledge or speculation that might be expected. Moreover, the suddenness initially allows it to escape a cognitive frame that would make it a conscious, mediated experience that could be rejected. If it is sudden, it is not able to be predicted by intuition, is unrelated in fact to any known process, and in essence is the unexpected appearance of alterity: the complete other. It theoretically creates a boundary between this psychic phenomenon of the irruption of the other and the known, which is normal consciousness. This very much confirms Jung's construct of a limited ego, with the unconscious having a greater, hidden depth.

As all spiritual traditions require prior knowledge, training, or insight, Jung is describing an unmediated experience not within the purview of mystical discourse. By its nature, it is not reliant on ethical behaviour, contemplation, or meditative practice. It is therefore unique as being without a formulated process or path – a pure subjective experience – and is therefore controversial in mystical commentary (Katz, 1978; Forman, 1990; Komarovski, 2015) as it is contrary to all spiritual hierarchy and teachings. In the context of these spiritual traditions, there are social, religious, and linguistic elements that form the basis for the eventual realisation of the ME, and Jung instead speaks of direct perception.

This theme that a change in consciousness may occur by a sudden, over-powering experience is expressed in many other ways in his writings. For instance (Jung, 1928b, para. 323; emphasis added): "only in moments of overwhelming *affectivity* can fragments of the unconscious come to the surface in the forms of thoughts and images." The emphasis in this orientation is the introduction of something unexpected (otherwise it would not overwhelm) that has such a powerful effect on the conscious mind that it feels over-whelmed by the affect that it brings.

The *affectivity* Jung mentions arises from the irruption of unexpected, unconscious elements into normal consciousness. Jung's (1921, para. 808) characterisation of affect is that it occurs where there is a failure of adaptation, which means that it is impossible to adapt to an occurrence because it is unconscious and therefore the effects cannot be mitigated. The means by which the experience becomes overwhelming and an irruption is when the libido is "dammed up and explodes in an outburst of affect" (ibid.). The libido, in Jung's terms, is the flow of life energy that he compares to the flow of water, so transformation as a bursting through occurs "by the damming up and regression [of libido], its changed character being indicated by the new way in which energy now manifests itself" (Jung, 1928a, para. 72). For a numinous experience, this is an explosion of unconscious energy that cannot be mediated so it is an affective overwhelming.

The need for revelation of the contents of the unconscious is, in fact, the basis for psychoanalysis; it is the manner in which the limitations of the ego structure can be overcome. If it is not a revelation of unconscious contents, which by definition is other than the ego, then there is nothing to shift the ingrained personal and inter-generational patterns and complexes. However, the usual activity of psychoanalysis does not demand a sudden, unmediated, overwhelming experience. The normal pathways – developmental or rela-tional – suggest a gradual unfolding of the unconscious resulting from the difficult engagement with early childhood or transference. The numinous experience is therefore a special category for psychoanalysis as it suggests an atypical, rapid realisation and revelation by an overwhelming outburst. Its basis in psychoanalysis is that the strength of the revelation will be a har-binger of its possible effect on those patterns, opening up other explorations and giving hope that the limitations may be overcome. It is not necessary to psychoanalysis, but, when it occurs, it offers a possible indication of an acute realignment of the conscious position.

In accordance with this theoretical framework, Jung's explanation is that a numinous experience is a subjective feeling of being suddenly overwhelmed by a force that is alien to the ego, which – by the resultant, powerful affective nature of the occurrence – yields a change in outlook. It has been argued (Dohe, 2016, p. 65) that this framework had a specific origin for Jung based on an absolute need for new revelations as he believed that Christian symbolism no longer had any real effect on the populace and was incapable of creating a new orientation in consciousness. In lectures in 1925, Jung (1989, p. 80), proposed: "So our way has to be one where the creative character is present, where there is a process of growth that has the quality of revelation." Most importantly, he adds (ibid.): "Analysis should release an experience that grips us or falls upon us from above, an experience that has substance and body, such as those things occurred to the ancients." Dohe's (2016, pp. 78–79) argument concludes with the idea that the influence of those who established the predicates of the nature of the unconscious (including Fichte and Shelling) were the real basis for Jung's approach to this need for revelation, and therefore:

> [Jung] presented his psychological theory as originating from his own personal encounter with the numinous character of the archetypal powers of the collective unconscious, rather than through systemizing in a new way the knowledge that had been taught to him by his instructors.

The implication is that Jung's attention to the revelatory power of a numinous experience may have been triggered by what he learned from his predecessors rather than his own personal experience. This is incorrect and deserves brief comment if we are to look to Jung as offering a glimpse into the nature of a ME. Dohe's argument ignores a deeper contextual understanding of *Seven Sermons to the Dead* (Jung 1998, Appendix V). In this work, which Jung revealed to only a few associates under the pseudonym of the gnostic Basilides, and which ended with an epigram of his name, he made the critical choice of adopting the language of Basilides and not the central, gnostic writers of the time (Stein, 2015). The particular language of Basilides was of a phenomenon of a ME where the divine merges with an individual to observe its own creation. It was an orientation towards MEs that made sense only to one *who had that experience*, as it was not within the mainstream Hindu, Taoist, and Buddhist philosophies with which he was familiar. This type of experience does arise in Sufism and Tantra, but Jung had very limited knowledge of both of these traditions (Stein, 2013).

It must be assumed that whatever the role of his mentors, Jung had some means of understanding that it is an overwhelming, affective experience that can cause a change in consciousness as it produces a revelation. He, of course, mentions many such experiences that occurred for him in his autobiography, *Memories, Dreams, Reflections* (Jung, 1998), but it is not at all clear which offered a spiritual revival. The same is true of the mystics I interviewed, who could not pinpoint a moment when they became aware that they had a tendency towards revelatory experiences and first encountered some other force within their psyche that altered their consciousness.

The reality of a numinous experience as revelatory is that it will be, by its nature, overwhelming, because it presents a moment where normal, waking consciousness is supplanted by a different, non-logical event, alien to the ego. The word "alien" is appropriate for the presentation of the archetypes of the unconscious to the conscious mind: "The association of a collective content with the ego always produces a state of alienation, because something is added to the individual's consciousness which ought to remain unconscious, that is, separated from the ego" (Jung, 1920/1948, para. 590). The reason the non-ego forces appear alien is that they seem to "come from the outside" (ibid., para 591). When the contents are not already part of the ego consciousness, they can be viewed as an object or, more accurately, a distinct subject matter of interest to be examined.

The existence of an object suggests a relationship in which it is regarded by the ego and has introduced some new knowledge. In a structure that relies on the revelatory purpose of a numinous experience, the contents of the experience are then relevant only to the extent that they present an object that has sufficient meaning or is capable of becoming an object upon reflection in order to influence or form an impression upon consciousness. Most importantly, that object must be imposed by such force and effect to impact the consciousness so it becomes recognised as novel. It therefore, in this purview, has the dual qualities of intensity and uniqueness, as to which a ME is a prime example.

There is an assumption in this view that the numinous experience will evade the resistances in the cognitive mind as it is so sudden and powerful that the subject is bound to encounter the other. Jung avoids the explanation of the force needed to break through and instead creates a condition for a numinous experience: that the consciousness is being overwhelmed by a force alien to normal ego functioning *and* the occurrence causes a change in consciousness. For the purposes of Jung's analytical psychology, its predicates and its purpose, an experience that does not alter consciousness is *not* a numinous experience as it has no function in the individuation process even if it is overwhelming and of great force and effect. However, in the same way, an experience that alters consciousness, such as a dream or a resultant insight occurring in a regression, is not a numinous experience in this definition as it is missing the quality of an overwhelming non-ego force.

Otto's numinosum

It is in the Terry Lectures on "Psychology and Religion" that Jung (1938/1940, para. 6; original emphasis) first uses the term "numinosum" in a specific context as the touchstone for his concept of "religion": "The *numinosum* is either a quality belonging to a visible object or the influence of an invisible presence that causes a particular alteration of consciousness."

There are two parts to the numinosum: the quality of the visible object that contains a holy or a non-logical appearance, such as an emotional reaction from being in a church with powerful iconography, or the effect of an unseen presence that causes an alteration of consciousness, such as a ME. Jung's use of the term is based upon his adoption of "numinosum" from Rudolf Otto's *The Idea of the Holy*, where Otto's emphasis was on the emergence of a quality other than that which is within existing religious knowledge structures. In this work, Otto (1923, p. 6) contrasts existing, doctrinal ideas of God with a unique emotional, non-rational, extraordinary experience. He names this experience a "numen" (ibid., pp. 6–7); hence the adjective "numinous." Jung adopts the latter term as the basis for all experiences or objects that retain an ineffable quality.

The use of the word "numinous" as standing for sacred realities is not common historically and owes its modern usage to Otto and Jung. Due to its connection with Otto, it may be taken to have a religious, Christian character and thus could lead to a distinction between numinous experiences that are religious and those that are characterised by a direct perception outside a tradition. As to the former, Otto explains that they are characterised by "outer and thunderous" qualities (Smart, 1974, p. 13). The "thunderous" quality is gained by a vision of the godhead or a divine connection – the "outer" – and not by a direct, subjective experience without a religious connection or orientation (Sarbacker, 2005, pp. 32–33).

The tie between the term "numinous" and religious experience naturally flows from the etymology of the derivative word "numen" as "a nod" that was expanded in several cultures to mean a display of "divine power" by the nodding of a God when it is questioned. As Otto points out, it has been used historically to refer to the highest, most majestic form of divine power and means a relationship or contact with that power through an experience. It is the divine power being brought to an individual by a nodding of the transcendent God in answer to a question, which perhaps is an unformed, unarticulated longing or desire.

In order to offer a more precise understanding of what Otto intends by his use of the term "numinous," he sets out the characteristics of a numinous experience. As Jung derived the term from Otto, an investigation of the qualities that were Otto's focus is necessary to clarify both the term and its scope.

The first quality is what Otto calls a "creature feeling": being overwhelmed by one's nothingness "in contrast to that which is supreme above all creatures" (Otto, 1923, p. 10). It creates, he says, an "uncompromising judgment of self-depreciation" (ibid.). The concept of self-depreciation arising in relation to a transcendent God very much echoes religious doctrine, especially the seventeenth-century Puritan theologian Walter Marshall's (1954, p. 27) concept of "sanctification," which suggests that the human heart is weak and incapable of overcoming sin until there is a revelation brought about by union with Christ, "receiving it out of Christ's fullness."

The maintenance of the duality of a divine–depreciated creature feeling is contrary to the idea in the mystical canon that a ME is unitive, with a *loss* of duality. A critique, most notably by Smart (1974, pp. 12–13), is that Otto's duality conflates a religious experience with all numinous experience, denying a separate ME. Those interviewed for this work reported no "creature feeling" but rather an elevation to a higher level by the revelation of the presence of the divine in a unitive state. The humbling experience was not noted; rather, the experience was perceived as a blessing or gift that was anything but depreciating either at the time or upon reflection.

The second quality of the numinous experience for Otto is "*mysterium tre-mendum*": the overpowering dread, terror, and awe that arise from the experience (Otto, 1923, p. 15). The use of *tremendum* as consisting of two negative emotions (dread and terror) and one positive sensation (awe) arises from the particular orientation of Otto (ibid., ch. 4) where he is concerned with different levels of terror arising from basic, human fear distinguished from that which arises in the experience of dread. Accordingly, *tremendum* is, he says, "terror fraught with an inward shuddering" (ibid., p. 14). The physicality of the experience appears to be equated with biblical terror relating to the wrathful God of the Old Testament (Ware, 2007, p. 54). This biblical reference is not in accordance with many mystical traditions; for example, in the Vaishnava tradition of Hinduism, terror is not a recognised emotion or mood in relation to an experience of the divine. That tradition is based on devotion, where God is a loved one so that terror is a barrier rather than a consequence (Kakar, 1991, pp. 17–18).

The possible reality of a physical reaction to a ME – the *tremendum* – to the extent that it exists, must relate to a possible jolt from the sudden, unexpected immersion into a state that is non-logical or alien to consciousness. Underhill (1990, p. 9) explains: "Consciousness shrinks in terror from contact with the mighty verb 'to be.'" It is an encounter, then, with a state that is outside any aspect of normal waking experience and may therefore, by the shock, create moments of physiological effect. The Book of Enoch, as an example, recalls his vision (1 Enoch 4:14–15) and how, when he entered the house of God, he was in a state of complete terror and experienced hot and cold at the same time.

James (1909/1979, p. 94) calls these feelings of panic or terror "diabolical mysticism" and contrasts them with benevolent experiences during instances of reverential religious MEs:

> The same sense of ineffable importance to the smallest events, the same texts and words come with new meanings, the same voices and visions and leadings and missions; the same controlling by extraneous powers, only this time the emotion is pessimistic: instead of consolations we have desolations; the meanings are dreadful; and the powers are enemies to life.

The argument has been made that these negative feelings described by James may arise more commonly than suggested (Kukla, 2005, p. 124). As they may not be reported or are shunned and rejected, they could skew the traditional understanding of the expected contents of a ME as beneficial and blissful. There is no reason to deny this insight. It is logical that negative feelings and perhaps a physical reaction may occur by an impact on the very structure of the conscious mind when it receives new stimuli that leads to a diminution of existing conceptual ideas and a rise in others that are just as likely to be negative (Deikman, 1969, p. 43).

Physical reactions to a ME are reported historically but not in more recent revelations; for instance, as an aspect of the initiation into the Eleusinian Mysteries: "then come all the terrors before the final initiation, shuddering, trembling, sweating, amazement: then one is struck with a marvellous light" (Plutarch, 1961, p. 202). Not one of the interviewed mystics reported any negative physical component, such as shuddering, as an aspect of their MEs. In fact, they consistently reported a disconnection from their bodies, as if they no longer existed on the normal plane of consciousness. As a Western mystic in Pushkar, Rajasthan, explained: "I was just not there to experience any physical reaction. When it started to fade and I was able to begin to comprehend what occurred, my body still felt like it was left behind."

The reason why physical reactions are not a modern statement for Western mystics is not known, but several factors can be the subject of speculation. The first is that the separation of the spirit from the body, as Jung explained repeatedly in his analysis of Christianity, causes a disconnection between the subjective experience of the spirit and physicality because "the spirit has been brought into the psyche and been identified with the function of the intellect" (Meier, 2001, p. 116). Another reason is body loathing and physical mortification, which is common historically in the descriptions of the experiences of female Christian mystics (Lochrie, 1991; Finke, 1998, p. 408), so that physical reactions are more likely. Generally, for Eastern mystics, this lack of terror or negative sensation may be a result of conditioning related to the importance of the experience and therefore a lack of shock when the experience occurs.

There is, however, a relationship between a numinous experience and the physical in that realisation implies more than a cognitive or a perceptual knowing by an embodiment that operates at an instinctual, inaccessible level that integrates experience. It is the embodiment that provides the sense of the revelation so that it is experienced by the whole being. Jung (1988, pp. 967–968) states: "Since we have a body it is indispensable that we exist also as an animal, and each time we invent a new increase in consciousness we have to put a link in the chain that binds us to the animal."

It seems more probable that a sense of terror or the occurrence of a physical tremor is a sign of an isolated, pathological reaction to an experience where there is no cultural context. Physical distress is an aspect of a pathological possession and arises if there is no setting or culture for the event, making it totally inexplicable and unable to be assessed. Stephenson (2017) examines possession historically and as a diagnostic category of pathology "relegated to the Other," as it arises outside any known milieu. A cultural attitude to a ME was the basis for the interviewees, all of whom have a mystical tradition, not to feel as if they are possessed, even if they were overwhelmed. In that cultural context, a ME is always an affirmation: "No mystical tradition considers a transcendent source evil. Indeed, both introvertive and extrovertive mystics often have a sense that there is a fundamental rightness to things at the deepest level" (Jones, 2016, p. 322).

It is convincing that a cultural attitude or familiarity with a spiritual tradition will reduce a physical reaction. Accordingly, if there is a possibility of a numinous experience being of a more general, non-mystical or non-religious occurrence, then a creature feeling or a physical reaction may occur. The fact that Jung did not incorporate the creature feeling for a numinous experience that has no cultural referents, where indeed it may occur, may be related to the writings of Gerhard Dorn, the alchemist he believed most echoed his psychological process of individuation.

Dorn refers to alchemical stages that parallel the psychological individuation process (Von Franz, 1979). The first stage that is most relevant is that the spirit must free itself from the instincts found in the body, because, as Jung (1935a, para 104) puts it, "they had to loosen the age-old attachment of the soul to the body." The reason is: "to free the mind from the influence of the 'bodily appetites and the heart's affections,' to establish a spiritual position which is superordinate to the turbulent sphere of the body" (ibid., para 672). The numinous experience is a basis for transcending the body in this interpretation so that it takes the subject out of, not into, the body.

The third aspect of the numinous experience, according to Otto (1923, pp. 16–19), is a fascination with the experience: the "*mysterium fascinosum.*" Merkur (2006) provides a necessary distinction between the *tremendum* and the *fascinosum*. He points out that Otto (1923, p. 34) describes the latter as a "Dionysical element" that arises as a source of elation through metaphor, as it draws in religious comparisons. On the other hand, Merkur proposes that the *tremendum* is a trance that does not have immediate associations with religious or transcendent meaning. The trance allows a direct experience with no time perception, logical associations, or attention to anything other than whatever takes place within the trance. The potential existed for Jung to make use of this distinction, with the *tremendum* as the overwhelming experience and the *fascinosum* as an effect on consciousness.

Jung's "numinous experience"

Jung does not rely on the *tremendum* and *fascinosum* as a foundation or criterion for a numinous experience but willingly accepts that his own broad concept contains these two elements. He states:

> I am in the last resort encountering an aspect of God, which I cannot judge logically and cannot conquer because it is stronger than me –

because, in other words, it has a numinous quality and I am face to face with what Rudolf Otto calls the *tremendum* and the *fascinosum*. I cannot "conquer" a *numinosum*, I can only open myself to it, let myself by overpowered by it, trusting its meaning.

(Jung, 1959a, para. 864)

There is no direct reference in this statement to Otto's "creature feeling" of self-depreciation, and he describes the essential element of the experience as being overwhelmed by an aspect of God that is "stronger than me." It is written as surrendering to a force that is stronger and cannot be conquered rather than a depreciation of one's being in the face of the numinous. This combative approach of conquering or eventually surrendering arises perhaps from his conception (Jung, 1912/1952c, para. 551) that fear and the resultant negation are "the spirit of evil" and "only boldness can deliver us from fear." In this context, one can only be overwhelmed by a stronger force, as normally an intrusion would be resisted. Thus, the strength of the numinous experience overwhelms all defences, likely ensuring that it has an effect on consciousness.

This overwhelming nature of the experience, necessary in Jung's language for psychological change, is the touchstone of the numinous experience, which is then evidenced by the *tremendum* and *fascinosum*. The physicality of the experience by shuddering or any other bodily experience is not mentioned or suggested in any context. Instead, Jung (1942/1948, para. 275; emphasis added) is oriented specifically to the effect of the experience on the psyche: "The numinous character of these experiences is proved by the fact that they are *overwhelming*." In the *Zarathustra Lectures* (Jung, 1988, Vol. 2, p. 1038), he explains that the overcoming is historically the basis for creating the idea of a "divine" object in consciousness:

> The idea of God originated with the experience of the *numinosum*. It was a psychical experience, with moments when man felt overcome. Rudolf Otto has designated this moment in his *Psychology of Religion* as the numinosum, which is derived from the Latin *numen*, meaning hint, or sign.

This "hint, or sign" that is contained within the definition of "numen" is of a divine power, which is consistent with the religious exposition of Otto. However, Jung does not make any use of this aspect of "numen" as a hint or sign in his definition of "the numinous," even though he was aware of the similar manner in which Cicero and Pliny used those terms as meaning intimations or hints of the existence of a "Divine Mind" (e.g. Cicero, 1923). Elsewhere, Jung (1938/1940, p. 51, n. 15) relies upon Cicero for his definition of an archetype, and no doubt understood the connection of a hint as a divine revelation, but he chose not to incorporate it in his exposition of numinous experiences because his concern was not religious or mystical but psychological.

The use of the words and phrases "overwhelming," "overpowered," "over-come," and "stronger than me" describe the first essential quality of the numinous experience. An experience that does not have this character *would not be a numinous experience*, even if it were unique, unintelligible, alien, offered a hint of the divine, advanced the process of analysis, or was replete with insight and meaning. An example of this might be the appearance of an archetype in a dream that does not overcome the dreamer or even a lesser ME. It follows that the numinous experience must therefore contain sufficient force or power to produce an effect on consciousness, because it is overwhelming.

To be overwhelmed is often linked to trauma as it passes the historical psychological test that the experience is abnormal and would be considered traumatic to the majority of people as it is difficult to recover from the impact. A numinous experience differs from trauma in terms of overpowering because the affect and force of a numinous event arise solely as internal, psychic phenomena; they are not connected to an external event. It therefore exists fundamentally as a purposive function to present a non-ego position to consciousness; it is, in essence, a benevolent or healing function.

As a numinous experience is purposive (having the quality of being overpowering for the purpose of altering consciousness), Jung is satisfied with this dual, inclusive quality (overwhelming and altering consciousness), so he feels it is unnecessary to draw on any other refinements, examples, or theories. The numinous experience requires that both the subject (by receptivity) and the object (by its overpowering nature) meet at a singular point that constitutes the occurrence.

The content – images, symbols, setting – of the numinous experience is *functionally irrelevant* as its purpose in psychoanalysis is derived from it being sufficiently overwhelming to introduce and impress the subject with a position that is novel and to introduce a previously unknown quality of the psyche. The image or feeling of a union with the divine or the description of a vision does not need, theoretically, to be considered. Jung was certainly familiar with the revelations of many mystics: at the time of adopting the concept of the numinous experience, he had access to the work of other writers on MEs, such as Underhill (1990). He also had knowledge of William James's ideas and his more detailed indicia of a ME, although he did not discuss them. This is significant because James was perhaps the first writer on mysticism to focus on the experiential, subjective nature of mystical states (Tyler, 2011, pp. 8–13). Prior to James, the attribution of these experiences was to "orientalism" – mysticism being a particular Eastern cultural phenomenon – without examination of its subjective influence. The reason that Jung chose to bypass James and others in his enunciation of the numinous experience is that he was interested only in the revelatory power of the experience on consciousness, not in its content.

The indicia of James (1902/2008, pp. 278–279) are in fact logical and consistent with reports of MEs in spiritual traditions. He states that a ME is ineffable, has the "noetic" quality of a revelation, is transitory, and there is a loss of individual will. These underlying criteria are subsumed by Jung on the simpler basis of a numinous experience as an overwhelming, affective force that is received into consciousness. When looked at in terms of the impact on consciousness, the fact that an experience may be ineffable or is transitory is less relevant than if it is overwhelming. If it has an affective force that is stronger than the conscious mind, the impact of the noetic revelation on consciousness appears likely. It is in that formulation an instrument of change, while if, as James puts it, it merely "offers" a new frame of reference, the impact is more speculative. Jung (1942/1948, para. 274) was directed to such a likely change, not just a possible alteration: "It is clear that these changes are not everyday occurrences, but are very fateful transformations indeed."

The use of "overwhelming" as the criterion implies a likelihood of a change in the psyche but does not require a unitive experience. This is not only because, as mentioned, there are no cultural, mystical, or religious referents in his numinous experience; there is also a distinct lack of consideration of such referents as germane. This distances Jung from the hallmarks of the highest definition of a ME, where there is a strict insistence on the union of subject and object, so that the possibility of a non-unitive realisation is considered imperfect (Jones, 1996).

A unitive ME will always be a numinous experience. In historical expression, it is to the specific – higher-order – content of the revelation that mysticism turns: "An experience is mystical if and only if it contains a direct, vivid yet imperfect and always one-sided experience *of the divine itself*" (Walther, 1955, p. 22; emphasis added). This makes the appearance of the divine an overwhelming experience because it is "an original phenomenon" (ibid., p. 21), arising from the "divine itself" that therefore *must* change consciousness. This vivid occurrence of a direct fact, it has been suggested (Mezei, 2017, p. 221), is referring to an active force that identifies and declares itself, delivering a "radically personal message." It is the self-identifying revelation that is then overwhelming as the object, and in the case of a unitive experience, is irrefutable.

Because of its profundity, the content of even a lesser ME may provide a gripping encounter with a non-ego force that is the basis for an alteration in consciousness. The ME will appear to come from outside because, as Jung (1955–1956b, para 786) explains, numinosity is the equivalent of autonomy. The force generated by the surprise and power of the object is likely to require the ego to become aware of something other than its limited perspective. As it is sudden, overwhelming, and gripping, it offers a revelation or an awakening from what Sri Aurobindo (Ghose, 1970a, p. 1) calls a "somnambulist whirl."

Jung (1942/1948, para. 274) provides examples of numinous experiences: "conversions, illuminations, emotional shocks, blows of fate, religious or mystical experience, or their equivalents." The reason for this group of examples is to indicate that there are certain types of experience that are so powerful that they are likely to create an alteration in consciousness. As can be seen in the case of MH, who rejected an experience, it may be stripped of its numinous experience quality if it is rejected. However, the overwhelming nature of the examples is that they are likely to have the necessary effect of altering consciousness and therefore comprise a special category.

Prior to examining the examples, it is important to ask if there can be a numinous experience without an object with which to relate, such as the divine or even nothingness. The experience may be overwhelming and have an effect on consciousness, as can a lesser ME, but what then is received into consciousness? It is the effect on consciousness that is most relevant, and *something* must be revealed. The concept of *gnosis*, as used from ancient times, is that knowledge is revealed of a universality that reorients the subject by uniting the contents of the conscious mind to focus on what is revealed. The questions that it answers are: "Who are we? What has become of us? Where are we? Where are we going?" (Peck, 1968, p. 252). "This solution is found by situating ourselves within a vast system having our present situation as its center" (ibid.). The object of a revelation is not as specific as meeting the face of the divine or immersion in the black emptiness of the void; rather, it is the realisation of a non-ego force that is objectified by its otherness. The experience may reveal a specific object, such as the Virgin Mary, but the object to which the ego must relate is that of the "vast system" or the presence of a mysterious other. A specific object may be the doorway, but its significance is to open to that which lies beyond limited consciousness.

Each of Jung's examples has a "numinous character" because they are overwhelming (Jung, 1942/1948, para. 275). The use of "numinous character" is confusing here, because Jung also uses this phrase for experiences that are not congruent with the examples, such as the numinous character of each stage of life and the "numinous aspects of the moment" (Jung, 1953, Vol. 2, p. 209). The definition of "numinous character" is therefore broad, and invoked by Jung (1947/1954, para. 405) in relation to the appearance of an archetype as that "which can only be described as 'spiritual,' if 'magical' is too strong a word." He gives the example of an appearance of the archetype in the form of a spirit in dreams or fantasies, or as a ghost, and adds that it then has a "mystical aura" and a corresponding effect on the emotions: "It mobilizes philosophical and religious convictions in the very people who deemed themselves miles above such fits of weakness" (ibid.).

The choice of examples seems logical as a special grouping of experiences with a numinous character. However, although each category has a numinous character because it is overwhelming; an experience with a numinous character is not necessarily a numinous experience, according to the chosen examples. What is different is being overwhelmed by a numinous experience, not the spiritual or magical quality of that experience. The distinction is focused on the intensity, force, and power of the experience, which brings it into the higher–order category, as well as the degree to which it has an effect on the consciousness of the subject. In the case of MH, his vision had a numinous character but it was *not* a numinous experience because he rejected it. Jung recognises this in his discussion of the numinous character of the archetypes: these appearances may "be healing or destructive, but never indifferent, provided of course that they reach a certain degree of clarity" (ibid.). The "certain degree of clarity" means that they are likely to effect consciousness.

This may seem to be a distinction without a difference, but it is a functional and necessary refinement. A common mistake when analysing numinosity is to equate its appearance with the presence of a numinous experience. For instance, Corbett (2006) conflates numinosity that may appear in a dream with a numinous experience. This misunderstands that a numinous experience has numinosity because it is overwhelming and is likely to be received into consciousness, causing an alteration, not because it has a numinous character. This often overlooked distinction isolates the numinous experience as a particular and distinct form of subjective experience that is more than that which touches the spiritual or magical quality of the unconscious.

Each of these examples reflects references in other parts of Jung's opus that indicate and confirm the true nature of a numinous experience. They are not exhaustive but establish a genus of experience that has internal consistency and appears to be chosen carefully for this explanation. There is no mention of examples of the numinosity that appears in dreams or in relation to a symbol, only those that offer a direct route to revelation by the likelihood of profoundly altering consciousness.

Jung (1928b, para. 270) explains that a "conversion" – the first of the examples – is a religious conversion that may be triggered by suggestion, contagion from a group, or "independent interior processes culminating in a change of personality." The Catholic conversion of, say, Bernard of Clairvaux, is how the term is usually understood: a process that is brought about gradually by God's will (Bernard, Griffin, and Evans, 2005). Conversions are considered a form of religious rather than mystical experience because they are emotional, signifying some moving relationship with God (Dewey, 1969). For Jung, conversion may be triggered by suggestion and contagion, both of which work on the conscious mind, or by an inner process in the psyche; but the actual conversion event occurs *suddenly*, when the conscious mind is "flooded with extremely strange and apparently quite unsuspected contents" (Jung, 1928b, para. 270). The notion of being "flooded" is consistent with his definition of numinous experience as an intra-psychic, overwhelming event that is unrelated to its religious content or an external presence.

Conversion, as a particular form of numinous experience, therefore arises as an irruption – suddenly – although it may have been developing over a long period. Jung (ibid.) states:

In reality the irruption has been preparing for many years, often for half a lifetime, and already in childhood all sorts of remarkable signs could have been detected which, in more or less symbolic fashion, hinted at abnormal future development.

This preparation occurs in the psyche and is evidenced by signs, meaning that there is a continuing process of psychic build-up. The idea that there must be preparation for this particular form of numinous experience is not unique to conversions. Illumination, another of Jung's examples, refers to an illumination of consciousness that requires the "aggregation of many sparks" to provide the light of nature (*lumen naturae*) (Jung, 1947/1954, para. 391). His statement about preparation indicates that these forms of numinous experience are more than just disconnected, spontaneous occurrences; rather, they are the result of a gradual build-up of forces within the psyche that then break through. However, the emphasis in each example is not on how they were brought about or why they break through, but on their irruption or overwhelming nature and therefore their impact on the subject.

James (1902/2008, p. 168) adopts the idea that spiritual illumination is a form of conversion experience. Maslow (1970) suggests that "illumination" is in fact the peak experience, so it is an aspect of a conversion and a ME. Jung (1944, para. 11) approaches illumination as revelatory, as "an illumination of the soul," as "enlightenment," and as a non-rational "lighting up" of the unconscious (ibid., para. 68). It appears to be a more generalised state that is reached when revelations occur and have an immediate effect, as could be expected of a lighting up of the soul or an enlightenment experience. Illumination emphasises the existence of an alteration in consciousness more than the overwhelming aspect that is likely to have that effect; it is the end-product, not the means.

Emotional shocks – another of Jung's examples – are not just surprises that make one emotional, such as the loss of a loved one. In Jung's (1961, para. 595) terms, they are conceived as profound revelations of archetypal contents, which represent "emotional powers or 'numinosities.'" They are a reference to a breakthrough of powers that overwhelm and are likely to alter consciousness. These are not concerned with the appearance of an archetype, as may occur in a dream, but rather confrontation with the underlying archetypes of the autonomous, collective unconscious. The collective unconscious is an independent actor, and when it gives forth its contents, it may do so in a manner that irrupts overwhelmingly into consciousness. By their overwhelming nature, they are emotional and can produce a shock.

Archetypal contents are the primal unconscious forces within the psyche that by their nature are overwhelming when revealed. To confront the archetype is to be flooded by its power because, in normal circumstances, it stands hidden behind symbols and signs. This makes it an extraordinary event that highlights a breaking through into consciousness. The emotional quality is the after-the-fact conscious assessment of what has occurred: what Jung calls the "value" of an archetypal event (ibid., para. 596). It is not only the power of the archetypal event that causes the numinous experience in this case but the effect of it through the value it is given.

Jung (1945, para. 443) explains that revelation of the contents of the unconscious is not a minor experience but one that always has an effect on consciousness. He explains this in relation to the "shadow," the intransigent, unexpressed, unknown dark side of the personality:

> The question remains: How am I to live with this shadow? What atti-tude is required if I am to be able to live in spite of evil? In order to find valid answers to these questions a complete spiritual revival is needed ...
> The eternal truths cannot be transmitted mechanically, in every epoch they must be born anew from the human psyche.
>
> (Ibid.)

There is no comparison to be made between a unitive ME and an emotional shock in terms of content. In effect, the shock is less likely to reveal an absolute truth or have divine presence, although it may change the conscious attitude. However, in calling for a "complete spiritual revival," Jung is oriented towards a more profound awakening triggered by one of the examples rather than a slight or transient alteration of consciousness. There is, though, no call here that an individual must have a ME or undergo any of these revelations. An inter-textual reading reveals only that Jung was keenly aware that the weight and density of the conscious mind contain the seeds of our destruction and the unconscious can be the corrective. The numinous experience is closer to the spiritual revival, and how the numinous experience occurs seems secondary to the effect.

Blows of fate – another of Jung's examples – are, for him, a "determining power" that is the daimon or, expressed in another way, the will of God (Jung, 1951, para. 5). To experience a "blow" is to be overwhelmed by an undeniable power, and that implies an imprinter or God. A blow of fate is not expressed as a worldly event, such as the loss of a job or meeting a potential partner, but as an event so profound that it can be attributed only to divine will. Jung (1953, Vol. 2, p. 311; emphasis added) clarifies this in a letter about how to deal with the "blow of fate" of giving birth to a mentally defective child: "the question at once arises: Does the event have a *meaning*? Did a hidden purpose of fate, or God's will, have a hand it, or was it nothing but 'chance' or a 'mishap'?" In commenting on this letter, Edinger (1996) speaks of destiny that is ordained above gods and men so that it comes about by the exposition of God's will. Such an experience has the characteristics of being overwhelming and capable of altering the conscious mind by seeing God's will, even though the consequence may be devastating.

In all of these examples, an experience is overwhelming because of the breakthrough of an archetypal force into consciousness that is experienced as such. Jung does not include lesser experiences in his examples – such as a feeling of peace when in nature, heightened emotion when listening to music, or a sense of vastness when looking at the stars – even if they have a meaningful effect on consciousness. In referring only to the most profound examples, he is clearly making the point that a numinous experience is a more direct occurrence of a breakthrough from the unconscious that will thereby effect a permanent change on consciousness because it is of sufficient force to supplant the previous conscious position.

The Self, individuation, and the numinous

The construct of the Self is at the core of Jungian psychology as the emergence of the intimation of essential wholeness that lies within the psyche. Its realisation is a process of the introduction and understanding of a non-ego, central object in the unconscious. It arises gradually during the therapeutic process by the resolution of conflicts and the consequent integration into consciousness of the contents of the unconscious. The sense of unity that develops appears in dreams or other aspects of the analysis in the form of balanced symbols, such as a mandala or a cross. This wholeness, Jung (1951, para. 59) adds, "is thus an objective factor that confronts the subject independently of him." In his terms, the Self is an archetype of a totality or unity. He offers Christ on the cross as a primary Western symbol of this archetype.

The conflation of the Self with Christ proves, as Jung (ibid., para 305) explains, that "it has a numinous character." However, he is clear that this connection is not an actual unity with or experience of God, merely the appearance of a symbol of psychic wholeness, so it should be taken symbolically, not concretely. In explaining the Self, Jung (ibid., para 348) chooses to draw on the notion of Brahman and Atman – the Hindu ideas of an all-encompassing divine and the aspect of the divine that is within each individual. There is no question that he equates the Self with the divine essence and that there consequently exists a relationship with God that can be realised as a sense of wholeness (Stein, 2012).

The realisation of the Self is perceived as a connection with the divine and, in that sense, approaches a revelation that may be *parallel to* the outcome of a numinous experience. In describing the archetype of the "hero," Jung (1912/1952e, para. 612) adds that the "Self is numinous, a sort of god, or having some share in the divine nature." He is describing a numinous "quality" of "highly fascinating unconscious content which, like all contents, exhibits a numinous 'divine' or 'sacred' quality" (Jung, 1937, para. 448). The Self, however, is an ongoing process, a "circular opus" (Jung, 1951, para. 419), not a sudden, overwhelming experience, although its intimation is not precluded from arising in a ME. It is, he adds (ibid., para. 418), most importantly, "a step by step development of the self from an unconscious state to a conscious state."

The lesser forms of a ME may arise as intimations of the Self experienced as wholeness or peace that occur as insights in the course of the analytical process, but they do not have the same qualities as a numinous experience. These experiences may also have aspects of the Otto criteria, but they lack the impact of a conversion, illumination, shock, or blow. They may have the same effect over time of shifting the conscious position, but they are not numinous experiences because they lack the sudden, overwhelming quality that bypasses the process and creates a direct, affective engagement with the other.

It is not easy for an analyst to draw a distinction between higher-order numinous experiences and Self experiences of a lesser quality. For example, the Jungian analyst Dreifuss (2001) describes two early adult experiences: feeling oneness when listening to Schubert during a concert, and a realisation of the overpowering power of the Alps while hiking. He explains his path in life, with these experiences playing formative roles. In Jung's conception of the numinous, such experiences are related to *intimations* or symbols of a unifying principle in the psyche – the Self. They are not within the ambit of a numinous experience, no matter how profound. Self experiences do not possess the primordial force of any of Jung's examples, although they may contain the inherent possibility that they will be transformative. Jung's examples are so powerful that they *must have* – or at least *are highly likely to have* – a direct, immediate impact that changes the personality. It is the actual, embodied degree of power of the archetypal forces that makes their reception inevitable, thus conflating the nature of the numinous experience with its reception and creating a meaning event of the highest value.

Jung's examples are also not at all dependent on a realisation of God or the Self, although the fact that the experience comes from the archetypal contents of the unconscious suggests that, as he puts it, it comes from an "aspect" of God. In his terms, God is of a different quality: "God is the name by which I designate all things that cross my wilful path violently and recklessly, all things that upset my subjective views, plans and intentions and change the course of my life for better or worse" (Jung, 1953, Vol. 1, p. 525). The numinous experience is an experience of that aspect of God as it upsets subjective views, plans, and intentions and changes the course of life.

The examples of numinous experience are all derived from a primordial, archetypal force that breaks through into consciousness and not from the presence of a particular symbol or the existence of a state that carries an intimation of the Self or God. The connection is with the power of the archetype. In a discussion of instincts, Jung (Jacobi, 1959, p. x) refers to archetypes as having an autonomous nature, "that is to say, they are 'numinous.'" It is the evocation of the archetypal, numinous elements that creates the numinous seed of the numinous experience.

The best explanation of a numinous experience is therefore that it must be of such powerful, archetypal force and effect that it will be irresistible and cause a change in consciousness. The archetypal force is that which is primordial and carries with it profundity. Jung (1938/1940, para. 6) refers to an archetype generally as that which "seizes and controls the human subject, who is always rather its victim than its creator." This is consistent with his explanation in the Terry Lectures that such an experience causes a change in consciousness for the "victim." A dream image or an object may have numinous qualities that facilitate the possibility of an engagement with the Self, but a numinous experience is "a particular alternation of consciousness" (ibid.) brought about by a force that arises from the depths of the unconscious.

In his list of examples, Jung (1942/1948, para. 274) refers to "religious or mystical experiences." The disjunction has significance only in that the religious experience requires a link to a divine being or creator God and is therefore extroverted, rather than just an internal self-reference (Smart, 1974, pp. 366–367) or one where there is no conception of God. The distinction can be made clearly in the case of Theravada Buddhism, where numinosity arises when there is no conception of a transcendent God. It has been suggested that, except for this form of Hinayana Buddhism, there is really no difference elsewhere between the description of religious and mystical experience because the presence of the divine underlies all experiences (Jhingran, 1981).

Nothing turns on the distinction between a religious and ME because the nature of either is that it is overwhelming in that it "convince[s]," as Jung (1938/1940, para. 167; original emphasis) points out in relation to affective symbols: "They are *overwhelming*, which is precisely what the Latin word '*convincere*' means." They do not convince because a choice is made that it is a good idea to accept what has happened; rather, the experience itself causes the result without any possibility of resistance.

Consistent with this concept, Schlamm (1991) has defined "mystical experience" as a particular form of numinous experience that emphasises the *tremendum* quality, while Neumann (1948/1969, pp. 380–381) has asserted that the two are in fact one experience: "Every numinous experience, whatever form it may take, is mystical."

The relationship of a numinous experience to the process of individuation raises the question of their consistency as the former is elevated to an unusual, atypical event. The process of individuation (Jung, 1921, para. 732) is concerned with becoming a psychological individual who is distinct from the general, collective psyche; it is the "extension of the sphere of consciousness" (ibid., para. 762). Conceived widely as the goal of personal development, it would include, when they occur, numinous experiences. These experiences in this context would be perceived as accelerating or sudden transformations of the widening of consciousness.

Jung proposes various directions for development in the individuation process and feels the alchemy of Gerhard Dorn provides a useful explanation of its various phases. The initial aspect of the first phase is the development of an ego that is sufficient to relate to unconscious revelation. This is very much a task of the first half of life. Dorn (Jung, 1955–1956b, para. 671) proposes that to attain the "unio mentalis" or interior oneness, the mind must be separated from the body "to establish a spiritual position which is subordinate to the turbulent sphere of the body." It arises in psychoanalytic practice by the realisation of affective states so that the instincts become crystallised as psychic objects and no longer operate autonomously at deep, unconscious levels. This initial task of interior oneness with the instincts – or, as Jung (ibid., para. 675) describes it, "the attainment of full knowledge of the heights and depths of one's own character" – is rarely completed, because, as he points out: "A permanent and uncomplicated state of spiritualization is ... such a rarity that its possessors are canonized by the Church" (ibid., para. 672).

The second aspect of this first phase is withdrawing the soul from the body. This is very much grounded in the idea that the spirit must free itself from matter and partake of the possibility of higher wisdom. This is a difficult stage because there is, as Jung (ibid., para. 674) suggests, "a conflict between the natural and the spiritual man." The second phase is the reunion of the spirit with the body: the "reuniting of the spiritual position with the body" so that the insights "should be made real" (ibid., para. 679). The final phase is the union of consciousness with the *unus mundus* – the "complete conjunction" (ibid.).

Perhaps the most significant phase, which Jung does not emphasise, is making the insights real by embodying them in the body. This is the form of realisation arising from Dorn's stages that suggests a new form of consciousness becoming permanent because it is grounded in the body. This is a reference to either the process or the result of solidifying the Self or having a deeper relationship with the centre of the psyche by embodiment. In this context, a numinous experience is a vehicle to deliver the insights that are part of the process of individuation, perhaps in intense, condensed form that are embodied. It allows the primordial archetypal constellations to break through, adding to previously gained insights, and, because of the overwhelming character of the experience, there is a stronger possibility of it becoming part of the "Real." Sri Aurobindo (Ghose, 1973, p. 117) explains that there are different ways in which this may occur:

> [W]e may say that the Real is behind all that exists: it expresses itself intermediately in an idea which is a harmonised truth of itself; the Ideal throws out a phenomenal reality of variable conscious-being which, inevitably drawn towards its own essential Reality, tries at last to recover it entirely whether by a violent leap or normally through the Idea which put it forth.

The goal of the individuation process, in these terms, is the transmutation of the Ideal to the Real. This may be accomplished by stimulating the archetypes behind the Ideal and bringing them to consciousness through the phases suggested by Dorn or by a numinous experience that is a "violent leap."

Preparation for a numinous experience

Jung indicates that in the example of conversion, the "irruption" was building up over many years. The same is hinted at for illuminations, but not for emotional shocks, blows of fate, religious experiences or MEs. Preparation is not a *requirement* for any numinous experience, as described by Jung, because it is impossible to know what will trigger it or even create a state where it might occur. Instead, the emphasis is on the autonomous unconscious acting without conscious control so there are no necessary plans to make and execute. In commenting on the notion of "self-liberation," Jung (1942/1948, para. 284; emphasis added) states:

> If, through introspection and the conscious realization of unconscious compensation, it is possible to transform one's mental condition and thus arrive at a solution of painful conflicts, one would seem entitled to speak of "self-liberation." But ... there is a hitch in this proud claim to self-liberation, for a man cannot produce these unconscious compensations at will. He has to rely on the possibility that they *may* be produced.

A numinous experience cannot be expected by conscious acts of preparation. This applies for Jung also to attainment of a perfected state by stages on a spiritual path. He insists that enlightenment or a completed state of absorption through religious or spiritual practices is unavailable because the Western mind is focused on the one-sided, outer dimension of conscious objectification. Accordingly, that complete merger with a non-ego force is only a "meaningless dream-state" (Jung, 1935/1953, para. 785). If there is no path to enlightenment and no practical way to trigger a numinous experience, the build-up in the case of conversion is of a non-directed series of occurrences arising from the unconscious that had that effect. However, this cannot be achieved by conscious religious or spiritual practices or any deliberate strategies. This applies to all numinous experiences, including MEs.

The basis for religious and mystical experiences is in fact that preparation is indeed the essence of all traditions, and the experiences are the end products. Accordingly, prayer and meditation receive prominence in the narratives that explain the achievement of such experiences. This is based on the clear idea that the mind can be trained to loosen its conceptual obsession to permit a more direct perception of underlying reality. For example, in the Buddhist practice of *anapanasati* – or awareness of the breath – the effect is to make the mind sensitive, still, focused, and present so that it will reach a purified, non-cognitive state that confers insight. This occurs because the concentration on the breath inflowing and outflowing provides a refuge from the normal cacophony of the mind from which awareness then grows.

From a psychological viewpoint, as the Jungian analyst Walter Odajnyk (2011) explains, meditation practice offers the possibility of states of consciousness not otherwise available to the day-to-day mind, and, in psychoanalytic terms, provides the space that activates complexes and archetypes. The activation of complexes and archetypes – a psychoanalytic concept – when it occurs through meditation, has the effect of offering a process of subtle awareness and reflection. A breakdown of the stages of meditation in Tibetan Rigpa Chog-zhag meditation suggests how this can occur (Lutz, Dunne, and Davidson, 2012, ch. 19). In the first stage of practice, there is concentration on an object, such as breathing, a mantra, or a visualisation. In this early stage, it is in the nature of a mental exercise that may, for that reason, result in drowsiness or distraction. It is a necessary, preliminary stage, however, as it strengthens the capacity of the mind to concentrate. In the next stage, there is an awareness or observation of the activity of the mind and therefore the development of reflective awareness. The importance of reflective awareness is to turn the mind inwards and to perceive the mind as an object that is always thinking. The third stage is where the thoughts are able to be rejected before they occupy the mind. The final stage is where consciousness alone turns completely inwards, meaning there is no subject or object.

If this is the operational effect of Eastern practices, analysis is another form that causes reflection by, as Jung (1936c, para. 875) explains, continuous confession in an analytic session that helps "the unconscious to reach the conscious mind and to free it from its rigidity." Both of these processes – Eastern and analytic – yield a lessening of the dominance of ego consciousness and a distancing from the operation of the mind, leading to a possibility of holding and therefore resolving the existence of opposites. That resolution leads to a recognition of the importance of a non-ego force and an awareness of the weakness of intellectual reasoning, as Sri Aurobindo explains: "I never admitted a truth in the mind without simultaneously keeping it open to the contrary of it. And the first result was that the prestige of the intellect was gone" (Ghose and Purani, 1995, p. 199).

Jung's focus in reference to preparation for conversion reflects the possibility that repeated exposure to the moral conflicts inherent in religion creates a tension of the opposites and consequent reflection. In this sense, the idea of preparation for a ME by meditation or by reflection on the nature of mind is therefore theoretically consistent with Jung's notion of the inward direction of psychic energy to its internal source, where it builds to create a breakthrough. The reversal of the instinctual energy comes about because of reflection, where the libido or life energy acts to resolve conflicts. According to Odajnyk (2011, p. 146), it is when the concentration of energy is focused inward by meditation that "consciousness begins to accumulate."

The idea that preparation through meditation will, at a particular stage, result in increased reflection and therefore the accumulation of psychic energy is, however, inconsistent with the notion that the unconscious is completely autonomous and impervious to manipulation into a particular position to trigger a numinous experience. As Jung (1935/1953, para. 782) explains, the unconscious may fail to cooperate even though it is activated by the inward concentration of libido. In speaking of meditation, which he does in relation to the contemplation practices of Ignatia Loyola that were focused on placing oneself in a scene from the Gospels (Jung, 1943, para. 937), he concludes that outside this particular form of meditation, "the thing does not as a rule work, or it may lead to deplorable results" (ibid., para 939) because it activates the chaotic aspects of the personal unconscious.

If these different ideas may be summarised, Jung's view is that the unconscious may be activated by meditation and its contents are then blended when consciousness dims so that there is a feeling of indistinctness and therefore oneness, which gives practices the appearance of efficacy. The activation of the unconscious *may* occur by an inward accumulation of psychic energy through analysis and reflection during meditation, but the occurrence of a numinous experience is not enhanced by deliberate practices. In this arrangement, the numinous experience is a manifestation of the unconscious breaking through unexpectedly, regardless of preparation, to deliver a view of itself as revealing a distinct other.

Jung's ideas were explained in the 1930s when there was no Western concept of preparation for a ME. This was probably because there were no established Western equivalents of the states reached, few Western mystical explanations, and linguistic difficulties in describing the phenomena (Yaden *et al.*, 2015). The Western need for specificity has since searched for rational definitions and standards to describe the endpoint but not preparatory practices. As an example, the "Mystical Experience Questionnaire" was developed using the insights of James (1902/2008) and the operational definitions of Stace (1960) for research into the nature of psilocybin mushrooms (MacLean *et al.*, 2012). The contemporary result is appropriation of Eastern preparatory practices by those who are not part of the esoteric and subtle teachings of the meaning of various states and their appearance in the hierarchy of experiences. As a consequence, the effect of Eastern preparatory practices on the development of a ME for a Western subject is unclear.

It is now beyond doubt, however, that there is a strong belief that a ME may be triggered by various events. James (1902/2008, p. 293) asserts that a ME may be brought on voluntarily through ritual and practices of various traditions. Accordingly, it appears there *may be* experiences where preparation will yield a numinous occurrence, but there are others where preparation in a particular, overt way is not responsible. The possibility of preparation as a triggering factor does not preclude the occurrence of a process that is based on, given the ideas of Jung, an intra-psychic build-up of psychic energy that yields a breakthrough of consciousness. The preparedness in this formulation is then on the unconscious level, not necessarily reliant upon external forms of practice or spiritual teachings, although these may add to the build-up.

Preparation on an unconscious level by meditation is not necessarily causal in conjuring a ME, but it does create other important effects. It may, for example, create a familiarity with introspection; it could make a subject more comfortable with a confrontation with repressed elements; or it could create that gap in consciousness between an event and a reaction. From a psycho-analytic perspective, it is a *skilful* practice that does not lose its efficacy because it may not cause a numinous experience.

In describing a numinous conversion, Jung does suggest that preparedness is a build-up over time of the necessary energy so an irruption into con-sciousness of an unconscious force may occur. He is not expressing it as acting causally so that there may be said to be a sequence leading in a progressive manner to a numinous experience. The numinous experience *may* take advantage of the build-up of psychic energy, but it *must* arise from somewhere else to break through into consciousness. That something else arises within the unconscious acting autonomously, removed from all other factors, to reveal itself in this manner. Jung's best approximation is that it comes from the force of the indwelling, historic, collective unconscious and not from the personal unconscious: "The unconscious is prodigiously strengthened by this reflux of libido, and through its archaic collective contents, beings to exercise a powerful influence on the conscious mind" (Jung, 1917/1926/1943, para. 150). In this explanation, the unconscious is "strengthened" and begins to exercise an influence, but the breakthrough is not by that factor alone; it requires activation of the primal archetypes of the collective unconscious. The exact cause of the activation at a particular point in time is speculative. Jung (1921e, para. 427) initially postulated a "transcendent function," or the tran-sition to a new attitude when the libido rises up from the unconscious and provides the revelation of the "original, potential wholeness" (Jung, 1917/1926/1943, para. 186). He is clear that this process has "nothing mysterious or metaphysical about it" (Jung, 1916/1957, para. 131). To describe the actual manner in which this happens at a particular time, however, he explains the alchemical need for the "balsam" or "caelum" (Jung, 1955–1956b, para. 691) – the heavenly substance that brings about the transition. He uses the term "Mercurius" to describe "the process by which the lower and material is trans-formed into the higher and spiritual and vice versa." This is a "reflection of a mystical experience of the artifex" (Jung, 1943/1948, para. 284), the latter being the alchemist who attempts to reconcile the coincidence of opposites.

This resort to another force – be it described as balsam or Mercurius – to bring about the transition requires an immersion into a mystery that is incompatible with psychological theory. The lever for the actual experience is not the build-up of psychic energy but rather a hidden, indescribable power that causes the activation of the archetypes of the collective unconscious and the breakthrough. This is convincing because the unconscious is not personal but rather autonomous or "objective," meaning that there must be a moment when it is triggered independently of the subject. Accordingly, it is difficult to say that it can be coaxed through preparation into activating that lever that creates the actual breakthrough. All that may be said is that preparation by the indwelling of libido makes for *possible* activation of the unconscious ele-ments or creates a unique conglomeration of elements that needs a spark for them to ignite. This is consistent with Jung's (1928b, para. 204) idea that the "unconscious is never quiescent [at rest] in the sense of being active, but is ceaselessly engaged in grouping and regrouping its contents."

As all of the mystics interviewed for this work had a meditation practice, the role of meditation in MEs was taken as given. However, for MH, there was no history of either meditation or prayer. He had an experience where there were no predicates as opposed to one that may have come from – or was at least consistent with – a cultural or spiritual tradition. The contents of the Virgin Mary may be explained by his Catholic upbringing and his continued attendance at Mass and Confession. What caused the breakthrough could have been aided by the continuous build-up of libido as he questioned his own faith, or maybe the work we did in analysis caused him to reflect on his psy-chic conflicts. But, equally, it may have been that the super-added ingredient of Mercurius or that indefinable heavenly substance acted on the psyche for its own purpose when there was a particular grouping of unconscious material.

Preparation does not guarantee a ME, but it can lead to altered states. In many instances, the promise of the pot of gold at the end leads the mind to rearrange an altered state to reach a feeling of congruence with such an occur-rence. This is not, however, a unitive, absorption experience. Even *samadhi* – absorption and loss of ego identity during meditation or prayer – does not necessarily yield a ME. There may be no overpowering revelation, merely a blanking out. There are different forms of *samadhi* in Hindu Vedanta. It is suggested (Sivananda, 1954, p. 137) that absorption may be easily disturbed so that real, full absorption requires a very subtle practice: "he who releases with an intelligent, calm, uniform force the mind that is slack ever so little from slackness and the distracted mind from distraction, drives it towards the goal."

The preparedness idea is attractive to psychoanalysis because it implies gra-dual appropriation of unconscious contents for consciousness. In an ego-based therapy, the cornerstone that the ego has primacy means that the unconscious is brought under control in terms of its mysteries. With the exception of Lacan, where the complete otherness of the unconscious means it cannot be integrated, the gradual unveiling of the contents of the unconscious in various steps is more appropriate so that it can be addressed and understood. The numinous experience described by Jung is therefore closer to Lacan than ego psychology because it requires an acceptance of the existence of that which is alien and autonomous. It postulates the absolute otherness of the unconscious that breaks through in a manner that is overwhelming to the ego and therefore incompre-hensible, requiring for its effect that it alters consciousness by its revelation. In fact, the claim that preparedness is unnecessary for a numinous experience is a radical statement for Jung because it undermines the concept that the indivi-dual is a unity within a predictable structure to which unknown parts are revealed over time. It is even an argument against mysticism, as it presents an unmediated form of revelation that lacks any special, theoretical underpinning. Leon Schlamm (2006) appropriately described Jung as a "post-religious or detraditionalised, western visionary mystic."

By not specifically addressing the question of preparedness or locating the experiences within a tradition or with writers of the time, including James, or discussing it in its own context rather than during discussions about another topic, it is clear that Jung is simply isolating a phenomenon of the psyche. It is a unique, unprecedented description of an event that is not pathological and falls within a legitimate psychological category. For Jung, this could be a reaction against Freud's (1930, p. 71) statement that such an experience is indeed pathological, as it is merely "a restoration of limitless narcissism" of the helpless infant. Freud drew the connection between mysticism and pathology in 1929–1930, while Jung proposed the power of the numinous experience in 1942. Another reason could be Jung's personal numinous experiences: Freud (ibid., p. 65) admits, "I cannot discover this 'oceanic' feeling in myself," whereas Jung (2009) certainly evidences his familiarity with an encounter with the other in his *Red Book*.

There is no real similarity between Jung's numinous experience and any other spiritual or religious tradition. Its closest analogy in terms of a psychological structure is perhaps trauma. Caruth (1996, p. 4) explains that trauma cannot be defined by the event itself or by a distortion of the event through discussion, but rather by its effect of returning to the subject as an uncontrollable phenomenon. As mentioned, trauma differs in many ways from a numinous experience, but it follows the same course of the ego being overwhelmed, leading to a change in consciousness. It is ascribed to an external event while the numinous experience is an internal irruption or breakthrough of accumulated libido.

By not basing the experience on preparation, Jung is able to avoid the forms of religious or mystical experience that are over-determined by a religious or spiritual tradition. Although there is a mystery attached to the final breakthrough, he makes it a psychological event that is concerned with the ego being overwhelmed by the archaic, embedded, archetypal core of the unconscious, occurring in a state when the ego consciousness is diminished. It is an act of supplanting the ego with the unconscious that does not result in psychosis but in a new, healing perspective.

It is hard to leave it at that when the final mystery of what takes the preparation (in the case of spiritual traditions) or a build-up of libido (in the case of a numinous experience) to the final breakthrough remains unresolved. The fact that its report is culturally determined or a psychological event still leaves open the question of how the experience unfolded at a particular moment in time. At best, it may be said that it is part of the "immense world forces in their perfect play" (Ghose, 1970a, p. 324); or, from the point of view of psychoanalysis, it is the autonomous working of the psyche. Nothing further may be added.

Chapter 3

Working with the experience

A ME, however described, and Jung's numinous experience have in common that they have the potential to change the conscious position by the revelation of non-ego forces. When it appears in analysis, it needs to be contained for its potential and also as it may be harmful by leading to an inflation because it is so powerful and offers a revelation of a previously unknown truth. It should be seen as likely that, to a greater or lesser extent, the one-sided ego consciousness will appropriate the experience, creating an object cathexis where the alien but profound revelation will add to the ego's grandiosity.

The mystical or numinous experience that is brought to the consulting room creates the opportunity to contain this exceptional psychic phenomenon within the analysis. To work with the experience, it is necessary, as the first condition, for both analyst and patient to treat it as a legitimate occurrence that is capable of being analysed. The paradox is that it is impossible to trace the content of the narrative to specific psychic forces as the primal archetypes are unavailable to be analysed, yet the material of the experience contained in the narrative arises within the analytic encounter. Bion was of the view that discussion of the contents of the experience was not the means to achieve a change in consciousness. Instead, it was useful for the patient to *be* the O. Jung was similarly clear that interpretation would in fact harm an experience. However, the narrative that explains the content is there in the session and cannot be ignored.

There is a case to be made for consideration of the contents of the experience, as this will bring material to light that appears to have importance for the psychoanalytic work, much as a symbol or figure in a dream. However, the clear limitation is that it is impossible to sort out any psychological issues that were the bases for the content and even how that content was amplified or altered during cognitive processing. The symbols and images in a unitive ME, unlike those in a dream, are not likely to be analysable because they are products of primal, collective archetypes that may not be accessible. The narrative, imbued with primal material, offers nothing that may be relied upon as useful for dealing with personal issues.

In the case of a unitive or numinous experience, the contents cannot be analysed but need to be explicated in some way to bring home the significance of what has occurred for the purpose of legitimising the experience and as a prelude to investigating the effect on consciousness. This inability to unravel the contents of a ME because it is informed by primal archetypes may not, however, be the case for lesser experiences, where a different approach is possible. In fact, it is most likely that a patient will not present a ME or numinous experience of an overwhelming, full absorption into a mystical object but rather will explain a lesser experience, such as an intimation of the Self, a connection with nature, or an emotional flooding from music. Merkur (2010, p. 206) suggests that these are the common experiences and even proposes that they should be considered MEs: "Everyone is a little bit of a mystic, some few of us more so." A lesser experience, although not traditionally classified as a mystical or numinous experience, will have some effect if it raises in the subject a new attitude towards the mystery and encourages further exploration. These fall short of Jung's examples and the common measure of a ME, but analysis is still feasible through the content.

Indeed, lesser experiences are more amendable to analysis than a full-blown unitive experience. For lesser experiences within spiritual traditions, a teacher is important to turn them into a direction where none may be apparent. The cryptic stories of Zen masters, as an example, offer a framework to enable the capacity to work with a lesser experience. Analysis, if the lesser experience is properly understood, may offer that possibility of providing a form or forum for the appreciation of what has occurred in psychological terms. If analysis is unavailable, the individual is more likely to begin to embrace a tradition in order to establish a path where there are understandable logical rules, standards, and moral observances, the most common being battling against the instincts. These are the spiritual hooks that await the first revelation and turn the lesser experience into a path. In Western patients, it can be observed by them reading from different traditions, seeking out teachers, or embracing Eastern practices before entering analysis.

If the analyst is unfamiliar with the tradition in which the content of a lesser experience is referable – be it Buddhist, Hindu, Sufi, or Kabbalah, to name a few – there is a danger that the contents of the experience may be misinterpreted or the mystery quality remains absent in the field. One patient reported that a former analyst had told him not to meditate with his palms up, as was the practice in his tradition, because it was making him too sensitive. This denied the patient the effect of having an experience in this way and eventually led to a breakdown in the analytic relationship. Accordingly, if the analyst has no interest in these experiences, they cease to be legitimate and are no longer a proper subject matter for analysis.

It is understandable that an analyst may have no particular interest in or knowledge of spiritual traditions for many reasons, such as a non-professional taint or a desire not to be marginalised. The absence of a tradition on the part of an analyst may, however, be beneficial for analysis for unitive experiences. A numinous or unitive experience – as a sudden, overwhelming occurrence – is outside a spiritual tradition and may have a greater likelihood of altering consciousness because it remains more alien to a patient than a mystical or religious experience within a tradition. For the analyst, it is "cleaner," less burdened by interpretation, and more open to a psychological rather than a spiritual explanation. Furthermore, the levels of the path in spiritual traditions may categorise what has occurred as a lesser experience, thereby deflating for the analyst the potential impact on the subject.

If a patient has no tradition in which to categorise what has happened, there is a greater danger of feeling overwhelmed and failing to report the experience as it may hint at pathology. Even if the patient realises that an experience may fall into the category of a ME, there is no quick explanation from a tradition or book or talk that they can immediately utilise to place it in a context because the descriptions are all as alien as the experience. In these circumstances, analysis may be the only way forward for full explication of the occurrence.

These concerns for the relationship of the experience to psychoanalysis suggest at least three relevant factors when working with a ME or numinous experience. The first is that the experience, whether within a tradition or outside one, must be made legitimate for the patient as well as for the analyst as a subject matter for analysis. The second is that the content of the lesser experience is relevant because it is admixed with cognitive evaluation and is not therefore necessarily blurred by the intrusion of the unknowable primal archetypes. The third is that for a unitive or numinous experience, emphasis during analysis should shift away from the content and towards the effect on consciousness.

Legitimacy of the experience

An experience will be made legitimate when it is accepted by the patient and the analyst as a truly mysterious phenomenon that has occurred. The critical importance of legitimacy is that it allows the experience to become an object that may be examined, discussed, and evaluated in the analysis. As with MH, or when there is an analyst who gives the experience no credence, it is weakened in its possibility of creating an alternation in consciousness as it is not a subject matter for elucidation.

If an experience has created a change in consciousness, that change will, in itself, become apparent and bring the occurrence into the consulting room as legitimate. This assumes that the experience has been positive. Mystical experiences that are framed within a tradition will be considered representative of a stage on a path and inherently positive. A negative experience may be reinterpreted in that context as part of the working through of the tradition.

Achieving legitimacy by amplifying the positive nature of the experience is not necessarily the case with various classes of numinous experience, such as a blow of fate or an emotional shock. It is possible that these will be bordering on pathological or merely unpleasant, bringing new material into the analysis but denying the experience itself. Jung, in statements scattered throughout his work, indicates that blows of fate and emotional shocks are evidence of the operation of divine will, but that does not prevent a person from having a negative reaction to them. In either case – mystical or numinous experience – the overwhelming experience may be analysed if it has created a change of consciousness. If it has not, because it is insufficiently overwhelming or the subject rejects the experience as it is too negative, it will probably not be analysable. If the experience is negative but not rejected, it must still be legitimised in order for it to be subject to analysis. In this case, the content may become even more important as offering a hint of what effect this has had on consciousness and the message that has broken through. However, it is important to understand that the cognitive aspect of the experience may have contaminated what has arisen, turning it negative, and that realisation can create a different direction for the progress of the analysis.

The issue remains as to the basis to be advanced for the legitimacy of these experiences when they are absolutely unique and not part of cultural norms or expectations. Agehananda Bharati was a distinguished, Western anthropologist who became an Indian monk – a sadhu, initiated into the ten-name (Dasnami) sect of Hinduism – and reported several unitive mystical experiences. He grappled with the question of how a ME may be proven, borrowing from the ethnoscience, linguistic approaches of "etic" and "emic," which are used to describe the bases of reporting cultural experiences (Bharati, 1976). An emic statement is one that is valid in terms of a standard used by a group of people, such as other mystics. Such standards are built up by that group and tradition over time and are regarded as accurate, legitimate, and real by the members of the group. Etic statements are verified when scientific observers, such as anthropologists, agree that an event has occurred. If a person proclaims that they have had a numinous experience, such as a oneness with the divine, it must be seen to be emically legitimate by fulfilling the criteria that are universally accepted among mystics and not just etically by some other psychological measurement. Accordingly, a person who continuously declares, "I am a mystic" and has had a "zero experience" (ibid., p. 25), *ipso facto*, has had a legitimate ME. The fact that they consider it a legitimate experience and then put it in the context of a traditionally explained ME makes it a real object from which an alteration of consciousness may be determined. Bharati (ibid.) proposes that the test of a full, unitive ME is simply a person's "intuition of numerical oneness with the cosmic absolute, with the universal matrix, or with the essence stipulated by various theological and speculative systems of the world." Accordingly, if a person describes a unitive experience – or one of the other forms of ME, such as the Buddhist realisation of nothingness – they have had such an experience and it is inherently legitimate.

The finding of legitimacy will arise for many patients who have had an overwhelming experience because there may be symbols or objects in the contents that allow it to be brought into the consulting room and classified as a ME, even if it is not unitive. That, in itself, does not mean that it will alter the conscious position, but it perhaps fulfils the basic first step of legitimacy that then allows the possibility of its evaluation after the fact.

Jung supports this position that the self-proclamation of a numinous experience – or perhaps any lesser experience – is, in itself, legitimate. He explains that an individual's insistence that they have had a religious experience must be accepted because it brings that conversation to an end: "What is the criterion by which you could say that such a life is not legitimate, that such an experience is not valid, that such *pistis* is mere illusion?" (Jung, 1935a, para. 167). The symbols arising in that experience are those that are convincing because they are overwhelming and have altered consciousness. Jung adds, "It must be a very real illusion, if you want to put it pessimistically" (ibid.). This reference to "illusion" should not be ignored as it relates to Freud's (1927, p. 31) definition of an illusion as derived from a belief resulting from wish-fulfilment. The fact that it could not be refuted because it arises from that source was Freud's basis for the "reality value" of the experience. It does not matter if, from the point of view of an outsider, the experience can be doubted; invariably, for the person who has and reports the experience, it is legitimate.

The importance of Jung's formulation to ascribe legitimacy to a numinous experience is to be understood in the relationship of that experience to ego consciousness. The conscious mind always has a need to dominate, and the intrusion of the unconscious leads to "disagreeable and intractable affects" (Jung, 1921b, para. 626). From this perspective, the ME obtains its legitimacy from its ability to overwhelm the ego in a positive or negative way, thereby establishing a relationship with the ego. This relationship is the fulcrum for understanding the effect on consciousness and therefore it should not be compromised by a failure to accept what is presented.

Jung made the ME legitimate for psychoanalysis, linking it with wholeness, the Self, and the process of individuation, but also placing it *within* analysis as a subject matter. In this sense, it is a relational concept that presents to the analyst an unintegrated, undifferentiated affective experience that is given significance because it is the ultimate revelation of the contents of the unconscious. This must be acknowledged by the analyst because it touches upon the evolution of consciousness and the role of analysis in the future of humanity.

There is no need for the subject to enter into a vitrified mystical oneness from which no slippage is possible in order to be recognised as legitimate. Legitimacy arises when there is an acceptance by the ego of the experience because an alternation of the conscious position may take place. If this is the case, an experience that overwhelms and potentially causes an alteration of consciousness may be of a lesser nature than Jung's list of examples. The latter is just that – a list of types of numinous experience with similar forms that are likely, by their nature, to have an effect on the ego. They constitute a class where the ego is most likely to be overcome and accordingly change its scope and realisation.

It is impossible to define the bottom line for an experience to qualify as within the realm of numinous or mystical and give it legitimacy on that basis because the test is the result that it had or is likely to have an effect on consciousness. A figure in a dream, a feeling of déjà vu, a hallucination, a synchronistic event, or any manner of experience that sets up a relationship between the ego and an overwhelming non-ego phenomenon may qualify if it has the capacity to alter the ego consciousness. To set rules or demarcations is to feign understanding of what is occurring and to diminish what has occurred. Hence, the only method of assessing a numinous experience is to accept that it has occurred *because* there has been an alteration of consciousness. For a lesser ME, it is accepted because it may have an effect. This is not a matter of degree but a statement that a change has occurred – or is likely to occur – that has some nexus with the experience and that this makes it legitimate as a subject matter.

This approach focuses Jung's limited class of numinous experience as a particular type of experience that cuts through the process of individuation; it is, by its force and effect, most likely to alter consciousness. However, when working with these experiences, they should be treated in analysis as just another form of unconscious revelation. They differ because of their intensity and the likelihood that they will accordingly alter consciousness. If they are lesser, but legitimised, they enter the analysis as one form of unconscious disclosure and, from that point, their content becomes relevant.

Cognitive evaluation of the experience

There is philosophical debate as to whether a ME is a pure subjective experience or essentially a cognitive event, where the thinking mind is always engaged. Merkur (1999) expresses reservations about whether a mystic can ever eliminate the psychic objects of consciousness and have a pure experience. In this view, every such experience is constructed or at least influenced by previous conscious elements. Forman (1999) is the foremost exponent of the ME as a pure event as there is no object existing during a unitive event. The only solution to this dilemma in understanding how a narrative of the content is constructed is to treat the experience not as a single event but as one that is made up of different stages. This approach is verified by the interviewed mystics' ability to break down their experiences into a *progression* of states – from beginning to end.

The difficulty with the philosophical debate is that it resorts for proof to the reports of historical and well-known mystics or their spiritual doctrines. Jung, for example, attributes the occurrence of conversions, illuminations, religious or mystical experiences to major religious figures, such as Moses, St Peter, St Augustine, Martin Luther, Joseph Smith, Ramakrishna, and others who have been hailed as prophets or recognised as mystics. These extra-ordinary or "mana" personalities, as he calls them, did not report stages of an experience but rather a singular, unitive event. Forman (ibid., pp. 20–21, 140–146) reports his own meditation practice twice a day as the basis of his observations of integrated non-cognitive experiences.

The literature has paid no attention to the stages and progress of a ME from its outset until its completion for various reasons. The stages of recognised experiences attributed to mana personalities are unavailable for this breakdown as they derive their significance from the concluded, focused revelation. There is little reporting of MEs for lesser mystics. Any mention of a ME in Western society starts a conversation about an oddity, the content of which does not accord with prior knowledge, discouraging logical assessment of the sequence that occurred. This is especially the case in Western religion as there are no direct biblical references to stages. The progress or state that arises during such an experience, being an atypical, one-off event, is therefore not recorded.

In support of the notion of different stages, in addition to the reports of mystics themselves, neuroimaging has indicated that many areas of the brain are active during a ME, offering a theory of "multisensory integration" where the information from various sensory inputs – such as vision, sound, and smell – combine. These inputs arise from external stimuli and the body and it is said that this "corroborates that a changed activation in areas involved in spatial and bodily processing may be at the basis of mystical and flow-like experiences" (van Elk and Aleman, 2017, p. 366). Accordingly, for different parts of the experience, there are various inputs as it is occurring, leading to specific, distinct activations.

Ignoring the stages of an experience and focusing on the whole limits what may have been the constructive, cognitive parts that mixed with the occurrence to create an overall narrative. The ME has relevance for psycho-analysis only to the extent that it is contained within a presented narrative that is constructed by the occurrence. For this to be explained, there has to be an emotional and cognitive response to what has occurred, and some means by which it has been digested in order for the narrative to form. This creates an opportunity to look at stages of the experience as aspects of a process that has occurred, or at least a pointer to some internal movements that may be recognised.

The full range of emotions upon having a ME are not usually described, other than in a common, positive way – ecstasy, bliss, or another feeling that is more a summation of the end product rather than the sequence of the

process. The Zohar lyrically speaks of delight and pleasure on attaining realisation (Hellner-Eshed, 2009, pp. 279–290), referable to the use of the term
"delight" in the Book of Isaiah (58:14). However, the actual change or variation in emotions during the ME is more complex as it depends on images
that are presented or the various states that arise in sequence.

The onset and passage of a ME may be perceived as transpiring over a brief
moment or a substantially longer period of time. Not one of the interviewees
was able to record the amount of time as the unitive nature of the experience
leaves no means to address the outward, worldly movement of surroundings
or people. It appears to the subject as one experience encapsulated within the
onset and end. However, further refined, there is an initial onset, the moment
after the onset has occurred, just prior to the experience reaching a peak, the
peak itself, coming off the peak and moving towards an ending, and the
ending itself. The onset and peak experience were treated as instantaneous by
two of the interviewees, but all of the others recognised an intermediate
stage of awareness just after it began. There was also a clear observation of
the experience fading – in some cases as quickly as it arose, and in others
more gradually. This parsing of the experience is not explained in spiritual
traditions because the experience is taken as a single blended moment with a
defined, understood nature.

The feelings or impressions about what occurred at each stage, as described by
the interviewees, covered a large range, complicated by linguistic differences and
means of expression. However, there appear to be some common elements that
were shared by all as the experience began and then ended, as well as in relation
to each stage. Having to describe the stages was unnatural for the interviewees as
the experience was expected to be explained as a single occurrence. In two cases,
as mentioned, a single unitive experience was indeed described as an instant
merging with a divine force, but others reported seeing different images, at some
stage having a divine force enter the body, disappearing into a hidden realm
before ending, observing the world around them when they opened their eyes as
without colours, and also witnessing bright light.

The overall impression gained by dividing the experience into stages is that
the onset is always overwhelming, even if the subject has had previous
experiences. It appears that memory of a previous experience is not a factor in
the experience of the onset or the passage of stages. There are no differences in
the intensity of being overwhelmed anew because the nature of the experience
is that the ego consciousness is pushed out of its prime position with a
resultant loss of identity; therefore, it is a single feeling. The likely explanation of the unimportance of memory is that when the subject had this
experience previously, it was subsequently integrated, forming part of the ego
consciousness. The fresh onset was described in all cases as a moment of slipping out of ego consciousness, including memory. If a subject had had previous MEs, they recognised what was occurring just prior to being absorbed.
However, this had no effect on the initial onset of an overwhelming force.

The moment after the onset is not entirely free of impressions as it may be recognised as the beginning of an altered state and immediately placed in a spiritual or cultural context. Thus, there is a moment of awareness following the onset where a cognitive evaluation may take place. This state blends into a pre-peak stage that sets the structure for the unitive, peak experience so that the subject enters the peak with some parameters. The distinction between the post-onset and pre-peak stages was slight, but there was a recognised difference. One Indian interviewee compared it to taking a dead body to be burned and turning the deceased's head to face the burning ground when the halfway point on the procession from home is reached. It was considered a turning away from the material world to the peak. The pre-peak is the setting for what is to come, when the surprise of the overwhelming after the onset of the ME gives way to what it portends.

The proposition of there being a universal, peak unitive state derives its force from the existence of an independent presence that is pre-existing and does not in any way relate to the structure of ego consciousness. Ramakrishna (1974, p. 736; original emphasis) explains: "Nobody knows what remains after the 'I' disappears. Nobody can express it in words. That which *is* remains." As it is a singular presence, it cannot have variations. The peak is a witnessing of that pre-existing presence that is unrelated to ego consciousness, so that "Whatever you meditate on, you are not that! Whatever you observe, you are not that" (Nisargadatta, 1996, p. 32).

Some of the interviewees reported that there are moments immediately prior to entering the peak state and on exiting that state where the conscious mind is engaged and may – because of linguistic, cultural, religious, and traditional fragments – attempt to interpret what cannot be interpreted. The engagement of the mind then recalls visual memories and appears to work in concert with these other linguistic, cultural, and personal elements in order to develop an explanation by providing a form of what occurred. The presence of the Virgin Mary is then a cognitive pairing with vision and memory to produce an interpretation of the peak experience.

This is *not* how MEs are usually described, because they would be demeaned as constructed by merely pre- or post-peak interpretation. It is a subtle issue because that moment of peak experience is non-cognitive and cannot be given a meaning as it occurs. Yet, the *sense* of merging with God or nothingness arises as a subject begins to enter the peak and afterwards, as the peak fades. There is this particular level of awareness of what is occurring in each ME because the peak experience provides a new revelation: "Even though its inherent nature has existed from the very beginning, you have not recognized it; Even though its clarity and presence has been uninterrupted, you have not encountered its face" (Odier, 2005, pp. 78–79).

If there is a revelation of an absolute truth as the essence of a peak experience, it consists of two parts. One is the phenomenon of the loss of ego and therefore a moment that has no cognitive dimension; the other is an awareness of a truth. When this was suggested to the interviewees, they were able to recall a sensation that differed from a physical sensation but constituted a knowing of a truth at that moment. It has been described by the early twentieth-century Jesuit Augustin Poulain (1996, p. 99) as a special mode of feeling, comparable to a sensation of smell, without image or object – as an interior touch – a variant of our normal senses.

It is possible that there is awareness within the peak itself, making it the experience of an undifferentiated sensation or perception. This is perhaps why it is often described visually as illumination or light, which is the non-specific sense impression around which various concepts have formed, such as a spiritual body and soul:

> Clement [the second-century Christian theologian] tells us that this light is essential – that is, real in the Platonic sense and not a mere sensory phenomenon. It is without shadow, but above the opposition of light and dark. It was first, prior to this dualism. It conveys adequate insight; it is comprehensive vision viewed as an act, and, as a result of this act, pure intuition.
>
> (Pulver, 1985, p. 252)

For Jung (1921, para. 795), "sensation" would not be the correct term as that occurs within conscious awareness; rather, it is *intuition* that arises and is characterised as unconscious perception. It would, in a psychoanalytic sense, fit that the subject could have an intuition of the revelation of a primal archetype or pre-existing truth at the peak moment. However, a closer examination of the experience reveals a different pattern in which the cognitive frame is active prior to the peak and frames the peak. There is, for all MEs, an initial entrance into an altered state: that is, one different from the previous conscious state. This is an awareness understood cognitively as the mind still operates when this state has been reached and perhaps intuits what it is to come. This blends into the pre-peak where the expectation is there as to what may occur and a frame is formed. Then there is the peak itself and a blanking out of the mind as it is absorbed. That blanking out results in a state where there is no longer a subject and *nothing* may be experienced: no sensation, no intuition, no light. It is only in the instant before consciousness is lost – or just after – that the frame arises and persists.

The only evidence for this rather mechanistic approach rebutting the idea of an intuition of a truth occurring during the peak is that each experience is so different when reported. If a singular truth were intuited, there should be some consistency. A Sufi mystic may perceive that God is looking through the subject's eyes to view His own creation; a Hindu will consider a merger between the Jiva Atman (the individual part of God) and the Brahman (the universal divine); and a Buddhist may experience awareness of non-self and "no thing" (*nirvana*). Unlike cognitive processing, the perception of a truth as an intuition does not require it to have different forms or contents. It is more likely that the truth derives its variations from the contents of the unconscious as it is brought to consciousness and assessed by the ego. It initially "comes to you" (Jung, 1935a, para. 69) as unconscious contents that arise "from the a priori inherited foundations of the unconscious" (Jung, 1921b, para. 659) – the archetypes. The archetypes therefore present in endless variations; and, in the case of a peak, with an underlying substrate of the archetype of wholeness.

Consistent with the idea of an underlying archetypal dimension, Ross (1992, p. 90) has argued that intuition causes the subject to perceive things holistically and therefore "discern a spiritual dimension in secular phenomena." This would suggest that the intuitive function would also operate in the peak experience to discern only the gestalt – wholeness – of the revelation, even if there is no cognitive assessment. There are indeed cognitive models of intuition (Larue and Juvina, 2016) that propose that, in the recognition of wholeness, the intuition is not pure. There are, it is suggested, three elements at play: an autonomous element for fast processing; a cognitive control process; and a deliberative event. All of these combine with intuition to provide information according to the current goal recognised in the onset or pre-peak that could suggest a more refined cognitive awareness during the peak.

In the interviewees' reported experiences, the intuition–cognition sequence is linked, so, at some point, the intuitive appreciation of a peak, unitive experience is deliberated upon and a decision is made in the peak to give it some form in order to make sense of it. Jung (1961, para. 577) accepted "One can understand and explain only when one has brought intuitions down to the safe basis of real knowledge of the facts and their logical connections." The sequence is likely to be swift because the subject matter is displacing the primacy of the ego and requires rapid interpretation because it can otherwise be expected to be subject to some negativity due to its alien presence.

It is only one explanation that the blending of intuition with cognition – perhaps one fast and the other not far behind – means that experiences that are unitive may sometimes be described as having other forms that do not reflect what occurred. This can arise when the perception or intuition of an absolute truth is immediately converted by cognition into a non-unitive story. The experience of the divine looking through the subject's eyes to witness its creation is the pinnacle of some traditions, but this does not suggest a loss of identity in merger; rather, it makes the subject a witness, perhaps rewriting the moment of the peak experience. The effect of the variations of experience in spiritual traditions has been to shift the emphasis away from the variation of the contents of a unitive experience to the singular perception of an absolute truth. That truth, in this example, may be the existence of the divine, one's relationship to God, and the nature of the world as God's creation. In the case of a Buddhist approach, it is the recognition of the lack of self and therefore of nothingness. It is therefore a case for assessing the experience in terms of an overwhelming experience – one that revealed an absolute truth – and it is this that changes consciousness. It may be that the alteration of consciousness is sufficient to prove the revelation, for, without it, there would be no change.

The common feelings of fourteen interviewees who commented upon each stage bears out this analysis. The reported feelings were:

- Onset:
    - surprise;
    - momentary confusion;
    - excitement (but not yet bliss);
    - disorientation;
    - feeling of loss of control of thinking;
    - fear;
    - in all cases, amazement; but
    - no bodily sensations.

- Immediately after onset:
    - cognitive awareness of an altered state characterised by peace, calm, and relief.

- Just prior to the peak:
    - cognitive evaluation of what was happening as a special experience and what may be coming next;
    - awe; and
    - further letting go into the experience.

- At peak:
    - knowing, intuition, or perception of – or connection with – a truth;
    - loss of any ego-based desire or will;
    - radiating warmth through the body;
    - "wide-eyed" openness;
    - absence of time;
    - bliss; and
    - fearlessness.

- Ending of experience:
    - immediate attempt at cognitive understanding;
    - feeling of connection with the divine, or that something had been revealed; and
    - feeling of being blessed.

- End of experience:

  - amazement;
  - continued feelings from peak, but lessened;
  - objects more vivid; and
  - formation of an explanation of what occurred.

The interviewees generally did not allocate these feelings to a process of deliberative thinking or detailed analysis immediately after onset, but rather to a bare awareness of peace, for example, or awe. Although this diminished awareness is an aspect of cognition, it also involves the "feeling function," which Jung (1921, para. 735; emphasis added) describes as a "kind of *judgment* ... to set up a subjective criterion of acceptance or rejection." This contains a cultural component related to shared values (Alho, 2009), meaning that it is not an intuitive knowing at this point but mediated by other factors that are extraneous to the experience. The wide range of reported feelings also suggests a blurring of cognition, intuition, and feelings that were present in some form at different intensities during the peak.

For all, there was a definite moment when a cognitive observation was made just prior to complete absorption. It was described as a momentary thought that an experience was unfolding that thereby produced a feeling of awe. It had no emotional content but rather was an observation – and explanation – of the magnitude of what was occurring in which the ego was still present and a dualism remained.

Several interviewees preferred to emphasise the existence of feelings during the event, denying any awareness of thought or classification. The onset was said to be characterised by a *feeling* of amazement and excitement mixed with an element of fear as the conscious mind becomes aware that it may lose control. The awe and fear were said to be alternating and in no fixed sequence. Even for those mystics who had many experiences, the elation or excitement was there each time; and fear, even if minor, was perceived. There was then, at that stage, an easing into a universally recorded peace as the ME continued, not so much from emotions relating to images but rather because of the weakening of cognitive assessment and evaluation as well as the feeling of either timelessness or a slowing of time. As one interviewee explained: "I could have been in that state for ten minutes or a minute but I was so focused on or lost in what was happening, I lost track of time." The gradual ending of the peak presented a clear chance for all interviewees to begin the evaluation of the event as full cognition entered, although the feeling of having been on a unique journey remained strong.

The interviewees were all self-declared mystics who had had previous experiences, some greater and some lesser. However, most significantly, they reported that each experience was as new as the next and contained the same series of stages, so that no previous occurrence or preparation prevented the initial onset experience of surprise and a similar pattern of feelings and cognition. Since they were, however, oriented to the benevolent nature of the experience, each occurrence was recorded as positive. Moreover, each peak experience was perceived to be different, revealing another aspect of an absolute truth. The revelation was not a refinement of a truth previously presented but rather a new truth that supplanted all that had come before. These new revelations all fed into the subjects' spiritual traditions, where others had previously recorded such revelations, but they were still revelations of what had not been previously understood or not yet made personal.

These are reactions to the unfolding of a ME but are not necessarily descriptive of an experience within a Western religious experience, strictly defined as occurring within a religious discipline. None of the interviewees could make that distinction as each interpreted what had occurred as a non-denominational, inward, subjective experience of a divine merging. They were, as Stace (1960) explains, "introvertive" unitive experiences as opposed to "extrovertive" occurrences of the revelation of truth found in the doctrines of others.

Beyond Jung's examples, a ME may not reach a unitive peak but still may reveal a revelatory truth that has an effect on consciousness. Unlike his category of "mystical experience," there are no known narratives that speak of the unfolding of an emotional shock or blow of fate in mystical terms. This suggests that, for psychoanalysis, the stages discussed by the interviewees are relevant in understanding how the narrative was formed: the constructs that were placed around the experience to create that explanation.

A prior orientation of an occurrence as mystical or religious, rather than an experience that is akin to a blow of fate or an emotional shock, may be the cause of the lack of negative experiences for mystics. Such an orientation comes from being part of a tradition that has, as its goal, the full unitive experience and provides the conditioning for the experience. These traditions become embedded in the psyche and form a psychic infrastructure against which any experience is measured and which is impermeable to other traditions. During discussions with Theravadin Buddhist monks in Thailand, Bharati (1980, p. 159) found it impossible to explain how they might reorient to his Hindu ideas because they had no concept of gods, and "entertaining such strange notions as 'Being' and 'God' is something pathological." Conditioning in a culture where MEs are the highest attainment and where the populace is regaled with the mystics' experiences embeds a view that not only ameliorates variations but also accounts for the loss of negative experiences and physical reactions. However, this is not necessarily the case where there is no connection with mysticism.

All of the interviewees, patients, and those who were examined as relatively contemporary mystics failed to report physical reactions when explaining their passage through the stages of the ME. In Otto's *tremendum*, the experiences were within a context in which a terror in the presence of God permitted such a reaction. This is not, as explained, a current context. This does not deny the possibility that the subject may experience what has been called a "painful sense of nothingness" (Hunt, 2007, p. 214) or some sort of physical reaction, but that a culture, or even a sub-culture, will have an orienting effect on the manner in which the experience activates an individual. This returns to the philosophical issue between "constructivism" (which takes into account the effect of culture on a ME) and "perennialism" (which accepts the existence of a universal ME as outside culture) (see Gellman, 2007).

All of the interviewees emphasised their non-cognitive explanations of their MEs to highlight that there is a mystery beyond our understanding. Imbuing a full ME or even lesser experiences with this mystery facilitates speculation that there is indeed "something" beyond our cognitive limitations or that what was understood or perceived involved a subtler process. It is that something we postulate that must exist prior to our interpretation of it, either imaginatively or symbolically. This has the result of forcing a conscious jump from an unknowable mystery to a workable explanation regarding what occurred after the peak experience. As a matter of timing, the jump is actually made earlier, as the experience begins to sink into one's being as disruptive of normal, waking consciousness and requires some resolution.

The peak experience offers an indelible truth that is outside consciousness and so, by definition, is reached without the intellect. James (1902/2008, p. 380) calls it: "States of insight into depths of truth unplumbed by the discursive intellect. They are illuminations, revelations, full of significance and importance … and as a rule they carry with them a common sense of authority for after-time." The proposition that the truth cannot be reached with intellect suggests that the narratives that follow may be *un*trustworthy, even though there is an intuitive perception. The complete removal of the discursive intellect from the revelation of truth as it is occurring means that it is hidden behind an impenetrable veil and can be reached only by subjective or perceptual awareness. It is only this non-cognitive form of perception that then offers a direct connection to the truth, even though it may be subject to a diluted or holistic cognitive glimpse. The mechanisms of non-cognitive perception are still subject to scientific debate (Block, 2011), but in all traditions the intellect is discounted because it diminishes the reality of the absolute truth. It was utterly rejected by all of the interviewees.

Lacan's insights are highly relevant to the nature of the revelation of truth. As a primary thesis, and expressed in various works, he believed that the unconscious was structured as a language. Accordingly, it uses the same fundamentals with rules of grammar that are the building blocks of the spoken word and writing and can therefore change one word or the exposition for the benefit of others to explain the same phenomenon. The subtleties of language would account for the different versions of what is revealed as truth, as it may be interpreted by perceptual awareness in endless variations of the language of the unconscious.

The nature of that truth, however it varies, is that which was pre-existing but previously undiscovered. It may appear in the course of the experience in the form of images that are foreign or bizarre, but it yields a certainty that what is being conveyed is a glimpse of a reality that previously could not be known. The truth is unrelated to any previous description that is available because it is novel to the subject; and, even though cognitive processing may still be present, it offers a depth that is unobtainable through intellectual analysis or explanation. The teachings of sages at this moment of revelation are irrelevant to the experience as the truth is entirely personal, even though it may subsequently be fitted within a tradition. As the truth is revealed, there are no analogies, no precedents, and no thoughts because the revelation is of something that comes as a complete and utter surprise. It is knowledge that has not been previously intuited, known, or anticipated.

We know the essence of these absolute truths because they have been explained in reports of countless MEs: we are all one; the divine is pure love; we must do God's bidding; the end of suffering is found in nothingness; we are pure consciousness and that is deathless. As Sri Aurobindo (Ghose, 1970a, p. 625) reminds us, "A thousand aspects point back to the One." Yet, the truth will not be delivered to us personally and it will lack the quality of revelation, unless it overwhelms the mind to supplant – for a moment – the intransigent, walled-in ego that has defined the world in a predictable structure. Accordingly, the peak experience delivers its truth for as long as is necessary for the ego to be supplanted. The ending of the peak begins only after the truth has been delivered, so continuation beyond that is not purposeful, meaning its duration is related to the time needed for its unfolding.

All of the interviewees saw the truth, when revealed, as self-evident, causing a common reaction of either laughter or bemusement. They reported that it had been there all the time, and was obvious when the reality was finally understood. In all instances, a narrative crystallised around the truth to bring clarity and produce "One small seed of spiritual certitude" (ibid., p. 499). Thereafter, further answers or revelations that were consistent with the revealed truth were sought. The wide-open not knowing becomes more focused and, although there were new experiences, they did appear to serve that same narrative by its expansion or subtlety. The new peak experiences did bring new insights, but these did not alter the earlier narratives.

The revelation of the truth presents an indication of not only what is important but also what is not. It leads to a denial of what was rational before and supplants it with what is initially a feeling of the paucity of that rationality. This dismissal of the rational may lead to nihilistic statements that are contrary to church or spiritual doctrine, such as those that resulted in the early condemnation of Meister Eckhart (Kikuchi, 2014, ch. 2). The feeling then reforms over time to become doctrinal as the new revelation is absorbed as part of a narrative. In the case of spiritual traditions, as the truth is grounded in a conceptual, shared position, it leads to it embedding in personal, subjective viewpoints. The counter-argument has been made (Jones, 2016, p. 38) that "mystics are not really interested in doctrines at all but only in attaining the experiences – the doctrines do not matter at all but are merely a raft to be jettisoned once we have the experiences."

In spiritual traditions, the revelation of the truth is only the starting point on the road to full absorption of a deeper truth that is both profound and doctrinal. This is because what occurred in the first experience develops into faith in the tradition as the peak confirms the established, traditional narrative. The tradition has concordance with the peak experience in all instances because the actual revelation establishes a new intra-psychic relationship with the mystery – the presence of the "silent nearness of the soul" (Ghose, 1970a, p. 502) that requires an explanation.

The imperative to start looking for an explanation or a point of view immediately after the peak experience arises because the revealed truth may at last offer a chance to be free of stultifying complexes, which requires that what has occurred must be compared to what has been. A problem could be that this discovery of a real truth in the midst of the failure of normal "truths" may yield nothing but illusions, as interpretations are the salve for the neurosis, as Nietzsche (1960, pp. 46–47) suggests. The truth thus revealed encourages many interpretations as it appears so real and indelible that it needs to be accessed through the conscious mind to ground it in thought so the ego can relate to it as an object.

The objectification of the truth by adopting an interpretation can turn the experience into a stagnant, psychic phenomenon after it has had an effect on the ego as it will lose force as time passes after the experience. The original experience then becomes a story that has marvellous qualities and accordingly fades in its impact on consciousness. This may explain why the revelation does not dissolve the longing in all cases; instead, it persists and requires more, as suggested by the gradation of MEs that fall short of full absorption. It could also account for the existence of a continuing path in spiritual traditions. The phenomenon of "longing" reinforces earlier, lesser experiences and provides the ego with an opportunity to carry the hopeful narrative forward. The longing also arises from that "nearness of the soul" experience that is the siren call for neurotic relief. Grotstein (2004, p. 1081) postulates a "truth drive" arising from what he calls the "Absolute Truth." This effect of the longing is true not in a mysterious sense but in a psychological frame because such a positive subjective experience, objectified into a narrative and no longer with the same impact as time passes, remains full of curiosity as to what has occurred and creates a search for more.

The ending of the ME is in two stages: the slipping away of the peak experience and then the complete secession of the experience. One of the interviewees reported: "It seemed that the divine had finished imparting what it wanted and then moved on to the next person, leaving me to figure out what occurred." There is a moment when the peak stops and it is at this point – just before the ME ends – that intellectual evaluation begins. The evaluation is initially a survey of what has just transpired followed by the process of setting up a framework of what it meant. The ending leaves a state of amazement at what occurred as well as lingering subjective absorption in the experience. However, as the subject returns to the reality of full ego consciousness and the absorption starts to fade, the search for a means to understand what has transpired intensifies.

The peak experience is therefore assessed by intellectual cognition both at the moment when the peak ends and certainly after the ME is over. According to Schlamm (1992, p. 550), this after-the-fact analysis of the experience brings in analogies and the need for an interlocutor who has previously processed such an experience:

> Often on first acquaintance they appear to the mind as inchoate, an elusive and tantalizing confusion, and thus we cast about for analogies for these confused religious experiences, which are provided by Otto's language about the *tremendum* and *fascinans* moments of numinous experience. We use the better known to elucidate the less familiar; and the moment of insight into the relatively unknown numinous feeling occurs at the same time as the choice of analogy for it, although it must be emphasized here that the choice of analogy can only be subsequently understood by someone who has already had a numinous experience.

The search for analogies assumes that they may be found, and here the subjects tend to resort to a spiritual or religious tradition because these are the only analogies that are available to them. However, if a subject is already or becomes conversant with a particular tradition, they will find analogies to follow, but these may confine the experience. Gershom Scholem (1941, pp. 5–6) explains:

> [T]here is no such thing as mysticism in the abstract, that is to say, a phenomenon or experience which has no particular relation to other religious phenomena. There is no mysticism as such, there is only the mysticism of a particular religious system, Christian, Islamic, Jewish mysticism and so on.

In this context, Schlamm's assertion that the understanding occurs with the help of someone who is already conversant with MEs makes sense: someone who has passed through an experience will be able to assist the subject with an understanding of what they have experienced. Previously, of course, the helper will have drawn on analogies and will have interpreted their own experience through the lens of a tradition. This limitation of the experience to a tradition or evaluation with the aid of someone who has already had such an experience may not be harmful to its reception in consciousness. The true meaning of the experience and its content are not accessible, so it is useful to develop a frame to carry it forward. In the absence of a frame, it would create unbearable loneliness and a possibility of crossing over into psychosis as the power of the experience on the psyche is then unmediated.

The choice of tradition with which to understand the ME is irrelevant. It is the experience itself that operates on the psyche, not the tradition, because the former offers a new object in consciousness that has the potential to alter the conscious position. It is beyond the scope of this work to explore why a Westerner might choose a particular Eastern tradition, but it may be said that there is a powerful necessity to place the experience within a context that takes MEs into account, and this is more likely to be found in ancient Eastern traditions. The truth that is slowly fading will continue to have an effect only if it has a context that is extraneous to the experience; otherwise, it will become corrupted by random information or ideas. Unless there is full, complete absorption into the experience, there will be a search for more. This is a never-ending process that will seek explanations wherever they may be available – in religions, spiritual traditions, esoteric teachings, cults, psychological orientations, and literature.

Full absorption is such a rarity that it will probably never arise in the day-to-day practice of psychoanalysis. It is the province of mana personalities and, even then, there is always a lingering question of the proof of perfected states from which there is no slippage. Sri Aurobindo (Ghose, 1973a, pp. 1061–1062) believes that our species is incapable of continuously holding the absolute truth and thus a new species is required, but "One might conceive of a number of individuals thus evolving separately in the midst of the old life and then joining together to establish the nucleus of the new existence."

Only one of the interviewees (an Indian monk interviewed in Pushkar, India) raised the possibility that he had no need for his waking consciousness – his ego – in order to have a relationship with the mystery as he was always in full, unmediated absorption. Whatever he was, he was beyond my understanding, and in answer to the question of how he became like that, he answered, "I was born this way." In response to the question I posed to a senior Buddhist monk of whether his fully absorbed state was available to me, he replied, "No. Not possible. I have a bricklayer's mind." For me, this raised the idea that the need to have a ME relate to the ego will always bring with it intellectualising and theorising beyond what is necessary to appreciate what has occurred. The discursive intellect is always vigorously engaged by educated analysts and patients in any discussion or presentation of a ME. The confusion of the spirit with intellectualisation, a complaint made by Jung in a letter to Wolfgang Pauli about Christianity (cited in Meier, 2001, pp. 116–117), has largely turned the understanding of MEs into a refined, philosophical object.

The role of the intellect for Jung's numinous experience provides a useful insight into the nature of this category. The process of cognitive evaluation is available not only for a ME or religious experience but also for a conversion experience. Ullman (2013) points out that a conversion can vary in intensity and may include the presence of a mystical revelation, allowing all of the stages of a ME. Furthermore, the effect of the conversion may arise by a process and not an event (Rambo, 1993), suggesting that it has stages, allowing cognition. As it is emotion laden, there is a period in which it will build to a moment where a truth is revealed that constitutes the pivot for the conversion. It therefore arrives at a peak, and after the event the subject enters into a cognitive assessment of the experience in terms of the tradition to which conversion is directed (Paloutzian, Richardson, and Rambo 1999).

The possibility of staging is different for emotional shocks or blows of fate as they are not so easily conceptualised after the fact because no particular framework is available. They both suggest a trauma that arises that may have different processes. As mentioned, there are indeed clear similarities and differences between the qualities of a traumatic experience and a mystical occurrence (Ataria, 2016). In terms of staging, a trauma may involve a bodily reaction – a non-cognitive result of an experience with no framework prior to that experience. It will not necessarily be transient as is a ME, it will be disruptive to the ego, and there will be no easy cognitive assessment that will alter consciousness in terms of presenting a non-ego aspect to consciousness.

The inclusion of blows of fate and emotional shocks in Jung's list of examples is very telling and indicates that his purpose in creating a generalised category of numinous experience is to disengage completely from the content of the experience and be concerned only with its overwhelming nature and, most importantly, its effect. The attribution of the source of the experience to God's will or other insights is not as straightforward for blows and shocks or as likely as those associated with all the other categories – conversions, illuminations, religious or MEs. Moreover, for a blow or shock, it takes not only cognitive assessment to alter consciousness but also greater receptivity for an event that has no apparent context. This means that the gap between the experience and the meaning event will be greater but the possibility of a change in consciousness is there in all events because of the numinous, archetypal power of the encounter.

Patients who enter analysis are too often subject to blows of fate or emotional shocks in the common sense, and there does not seem to be any direct connection between those experiences and a positive, significant alteration of consciousness. Instead, trauma, dissociation, or a loss of agency is more likely to occur, and there will be little evidence that the ego consciousness has become aware of the non-ego component of the unconscious. Their inclusion in the list of numinous experiences makes sense only on the basis that they are overwhelming and *offer the possibility* of a change of consciousness. This supports the thesis that a numinous experience exists only if it has an effect on the conscious position by revealing the not-I. If the experience occurs and is too difficult to examine, it may be barely a subject of analysis and will not, in itself, continue to have potential to alter consciousness.

Alteration of consciousness

The test of a ME is categorically that it has had the effect of altering the previous position of the ego by revelation of non-ego forces. The ego holds two fundamental positions in relation to the unconscious: it consolidates its position where possible to be the dominant structure in the psyche; and it resists any attempt to relinquish its ascendancy. As a result, the unconscious material that breaks through does not necessarily change consciousness because it comes into conflict with the ego as it represents a non-logical force that is always a threat. An alteration of consciousness is thus, at the basic level, the *successful* intrusion of the unconscious that changes the conscious position in some manner.

The ego is best described as that which operates by awareness of psychic facts provided by "a general awareness of your body, of your existence, and secondly by your memory data" (Jung, 1936, para. 18). It is necessary for the ego to develop a relationship with the unconscious because "nothing can be conscious without an ego to which it refers" (ibid., para. 17). The ego seeks dominance by abrogating the revelations of the unconscious for its examination. The revelations are hard won as it has a natural tendency to resist the appearance of a non-ego force in the unconscious.

A good description of the ego as limited and a cause of suffering is described in the doctrine of Tantra (Anandamurti, 1982, p. 192). It is explained that it is the source of suffering because the ego is subject to three powerful bondages that limit it and turn it into a walled-in system. The first is physical bondage, because the ego must contend with economic, political, commercial, and other mundane, material issues. These physical constraints are further divided into other barriers, such as the restrictions of dogma and the barriers of time and space, which impose limitations and exert pressure on the ego. The other two types of bondage are: psychic, such as mental clashes, complexes, doubts and confusion, and the resultant reactions; and spiritual, including the sense of failure due to the non-attainment of spiritual elevation.

The depiction of the ego as a closed system that is the source of suffering and limitation creates a belief that pervades all spiritual and religious traditions: that the answer will be found *outside* the ego. According to the contrary position of Žižek (1989, p. 44) in his discussion of Lacan, a person is always seeking a "secret supposed to be hidden in the Other." This arises because the subject is "excluded from the secret of the Other" (ibid., p. 66) and implies that the Other – the unconscious or the effect of spiritual attainment – contains the answers that are needed to relieve suffering. In Žižek's thesis, this cannot be found, as any experience will not provide what is required: "the Other itself 'hasn't got it' – hasn't got the final answer – that is to say, is in itself blocked" (ibid., p. 122). In this view, the search or longing is a never-ending source of suffering of the ego, as it gives rise to the desire for the ego to transcend its limitations but which is unavailable in the Other, be that God, nothingness, or the unconscious.

This concept of presenting a new, radical conscious position to the ego that can alleviate suffering is explained as follows: "A principle characteristic of this experience involves transcendence of one's personal identity and dissolution of a primary conscious force on or grounding in one's ego" (Levin and Steele, 2005, p. 89). The notion of transcendence – of finding a non-ego source – is offered through seeking the realisation of the transcendent truth of a divine figure with a resultant shift in the ego position: self-transcendence. It is fundamental to psychological theory and is an observable fact that self-transcendence is responsible for relieving neurosis. In all of the descriptions, this is necessary as the ego is envisaged as a "natural sloth" so that the "mental and moral sloth which keeps us so comfortably wrapped in unrealities must go" (Underhill, 1920, pp. 12–13).

The measure of the effect of a ME is in understanding the specific manner in which ego consciousness is altered to relieve neurosis. There is therefore no simple approach as to what degree of alteration is sufficient to constitute the psychological benefit needed from a ME to alter consciousness. This lack of certainty is essentially because a ME may have varying effects on the conscious position. In Zen practice, the *paramitas* – or parameters – of enlightenment consist of ten states, so the first awakening has a minor effect on consciousness and is only a foundation for the remaining nine steps "which goes on to develop the capacity to attain" the final enlightenment for oneself and humanity (Cleary, 2001, p. 632). In this formulation, the ME is germane as having an effect on consciousness when there is a lesser form of awakening but requires further capacity or receptivity for full attainment. The ultimate goal is therefore the ultimate alteration of consciousness as it is what relieves the ego's limitations.

The conclusion drawn in the explanations of the levels of experience in mystical traditions is that the first experience – or a continuation of many lesser experiences – does not necessarily have the power to shift the ego position, either because it is resisted or simply because it is too weak in energy. The idea of greater states implies that subsequent experiences are necessary because they are more likely to have a profound effect or perhaps that the experiences and related insights need to be cumulative. This suggests that the ego can be conditioned, meaning the force is the same but there may be less resistance through greater exposure, or there is a greater build-up of libido as one tries harder to bring on the next phase.

For the purpose of psychoanalysis, the test is not the particular stage that is reached along a possible path to final absorption but whether there is, in fact, a psychological alteration of consciousness. There is no conclusive answer possible because the experience may change consciousness or have an effect on one subject but have insufficient force to affect another. Accordingly, it is possible that a lesser experience or a step along the way of a spiritual tradition will have an effect on consciousness. On this reasoning, it appears that lesser experiences should be included as categories of numinous experience. The appearance of the Self, for example – the autonomous centre of the psyche seen in symbols of wholeness such as a mandala – provides a revelation that a non-ego force is at work. However, consistent with Jung's definition, this does not come upon an analysand with overwhelming force, as explained, but rather appears to drip into consciousness to reveal itself.

The distinction as to the relevant effect relies upon the *potential* of the experience to alter consciousness. The quality of an overwhelming or unique experience may offer something immediate and profound that has that potential. By requiring that it must be overwhelming, Jung is postulating a force that is unlikely to be resisted by the ego because it has revealed the existence of a truth. The overwhelming relates to a truth that cannot be denied, which appears in any of the myriad forms that have such an impact. As an example, when describing a mystical vision of Meister Eckhart during which he entered into an abyss "deeper than hell itself," Jung (1951, para. 209) comments:

> The centering of the image on hell, which at the same time is God, is grounded on the experience that highest and lowest both come from the depths of the soul, and either bring the frail vessel of consciousness to shipwreck or carry it safely to port, with little or no assistance from us. The experience of this "centre" is therefore a numinous one in its own right.

With the requirement that the "depths of the soul" are reached as the centre, Jung is dismissing experiences that are not of that nature as incapable of bringing the consciousness "to port." The aspect of the numinous experience that is relevant – as it can lead to the necessary attainment and alteration of consciousness – is that it submerges the individual in the deepest aspects of their psyche: the archetypes of the collective unconscious, wherein a truth is revealed. Jung (1961, para. 594) explains that these mythological, collective fragments (archetypes) have the capacity to cause "profound psychological disturbances, while in other people they can produce astonishing cures or religious conversions." Lesser experiences are irrelevant and what is required is a direct confrontation with the primordial archetypes of the collective unconscious.

In his commentary on *The Tibetan Book of Great Liberation*, Jung (1935/ 1953, para. 783) explains that an introverted attitude will call forth "the characteristic manifestations of the unconscious, namely, archaic thought-forms imbued with 'ancestral' or 'historic' feeling, and, beyond them, the sense of indefiniteness, timelessness, oneness." The collective unconscious has levels, and "beyond" all archetypes is the ultimate oneness or that which is the essence of the content of a ME. Jung's introduction of levels, and his description of a level "beyond" the primordial archetypes, indicates that eventually, at the bottom (or the top) of the archetypal structure lies the archaic thought-form of oneness, which is both real and ineffable but has the highest potential for alteration.

The significance of a truth revealed and the action of overwhelming the ego are the same: it is only the revelation of a truth arising from the primordial archetypes that makes it overwhelming. To be an overwhelming experience, in Jung's terms, what is revealed must be exposure to the core archetypes of the collective unconscious, a realm that is not available by conscious enquiry or indeed anything other than the bursting through of the autonomous hidden substance of the unconscious. This is not to deny the lesser experiences, but, again, Jung is referring here to the unique situation of a glimpse into what is unknown and hidden deep in humanity's collective psyche.

This is the highest standard of understanding and could mean that the ME is not relevant to psychoanalysis unless it reaches this level. There are several possible explanations for why Jung chose to depart from religious and mystical metaphysics and categorise the numinous (and mystical) in terms of its profound impact on consciousness through the revelation of the processes of the collective unconscious. These explanations are necessary because theoretically he could have explained that a ME, even if it does not change consciousness, could be one of those events that "hinted at abnormal future development" (Jung, 1928b, para. 270), which he suggested is a relevant sign when describing a religious conversion. A distinction could have been made by him of the relevance of loss of ego in the experience, and the effect that had as a primary experience of the Self. There seems more at play in his shift in emphasis to the highest level of the alteration of consciousness and away from the nature of the experience.

One possibility lies in his reluctance to describe the nature of a numinous experience at all because of the difficulty of explaining with any clarity the true nature of what has occurred in the psyche. To do so would have detracted from the espoused scientific nature of his work and his ability to elucidate psychic processes. This reluctance is evident elsewhere, such as when he describes dream interpretation as deciphering "hieroglyphs" (Jung, 1928c, para. 263), which leaves many "question marks" (ibid.). The difficulty of interpreting any communication from the unconscious makes the extreme nature of a numinous experience even more obscure. Jung's limitation is perhaps grounded in Freud's expressed inability to decipher the primal, central essence of a dream, or what Freud called the "dream's navel" that reaches "down into the unknown" (Freud, 1900, p. 111, n. 1). Jung does not criticise or even mention Freud's encounter with a point of limitation. However, it creates what Pruyser (1983) calls a "limit situation" in which it is impossible to discern the cause or reason for the occurrence and is therefore inconsistent with a scientific approach.

Another possibility that bears repeating is that Jung did not want to reveal or even hint at the content of his own MEs as this would diminish the scientific bedrock of his work, even though there is a strong argument that such experiences had a profound influence on him (Stein, 2015). As mentioned, the *Seven Sermons to the Dead* (Jung, 1998, Appendix V) was attributed to the gnostic Basilides and distributed only to friends, while and *The Red Book* was hidden from view in his lifetime. Hence, it seems reasonable to assume that Jung's legitimate concern with the authority of his work dissuaded him from attempting to clarify the evolution of a ME in the psyche.

This reluctance to explore the full content of the numinous or mystical experience is also understandable in terms of the potentially dangerous effect of the revelation of the mystical on those who are unprepared for its impact. In speaking about the effect on consciousness of a numinous experience, Jung (1947/1954, para. 405) explains that it

> drives with unexampled passion and remorseless logic towards its goal and draws the subject under its spell, from which despite the most desperate resistance he is unable, and finally no longer even willing, to break free, because the experience brings with it a depth and fullness of meaning that was unthinkable before.

This can lead to embracing an "-ism" that "works most successfully with those who have the least access to their interior selves and have strayed the furthest from their instinctual roots into a truly chaotic world of *collective consciousness*" (ibid.; original emphasis). The collective consciousness, as opposed to the collective unconscious, is the joining into the cultural ethos of religion and other oriented groups, resulting in a loss of individuality – a theme that Jung positions throughout his works as the most dangerous of results.

In reading Jung's account of the presence of God in man, the use of the concept of the Anthropos, his comments on the evolution of the God image, and his critique of God in *Answer to Job*, there is an unmistakeable feeling that his is a mystical endeavour. No analyst can dispute this feeling, and it has led many schools of psychoanalysis to exclude Jung. He is, after all, writing about those primal archetypes at the core of the psyche – concepts that are difficult to imagine and impossible to describe. The pull of the mystical in Jung's work and its simultaneous rejection have led previous and current Jungian scholars to return again and again to the mystical intimations of his work, even though he expressly denied such a connection. It is hard to slip away from the mystical and rest firmly on pure scientific proof when reading Jung. This makes it more awkward to decide why he did not explore the process of the sudden appearance of the archetypes of the collective unconscious in more detail, exposing specifically in one place at least why there will be a breakthrough and which unconscious archetypes are actually relevant. One can only be reminded of the noteworthy section of the Zohar, the central book of

Kabbalah, called the *Idra Zuta* or the Small Assembly (Matt, 2006, Vol. 9, p. 767). This describes the moment when Rabbi Shim'on decides to reveal the secrets of the universe. The room was filled with people, but just as he was about to speak, "they all left" (ibid., p. 769), which meant only a few who had proven themselves ready to withstand the power of the revelations remained and listened.

In contrast to Jung's reluctance to explicate the characteristics of the processes that crystallise a numinous experience, there is a need expressed in the Zohar to pass on the revelations because, if mystical doctrine is not spread, the fate of the world falls into the hands of those who may be destructive. The sense of the urgency is expressed when the rabbi says, "it is time to reveal everything." Giller (2000, p. 94) points out that the Zohar balances this urgency with the fact that the revelation is extremely hazardous, as three rabbis were immolated by the "orgasm of the cosmos" prior to the Small Assembly. Nevertheless, given the profound importance of the revelation in dark times for the future of humanity, gnosis must be revealed.

The best explanation for why Jung failed to explore the nature of the effect on consciousness and devoted no attention to the content is simply that there is no psychoanalytic language to describe the content of a ME. It has this critical limitation because a description requires an object of that experience, and Jung would have to name that object and make sense of it. Meister Eckhart, whom he frequently mentions, describes the object in many ways, including the opposites of both nothingness and the godhead (Eckhart, 1981, p. 206). When there is a theology as the reference point for a ME, there is an object. When the object is "nothingness," allowing no description, no words are adequate, yet an object is created. Sells (1994, p. 148) includes Eckhart's nothingness as an "unsaying" – or apophasis – that rejects the idea that the transcendent subject can be named, leading to it being an object based on what it is not. Jung's views on God are clearly of this type when he writes:

> All statements about and beyond the 'ultimate' are anthropomorphisms (that is just projections of human qualities) and, if anyone should think that when he says 'God' he has also predicated God, he is endowing his words with *magical powers*. Like a primitive, he is incapable of distinguishing the verbal image from reality.
>
> (Jung, 1953, Vol. 2, p. 260)

Although Jung did not deny the existence of a transcendent God, he makes it the nature of an apophasis, rendering it irrelevant to describe the content of a ME in terms of an object. There is then, in this specific context, no basis for attempting to explain that which cannot be explained. Mysticism and religious experiences are reduced to a psychoanalytic experience with clinical consequences and are not connected to philosophical, theological constructs or even to spiritual or religious traditions. This view of a religious experience being an aspect of a non-religious, numinous experience has been criticised on the basis that religious, numinous experiences absolutely create an identity with a transcendent divine – a "personal object of devotion" – while only MEs reveal a unity between subject and object, so there is no object (Smart, 1970, p.14). The grouping together of object-oriented experience and non-object experience augments the view that the actual experience is just a trigger for the more important question of the effect on consciousness.

As Jung deals with Eastern mysticism, it is incumbent upon him to comment on the claims of oneness of a ME. He accepts the existence of a feeling of oneness but not as a description of a unitive experience, thereby diminishing again the importance of the content of a ME. He adds that it "probably derives from the general contamination of contents, which increases as consciousness dims" (Jung, 1939b, para. 783). This is his particular, causal explanation of a ME where there are two parts: a contamination of contents; and the dimming of consciousness. These contents that are contaminated are of the unconscious as the deep, primal, archetypal forces he describes are "incredibly vague" (ibid.), as can be seen in the images that rise in dreams. They become "contaminated" from their pure state by being subject to images and also cognitive interpretations that mask their true nature: "Yet communication often tended to result in miscommunication or failed communication as a message was intercepted, misdirected, misinterpreted, corrupted, broken up or spliced with others in its attempt to reach its destination" (Ko, 2007, p. 744). The result is that when consciousness dims – as, for instance during meditation – there is nothing specific or clear to hold on to and it is therefore a natural phenomenon to perceive it all as an amorphous, unblended whole forming into a singular experience. Jung (1939b, para. 783) concludes: "Hence it is not unlikely that the peculiar experience of oneness derives from the subliminal awareness of all-contamination in the unconscious."

Elsewhere, Jung (1961, para. 511) explains that "subliminality" or subliminal awareness is related to a drop or weakening of the ego consciousness into the fringe of consciousness: "Subliminality corresponds to what Janet calls *abaissement du niveau mental*. It is a lowering of energic tension, in which psychic contents sink below the threshold and lose the qualities they possess in a psychic state." Subliminal awareness in this context of an experience of oneness is therefore a limited awareness of only that which is contaminated, vague, and not distinct in the unconscious. The weakness of the conscious mind allows the lowering of the threshold – or, as Jung (1947/1954, para. 382) puts it, the "marginal phenomenon" – where the archetypes may cross.

At the level of subliminal awareness, there is a contamination of the conscious mind by the undirected material blending below the threshold of consciousness and coming through as undefined. This feeling of oneness, the essence of a ME, is therefore not a unitive experience for Jung but one derived from a moment when there is a lowering of consciousness that is sufficient to make the unconscious quality of oneness rise up because the mind is no longer making distinctions.

It is clear that the sense of oneness in a ME is not relevant for Jung. Instead, the emphasis remains on what he calls an "alteration" of consciousness: when you remove the content or the nature of the experience, this is what is left. In considering the nature of the "numinosum" in the Terry Lectures (Jung, 1938/1940, para. 6), he invokes that term to refer to an experience that "causes a particular alteration of consciousness." It is a definition created by a "particular" alternation, and not the subject matter – and certainly not the content – of a ME.

With the phrase "particular alteration of consciousness," Jung clarifies that an overwhelming experience *must* produce a result – an alteration of consciousness – in order to be considered a numinous experience. It cannot merely be overwhelming in nature or offer a revelation. This leads to the position that an experience that is disregarded or ignored as it arises cannot be classified as an experience of the numinosum, even if it is categorised as mystical or religious. Accordingly, the revelation of an absolute truth is not relevant if it does not alter consciousness.

A "numinous experience," it may be concluded, is therefore a psychological term of art, which consists of an occurrence that has significance only because it contains a likelihood that it will be received and will create an alteration of consciousness. That is why the appearance of the "numen," as Jung (1988, Vol. 2, p. 1038) explains, is only a "hint, a sign," as it suggests the possibility that it will be received and absorbed, causing an alteration of consciousness.

The formula is better expressed, in this light, as an alteration of consciousness brought about by a revelation of the processes or content of the collective unconscious. A mystical or religious experience, no matter what the content, or the revelation of an absolute truth is included if it alters consciousness. This drives strongly to a purposive definition for experiences that do not necessarily bring a person closer to enlightenment or higher states but rather, in psychological terms, have a psychological effect. It is to the psychological effect that analysis must be directed. It is not related to a generalised result that blends within a tradition or is a curiosity to be enjoyed; rather, it is a specific subjective event that is important because it acts on the conscious position in a manner that adds to the therapeutic process.

As Neumann (1948/1969, p. 380) explains, the psychological effect and the requisite alteration of consciousness create an awareness of a *non-ego* power within the unconscious. This is the revelation that comes out of the unconscious and presents itself by its force and power to the ego. When this occurs, "It is characteristic that in it [the numinous experience] the ego cannot cling to its position in consciousness, but must expose itself to encounter with the non-ego." When such an encounter happens, Neumann states, the ego goes "outside itself" (ibid.) and will experience "a richness beyond the power of consciousness" (ibid., p. 381). The revelation has created the precondition of the alteration but is not determinative unless there is an awareness of the non-ego.

In this setting, equating the experience with a divine force may occur as the form and content are therefore attributed to such force and power. However, psychologically, this weakens the nature of the experience as it compromises its essence as an internal, unconscious force. The argument has accordingly been made that the greater the theism, the weaker the experience, as it takes its force from the purity of the occurrence, not from its translation (Smart, 1964, ch. 4).

Aniella Jaffe (1989, pp. 15–16) enlarges the psychological importance of encountering the non-ego:

> By rendering conscious the transpersonal influence on our psyches, through the experience of the numinosity, forces are recognized which underlie one's being and behavior in a structuring and autonomous way, as well as being behind the apparently random unfolding of events. One experiences or senses the wider context in which life is lived, and toward which goal it is striving.

Consequently, the realisation of the numinous in consciousness is a significant marker along the process of individuation. As Jung (1953, Vol. 1, p. 377) explains: "It always seemed to me as if the real milestones were certain symbolic events characterised by a strong emotional tone ... the numinous." The emotional tone in the case of a numinous experience (and the categories of a religious experience or ME) is the affect created by the overwhelming event: the revelation of a truth. It is not considered emotional because it is novel, exciting, or related to the spirit or a God, but rather because it reveals collective unconscious insights of the non-ego dwelling in the unconscious.

This approach clarifies the role of the ME for psychoanalysis and the requisite degree of an alteration of the conscious position. It will be an important marker in the process of individuation because it displays to the ego that there are forces that are not dependent on day-to-day thoughts and events. This allows the ego to contemplate that there is an alternative point of reference and, in this respect, the impact of merging with the divine may be a higher form but may not have any greater impact on the ego than a blow of fate. It all depends on the psychological realisation.

It should not be ignored that the power of a ME may create such an immediate, indelible impression that consciousness is changed for ever. These experiences are realisations that shift the locus to a non-ego object and consequently may create a reorientation that persists. A change of consciousness may also crystallise slowly or rapidly and take the subject to a new understanding of the non-ego presence. "The self slides gently, almost imperceptibly, from the old universe to the new" (Underhill, 1990, p. 177).

An alteration of the conscious position holds when it goes beyond a narrative and becomes a steadfast point of reference. It may appear that a patient has realised a truth but over time there is slippage and the insight disappears. This occurs because the unique nature of the experience requires it to be placed in a narrative and, when that occurs, the intellectual processes begin to contextualise and refine but also corrupt what transpired. There is, in Bion's terms, an interpretative, unwanted transformation of the O – or a readjustment of the revelation – to make room for the written or spoken interpretations of others. To have a lasting effect on consciousness, a ME must become embodied (used here to mean that it is felt as interwoven in the non-cognitive being of the subject).

This concept of embodied presence is familiar to analysts but not measurable because it is not cognitive. It is often transient and not always available to the subject. Also, because it is a feeling or a sense but not a narrative, it is subject to displacement by intrusion of the ego or an activation of complexes. As long as it remains as an altered conscious position, there has been a numinous experience. If it has faded and there is a return to the old position, the experience has led to no more than a fragile bubble of awareness.

The "real therapy"

In a letter written in English to the Jungian P.W. Martin, Jung (1953, Vol. 1, p. 377) establishes the critical importance of the numinous for analysis: "the approach to the numinous is the real therapy and inasmuch as you attain to the numinous experiences you are released from the curse of pathology." This categorical statement places numinous experience as *the* critical, "real therapy." This immediately challenges the normal model of psychoanalysis as requiring the interplay of many psychological dimensions, such as transference interactions and regression. Accordingly, Murray Stein (2006, p. 35) argues that Jung did not mean what he appears to say and suggests that a numinous experience is insufficient in itself. There is still a requirement for the traditional stages of individuation: "For modern and psychologically astute people, however, such a spiritual development might not signify more than a temporary Band Aid and by no means a definitive solution to the problems created by neurosis" (ibid.). He reconciles Jung's emphatic statement to Martin by asserting that a numinous experience is only a hint that larger non-ego powers are in the psyche, rather than an event that completely shifts the conscious position along the ego–Self axis, away from the ego and closer to the sense of wholeness. Stein derives this argument from Jung's observation in *Memories, Dreams, Reflections* that the numinous experiences Jung had were only *"prima materia"* and concludes: "In other words, the attainment to numinous experiences, while significant in itself, was not of final import; rather, it provided the essential ingredients for further stages of the individuation *opus*" (ibid., p. 45).

When commenting on the same letter to Martin, Gerhard Adler (1978, p. 2) suggests that the experience of the numinous is useful only as an aid to individuation as it offers an opportunity for something new to emerge in consciousness:

> The emphasis on the numinous does, of course, not mean that we do not have to work hard and conscientiously through complexes, resistances, defences, or what have you before we reach the motive power behind the screen of neurosis. St Paul's words apply here: *Per visibilia ad invisibilia.*

The "approach" to the numinous is indeed the real therapy because an analysis that orients to the gradual realisation of a non-ego power in the psyche is the essence of the therapeutic endeavour. This is the explanation of the first part of Jung's statement. It is a statement of the importance of the realisation of the autonomous nature of the dynamic elements of the psyche, or what Jung (1912/1952, para. 344) terms the "physics of the soul." The same approach occurs in the revelation of the Self as an organising principle within the psyche. This does not necessarily demand an overwhelming force but the Self is revealed through the progressive process of psychoanalysis as the *spiritus rector* – the guiding principle of the psyche. The gradual growth of awareness of the Self shifts the ego consciousness away from its vicissitudes to a central point of reference. The numinous is an intense, overwhelming experience of the Self but has the same fundamental purpose of revealing a non-ego power. The approach to the numinous is to attend to that which indicates the hidden, orienting principle that is not usually available to the ego. It is at the core of psychoanalysis as revealing the previously unconscious forces in the psyche.

In the particular context of trauma patients, Kalsched (2013, p. 203) explains how the approach to numinous experiences can lead to an ego–Self shift and be a basis for reorientation: "These [numinous] experiences were healing, partly because they restored a mytho-poetic matrix – a larger, archetypal story within which these patients' personal stories could find a place. The patients felt witnessed or companied from within and thereby found hope." Accordingly, it is the *approach* that is the *sine qua non* of the individuation process, and it is correct to say that it is the "real therapy." Without the gradual development of the Self or the sudden intrusion of a numinous experience, the ego pathways are hard to change. In the case of the Self, the process is long and arduous, requiring the reconciliation of the conscious and unconscious opposites. With a numinous experience, the process is accelerated as there is a sudden, profound alteration of consciousness, which must be an awareness of the existence of non-ego powers within the psyche.

The second part of the sentence in the letter to Martin articulates that *attainment* to the numinous is the cure. If one can "attain" to the numinous, the Self, the "soul," the divine presence, or even a non-ego force has been realised and this is the ground of being that becomes the guiding principle rather than the neurotic vicissitudes of the ego. It is truly a cure for neurosis if the non-ego force is accepted and becomes the permanent point of reference. Attainment is to achieve success of that goal and, if that occurs, there is no room for neurosis.

Neither Stein nor Adler properly considers Jung's statement in the Terry Lectures that a numinous experience requires an alteration of consciousness, giving the occurrence a definitive, psychoanalytic role. Such an experience, because of its affect, awakens the possibility of an alteration, arising from the hint of non-ego powers, thus creating the Jungian *vexillum excelsis*: an essential shift in the ego–Self axis. As Edinger (1972, p. 69) puts it: "the ego becomes aware, experientially, of a transpersonal center to which the ego is subordinate." That shift is the goal of individuation, and a numinous experience is one of the means.

The first part of Jung's statement on the approach to the numinous does not deny the importance of the stages of the analytical process, nor does it suggest that a spontaneous numinous experience is required. It does emphasise that the proper approach is to the process of revealing the non-ego power and the numinous experience is a prime, facilitative means to bring about that revelation. This is a statement about a perceptual shift. The numinous does not dispense with the ego or somehow diminish it: the other is in the ego and the ego is in the other. Rather, it offers that possibility of finding a new perspective, such as being comfortable with uncertainty, open to the mystery, or having less need to rely on logic or reasoning.

Theory of the analytic attitude

In overlapping articles Bright (1997; 2014), makes the case that the only possible analytic attitude when faced with the report of the psychoid phenomenon of synchronicity (an inexplicable, mysterious, non-causal event) is to treat all interpretations, comments, or amplifications as provisional, because the experience is

> secondary to facilitating the emergence of the underlying psychoid meaning and pattern, which cannot be fully comprehended, but which have their own power, independent of the ego, to contribute to the processes of the development of the analytic relationship and ultimately to the patient's individuation.
>
> (Bright, 1997, p. 632)

"Psychoid" is a reference to a level of the unconscious that is not accessible. Bright is implying that it is nevertheless possible to facilitate the emergence of a meaning and pattern. For a psychoanalyst, there is something in an unknowable occurrence that seeks explanation even though any interpretations or elaborations can only be tentative, as Bright suggests. It is impossible to make any sense of why the experience occurred at a particular point in time in relation to the analytical field or even on the individual's life journey. However, he expresses a truth that it is hard to resist provisional explanations or a premature hypothesis because the significance of the experience must have some rationale.

The attempt at understanding, even provisionally, has both a direct effect on the binding or limiting of the complete mystery of the event and removes its possible effect on the ego by construing it and giving it a psychological explanation. Every analyst is aware that providing an interpretation will reduce the potential of any insight. Bright (2014, p. 92) quotes one of Jung's letters (Beebe and Falzeder, 2012; Jung, 1953, Vol. 1, p. 30) in which he states that "understanding," like the devil, is a "devouring": a murdering of the soul. "With our patients 'analytical' understanding has a wholesomely destructive effect" (ibid., p. 31). Jung (ibid., p. 32) concludes:

> We should bless our blindness for the mysteries of others. We should be connivers at our own mysteries, but veil over our eyes chastely before the mystery of the other, so far as, being unable to understand himself, he does not need the "understanding of others."

Assuming Jung would have made this applicable to numinous experiences, it would suggest a reticence towards any attempt to understand why the event has occurred and how it might fit into the analytical progress of the patient. It must, however, be acknowledged that "veil[ing] our eyes" is only an ideal and close to impossible because it is a rejection of the teleology of the unconscious that forms the basis for therapeutic practice. It also goes against the rhythm of an analytical session where the meaning hangs suspended, waiting for its illumination, which is especially the case when there is a reporting of a unique ME. Merkur (1999, p. 68) records a patient who had previously experienced MEs yet rejected their most recent one, and asks, "Why should someone who has already successfully enjoyed mystical moments undergo a subsequent period of their nonoccurrence?" He concludes – as a conclusion is irresistible – that they may wish to remain "developmentally simple" and consequently fail to realise that this leads only to a "spiritual dryness" (a phrase borrowed from St John of God) of their own making.

If the discipline of the analyst means that no attempt is made to understand the experience, the content still appears to be of interest as every mystical or numinous experience will have symbols or an object. In the case of MH, it was the Virgin Mary, but it could be God, a feeling of peace, or nothingness. In psychoanalysis, there is a power in these symbols as objects that have been delivered by the unconscious as a form of communication. In the letter cautioning against the destructive nature of understanding, Jung (cited in Bright, 2014, p. 93) explains that "in the later stages of analysis," it is necessary to "help the other to come to those hidden and unopenable symbols." This implies that there is a stage in the analysis where the sanctity of the symbols is appreciated, although they remain untouched.

There is a difficulty in obtaining associations or amplifying or in any way making more of the symbols that appear within a ME. Associations are a way back into the personal unconscious of the patient, with all the defences, history, and patterns that create the personal narrative. There are no amplifications or analogies that can be made of the contents of the experience because they, by their nature, point to the highest level of references, which in turn are shrouded in mystery. A ME differs in this respect from a dream, where the true telling of the contents raises symbols that arise directly from the unconscious, hopefully unchanged. For the interviewees, there was a much narrower range of symbols than in a dream, perhaps because there is a concentration on a single, mystical object, such as God or nothingness. This indicates that the communication from the unconscious is, by its overpowering nature, delivering a singular message of the existence of a non-ego force within the psyche and does not need to convey it more gently or vaguely in complex symbols.

As the experience is so forceful and unique, yet unknowable and untraceable, it would appear, according to these theories, that an analyst should say nothing except attempt to legitimise the occurrence. Merkur (2006), however, indicates that the consequence of taking an active part in the discussion of the numinous is that we will ask patients to speak of feelings about such an experience and thus seek fresh emotions, even though we may be content to remain observers and not interpret. He suggests that an interpretation inevitably must take place because of the element of fascination – Otto's *fascinans* – and this awakens metaphors. "The verbal unpacking of the metaphor is, however, not part of the unconscious originating metaphor but instead constitutes commentary on its meaning" (ibid., p. 209). This, in turn, suggests that the patient can then "ponder the 'argument from design': the argument that the cosmos exhibits a plan or design that attests to an author" (ibid.). Merkur reports his own experience aboard the *Maid of the Mist* at Niagara Falls and concludes: "When wonderment at the fascinans is aroused, the limit situation facilitates thoughts of something more" (ibid., p. 212).

To bring the patient to the symbol or to a feeling is, in the context of a numinous experience, recognising the Self or the not-I in the psyche but nothing more. It establishes that there is a non-ego force, which is the key to the attainment of an alteration in consciousness. It is not a process of working with metaphors that then concretises the object. Analysis of metaphors or feelings when there is a ME will have the negative effect of channelling the libido – directed life energy, or what Jung (1912/1952b, para. 194) calls "appetite in its natural state" – as each of these is directed in some form to a figure (a teacher, a tradition, a god, an ideal), which Gershom Scholem (1941) suggests will become the inevitable imposed framework that arises by contexualising the experience.

This suggests a delicate balance in analysis between allowing the symbol of the primitive force to become an intra-psychic object (as the not-I) and allowing that to deepen, become embodied, or crystallise in another symbol. Jung's (1912/1952b, para. 259) concern is:

> The concrete reality of religious figures assists the canalization of libido into the equivalent symbols, provided that the worship of them does not get stuck at the outward object. But even if it does, it at least remains bound to the representative human figure and loses its original primitive forces, even though it does not attain the desired symbolic form.

He explains the risk that the primitive forces may be replaced by a new symbol of the projected object, leaving the power of the original experience diminished. It may certainly be the case that a guru or teacher, living or dead, or a god-like figure may offer by ideation some guidance as to the mysteries that have been unveiled, thus increasing rather than lessening the nature of the primitive forces. However, a change in consciousness is understood by reference to the introduction of a non-ego force *within* consciousness, unrelated to any spiritual or religious orientation.

Maintenance of a non-religious or non-spiritual viewpoint allows an encounter with the primitive, archetypal forces that may or may not take shape into one symbol or another. What is being presented to the psyche is an affect-laden experience that indicates that here is something unknowable that is not subject to interpretation, as would be a dream or projection. The analyst then has no reference point and no basis for any interpretation directly or by metaphor, and none should be attempted. The introduction of the intellect or the ego in interpreting is contrary to the utter unknowable mystery of the occurrence. In the words of William James (1902/2008, p. 307), the patient has "come face to face with facts which no instinct or reason can ever know."

The requirement of a ME to effect a change in consciousness requires that the ego must relate to the psychic object of the not-I. This is the analytic imperative and the touchstone for working with these experiences. Neumann (1948/1969, p. 382), in relation to the realisation of the non-ego, calls for "attention and devotion on the part of the ego, an aptitude for being 'moved,' a willingness to see what wants to appear." The devotion, aptitude, and willingness appear to be qualities of the *subject* – their receptivity – and all that an analyst can then do is bring the existence of the experience to attention, legitimise it, and open the possibility that it is the appearance of a non-ego force. An analyst is poorly served by attempting to create a context, or an interpretation, or by breaking down resistances.

This has led Bright (2014) and others to suggest a kind of wide openness on the part of the analyst that does not interfere with a psychoid occurrence.

It requires, in Bion's terms, that by the analytic attitude a patient can become the O. It leaves the analyst with no theoretical basis for dealing with the event that is brought into analysis, other than by a passive, meditative-like state, devoid of understanding or amplification. This makes the analyst only the witness to the event and places all of the consequences of a mystical or numinous experience on the receptivity of the subject.

The existence of receptivity as a critical concept proceeds initially on the basis that there is a sound ego that can relate and assimilate the presence of a not-I. According to Lacan (1988, p. 16) that ego is an illusion – "the mental illness of man" – and the unconscious is not the "other" with which there is a relationship. Therefore, the latter cannot be assimilated, only accepted. In this way, Lacan is closer to the appropriate position in relation to a ME of the importance of acceptance of the "other" as the proper orientation for clinical practice.

There are two theoretical positions as to the ego's relationship with the not-I, highlighted by Parsons (1999, ch. 6): the "adaptive school," which emphasises the healing dimension of MEs on account of the changes that result in the ego structure; and the "transformational school," which looks at direct, non-ego dialogue with the transcendent. The structural foundation of psychoanalysis, originating with Freud and extending to ego psychology and object relations, discloses the need to relate the experience to its effect on ego being able to have a healing function. Jung certainly falls within the category of ego psychology in this regard of making the unconscious conscious to the ego as the basis of a cure. Lacan does not accept the ego as an agent, only as a narcissistic fixation, a perspective that has been likened to the Zen Buddhist concept of no-self and therefore direct knowing. However, he also does not accept that we can ever know or relate to the unconscious: "For Zen this possibility (of enlightenment) goes unquestioned. For Lacan ... though we are compelled to seek such a realization, it is one we will never obtain" (Molino, 1998, p. 299).

The important theoretical issue for the analytic attitude is not that there is an ego to view the experience or that there is direct knowing; rather, from the viewpoint of psychoanalysis, there is a change in perception in the subject. In the interpretation of Jung and Neumann, having an ego structure is possessing the ability to be affected by the experience through an alteration in consciousness. In an analysis of Buddhist philosophy, Klein (2012) makes the case that in any event, the existence of a non-ego force is a conceptual thought that occurs *with or without an ego structure* as a subjective centre that leads to a change in perception that is liberating. If a ME is never free from cognition, as the stages of the experience reveal, the change in perception can occur even though the actual nature of the ego is undeclared.

These theoretical positions regarding a passive, analytic attitude are not useful, except in legitimising the experience, as they turn the analyst into a non-participant who is relevant only to the extent that their attitude can provide an open container for the subject. This means that there is little that the analyst can do on a practical level to keep a snippet or a version of a ME alive in the analysis. It is common in clinical practice to hear what amounts to some form of a patient's affective non-ego experience, always with some degree of fascination, only to have it discounted in the next sentence, without a bridge back to considering it further. MH is an extreme example, but references to feeling at peace inside a church, or recollections of a moment of unity with nature when a child, are heard from time to time and invite some connection with a ME. Knowing the potential healing capacity of a ME by a change of conscious position suggests that something should be done.

The primary, most important step is to ensure that the experience is at least in the analysis. It may not always be recognised as such as it appears as a random aberration, or embarrassing, or even bordering on the psychotic. It may be rejected outright by the patient (as it was with MH), and in such cases there is little that may be done to recover it in any useful way. If the analyst is then to retain the experience in the room, there must be a non-interpretative recognition of the emotional power of the experience. This is a noteworthy occurrence in the psyche that arises out of the details of the experience that have been expressed as a narrative. There is accordingly an opportunity to examine the after-effect of such a powerful phenomenon. This permits the experience to be part of the analysis and at least recognises it as a phenomenon that has occurred as a subjective experience.

The effect on consciousness is the critical factor, and it must be brought into the analysis; there may be a great effect or none at all. The focus on the passage of a ME from its occurrence to an effect on consciousness is then *solely* dependent on the patient's receptivity: their willingness, openness, and interest to consider it further and keep it alive in the analysis. If receptivity is limited, there is little an analyst can do to bring the experience into greater focus in this respect. If there is receptivity, the experience may be taken further by more deeply legitimising it, acknowledging its significance without interpretation, and helping it to be embodied as a significant psychic event that indicates the existence of the non-ego.

In determining receptivity and the possibility of expanding the experience, there is a point in time – a crossroads – where the progress continues or ends, as illustrated by two clinical case examples of two men in their forties.

Case I

PATIENT: I had this experience just as I was waking that the Great Mother came and started yelling at me. That was all. I wasn't dreaming or maybe I was. She was there at the foot of my bed.

ANALYST: What was the feeling associated with that?

PATIENT: Interesting, isn't it? Too crazy. My mom came to see me last week and was telling me that I am not earning enough. That really bothers me as I am in fact doing just fine. Maybe that's what it's about.

Case 2

PATIENT: I felt this overwhelming clarity last night – like everything was connected. I was sitting and watching the news and it came over me and it freaked me out.
ANALYST: You say "overwhelming." Can you tell me how that felt?
PATIENT: I saw that there was something – a force – that was bigger than me. Some uniting force. It felt like I had a new set of eyes and the TV and the curtains and the desk were all somehow connected to me.
ANALYST: Have you had experiences like this before?
PATIENT: No, this was the first and it scared me. What do you think it means?
ANALYST: I don't know. Let's explore it. Tell me what effect it had on you then and now.

In Case 1, the invitation to feeling is the only possible response as there is no alternative path of the significance of the Great Mother or the psychological nature of the mother archetype for this patient at this time. If it were a dream, it would be subject to associations and amplifications and would tie in with the patient's previous history. As it was on the border of dream and ME, it was tempting to treat it as a dream, but it was clearly a ME, so its meaning is not relevant and all that is important is the patient's willingness to open up to the experience and its effect on his conscious position. This did not occur.

In Case 2, the patient expressed an enthusiasm for further exploration of the experience. At this stage, the parameters of the experience can be explored and the recognition of the non-ego may begin. What separates the two cases is the receptivity, and no amount of discussion would make the patient in Case 1 amenable to opening up to what occurred.

The crossroads is brought into the analysis by calling upon the feeling of the occurrence. It is a call to go deeper into the exploration of an inexplicable event. The lack of receptivity could be tested by that question after a greater explication, but that would engender too much discussion, which would reframe it, either positively or negatively. Outside a tradition, the unfolding into a negative frame is just as likely as a positive reaction, so the patient's level of receptivity should be ascertained first as a guidepost before further discussion begins.

The case for expansion of the experience, when there is receptivity, is not to assail it with associations or amplifications but to keep it alive for the patient as a profound, mysterious occurrence. The experience does not fit within the normal frame of cognitive subjects and is so alien that there is a probability that it will be discounted after the fact. It therefore must be accepted that it is more likely to be treated as an aberration than as a meaningful, consciousness-changing event.

The means to keep the experience alive is primarily through the formation and repetition of the narrative of the experience and the reduction of the event to an image, such as the Virgin Mary, nothingness, a moment of peace. The purpose of the image is to have an object to relate to after the narrative, when the immediacy of the experience has faded. This is not to open up the examination of the symbolic but rather to create a placeholder for the experience. The image is derived from the overwhelming image of the experience or, if it is present, a somatic effect, such as a release of tension in the chest or a smoothing of the brow. It becomes a symbol of the nature of the experience so that it is "the sensually perceptible expression of an inner experience" (Jung, 1953, Vol. 1, p. 59).

This need to make the experience concrete requires the analyst to interact with the experience and not merely be the meditative receptacle for the patient. In instances where the subject has a passionate encounter with the object of the experience, the occurrence will be more amenable to image formation. However, a substitute placeholder is necessary as there is an inevitable turning point when the experience and image will remain only as memory, subject to slippage and eventual loss of effect.

Given the unknowable origins of the experience and its appearance as alien to the conscious mind, it is impossible to assist in the image formation by offering the patient a structure or containing it within a known philosophy or tradition. The experience should not be perceived as providing information about the details of psychic structure from which it is possible to extrapolate what it means in order to create a new symbol. It is rather an attempt to assist the patient to develop an emotional, physical, or even mental picture of the experience in order to place it, as much as possible, as a working object in consciousness.

The essence of the process is that the formation of a placeholder image as a condensing of the narrative allows a recall of the non-ego as alien, yet derived from the patient's unconscious. In this sequence, the first three steps are: legitimising the experience to bring it into the room as a valid function of psyche; testing if the experience can be explored based on receptivity; and introducing through repetition of the narrative of the experience an image or somatic effect that may be used as a reference point for discussion. The final step is to make that image represent a non-ego appearance to realise that there are such forces available in the psyche.

Case study: analysis of the experience

As I was about to write further about the analytic attitude, a patient began a session with an announcement that he had had a ME. It was a unitive experience of an overwhelming connection with a force of peace and the effect of letting go of his Gordian knot of anxiety. It was indeed a mystical or numinous experience, as it was sudden, overwhelming, and initially seemed to have had an effect on consciousness. For the patient – RN – it appeared to deliver a major breakthrough in feeling and a revelation of a truth that created an immediate and clear alteration in his conscious position. Meanwhile, for me, it was uncanny in its timing and gave me a chance to record how the session proceeded in light of the theoretical boundaries, the timing of my reactions, any mistakes that were made, and the outcome in subsequent sessions.

RN is a highly intelligent forty-two-year-old with an encyclopedic knowledge of spiritual and religious traditions. He spends much of his time tracking down obscure references and finding the spiritual needle in the haystack. He does this with a fervour that causes him anxiety as it is compulsive and allows him little rest. His presenting issue was anxiety and a damaged sense of self-worth (for reasons that are irrelevant to this discussion). Many years before, he was hospitalised after suffering a drug-induced dissociative experience that he describes as a "psychotic break."

I had no specific goals as the session began and he related his experience, except to avoid restricting or confining the experience and, if possible, to find a way to work with him to enhance the effect on his consciousness. I initially sought, as he began to speak, to eschew memory or desire so as not to undermine the experience. This proved impossible as the timing of the experience and its relevance to my research made me realise that there is no pure listening of such a momentous event, so it may potentially be tainted with cognitive material from the analyst. All I could do, at this early stage, was to remain extremely respectful of the experience and mindful that any comment, body posture, or facial expression may have an impact on its receptivity.

I realised that an analyst cannot provide a clear, consistent approach in the face of a ME but rather will have an active mind during the telling of the experience, given that it will be overwhelming for the patient and create awe and fascination for the analyst as well. As I listened, I reminded myself not to ask or even ponder the basic question "Why now?" both in terms of RN's life journey and the progress of the analysis. To do so, I sensed, would have taken something away from the experience and place it within *my* narrative, which comprised previous work we had done, hypotheses I held, and where the experience might fit in the particular arc of RN's analysis in terms of ego strength and his developmental background.

The experience unfolded in the analytical session through the delivery of RN's narrative, which provided details of his subjective experience:

> I was sitting down on the floor, feeling strangely unsettled. I tried to meditate and as I did I was overtaken by peace, pure peace. I felt how it operated on that part of me that keeps pushing and looking for more and

causing me constant worry and feelings I am not good enough. It took those feelings away for the first time I can remember. Before, as you know, the anxiety was this terrible tightness in my chest and it caused me terrible pain. For this first time, the pain went. I had no intention, no need to think things through or do more. I just sat there, completely peaceful. It was the breakthrough I have been hoping for all my life.

That experience has two possible psychological elements. The first consists of the internal processes that led to his experience; the second is the effect on consciousness that emerges from the narrative. These two elements emerge from the narrative because it represents the only material in the analysis. The narrative creates the subject matter by indicating the nature of the effect, which points to the fact that it was received by the patient.

As it was part of the narrative, the first element offers up the internal processes that were responsible for that overwhelming force, the way it descended, or from where it originated. This element cannot be analysed as it is utterly unknown. The truth revealed in the narrative, however, contains may theoretical markers for psychoanalysis. The question that emerged in the course of RN's explanation was whether the analyst should rely on these markers in any way to frame the experience for the session or, alternatively, consider them completely irrelevant as representing interpretations.

From a psychological point of view, RN had a profound event that was the revelation of a peace that *resides within him* that he was experiencing for the first time, supplanting his normal, ego position. It was the appearance of the "not-I" that provides the ego with a new, healing perspective. In Jungian psychoanalytic terms, this was the appearance of a particular, autonomous element that broke through to reveal what Jung (1912/1952, 344) calls "the numinous, structural elements of the psyche," which have energy and act as transformers to move from a lower to a higher form. Explained as an archetype, the element of his peace or being able "to be" may be viewed as an ancient archetypal force buried in the collective unconscious replaced by the ego ideal of doing. If it was that archetype, it would explain its novelty to RN and its connection with the collective unconscious: "Experience of the archetypes is not only impressive, it seizes and possesses the whole personality and is naturally productive of faith" (ibid.). All of the categories for his numinous experiences are defined by the workings of the archetypes that seize the personality and produce faith about or an introduction to a new orientation.

In the face of RN's numinous experience, it would have been useless and irrelevant to the analysis to address this first element, to dig for the archetype, or, I believed, to call it a mystical or numinous experience. Jung specifically does not make extensive use of the word "mystical" in defining the primordial archetypes or their appearance as he considers that the word has been "debased by sordid usage" (Jung, 1927/1931, para. 83). His only specific explanation of the process of a ME in these terms is in the Tavistock Lectures where he states, "mystical experience is experience of the archetypes" and "Mystics are people who have a particularly vivid experience of the processes of the collective unconscious" (Jung, 1935a, para. 218).

Of course, at this point, an explanation or discussion with RN of *any* theoretical underpinning of the experience would have been fruitless. His primary presenting issue was a dissociation caused by intellectualising experience, and discussion along these lines would therefore have destroyed the experience. In his case, there was also no need for any "educational" component or to structure the experience into a particular framework as he was replete with the structures of traditions. The first element of the narrative that suggests a process therefore cannot be utilised. In any event, even if it were thought to be relevant, a discussion of what occurred in psychoanalytic terms is not at all straightforward even if the theory can be explained because the particular archetype at play cannot be ascertained. This is because it is never a matter of naming a specific archetype for a ME as the processes of the collective unconscious are concerned with the grouping and regrouping of the universal archetypes that are outside normal conscious engagement. This includes a grouping of every level of human existence and history, including, therefore, the primordial archetypes of the fullness of a divine force or the nothingness of the universe. If one of these breaks through from a particular grouping into consciousness, it follows that it yields a momentary glimpse of the core archetype or the archetypal element of the feelings, including peace and oneness, that emanate from that contact.

It may be self-evident not to bring the theory into the analysis and to reject ideas of what occurred. I thought that it was also important for the analyst not to reflect on the theoretical position during the session, if possible. This is because it represents a change in the field where the mystery is no longer unsolved but is being brought to ground by the analyst, thereby removing its potential force. In the consulting room, whenever a ME is presented, there is a profound feeling of the unknown that mysteriously enters both the patient and the analyst; it is this feeling that should not be contaminated. For Jung, there are affects derived from the archetypal forces that cluster around the primordial archetypes that make up the psyche, including passion, ecstasy, and love and these are to remain and not be untangled.

I struggled to put aside my suspicion that this had arisen in the field between myself and RN, as I was writing a book on the subject and he was well read in spiritual traditions. I became aware that the rejection of these ideas as well as the theoretical underpinnings of the experience were having a positive and immediate effect of us both engaging with a deep feeling, opening up the mystery of the event. As I listened to RN (without interrupting), Bion's suggestion that the analyst can help the patient "be O" by providing an open space and meditative attitude came to mind. I was clear that this would not be achieved by me meditating or attempting to exclude thoughts but by continuously reorienting to the mystery in the room and struggling to keep open the space for it to unfold.

It was observable that RN was elated, open, curious, and wide-eyed during the telling of the narrative. At that point, any interpretation may have been taken up and could have had the effect of changing his story. This is because every patient who has such an experience is unsure of what happened and wants an explanation. I found it tempting at least to indicate that an element of growth has resulted from the experience and that somehow the threads of previous sessions have created a new direction. However, while it should be accepted that the experience is indeed a prime example of growth, this should not be mentioned, as doing so would take the experience in another direction.

RN mentioned that he had been meditating and that immediately made me think of the relationship of that state to the outcome. I was also listening carefully for any reference to oneness as he talked about the importance of having some peace. I started to consider, before I stopped this reverie about meditation, that peace is a necessary form – or result – of oneness. It was difficult not to reach further with this idea as the peace seems to fit a model of oneness proposed by Jung. The feeling of peace may have been derived from RN being in a meditative state or being tired at the end of the day (when the experience took place), as part of a depressive state (he had declared that morning that he had "had enough") and therefore was just an amalgam of vague contents circulating at the margin of consciousness. To take the component of "peace" out of the general narrative would be a mistake as it would offer no benefit in uncovering the significance of the experience.

I sat quietly through RN's telling of the narrative, even though my mind was very active, and, as it quieted through rejection of interpretation and continuous reorientation, I was able to relate to the experience as a feeling in the room. However, the more he talked about it, the more I began to sense that he was intellectualising what had occurred and that he was drawing on analogies from his vast understanding of the literature on spiritual traditions. I felt the power of the experience beginning to slip away. It was still there, but its power was diminishing as RN's detailed analysis of it became more abstract.

I asked him about the effect – the loosening of the Gordian knot – and how that had occurred. He put his hand on his chest and described it as a sensation of a loosening of the perpetual tightening that he had experienced since childhood. I asked him to take me into that tightness so I could understand what the feeling of peace did. This seemed like a good idea, because I wanted RN to connect more with the experience and it would open an opportunity for embodiment. However, it merely led back to one of our earlier discussions about the anxiety that RN had felt when he was younger. Not wanting to lose the experience, I asked him to stick with that feeling so I could better orient to what had occurred. Unfortunately, in a sense, it was too late, and the experience seemed to dart from the room as I wondered if it had

had any effect. I understood then that speaking of the effect was difficult and it may have been better to wait until that became apparent and instead concentrate on legitimising the experience and leaving the mystery intact and in the room.

In the next session, RN reported a continued easing of the anxiety and spontaneously declared that he had no need to put the experience into a spiritual or philosophical package. Then he began to open up about feelings of inadequacy and how the experience contrasted with his depressed state, highlighting the latter and dimming the former. I had the sense that the grandiosity of the experience in the room led to a more intense evaluation of his limited view of his day-to-day life and his inability to advance in his career.

The experience did have an effect on consciousness: it revealed to RN the existence of the not-I as an aspect of his psyche and allowed him to reflect more fully on his complexes. I believe that this was accomplished by keeping all theoretical or psychological insight out of the session, which allowed the experience to be itself, in all its mystery. However, this was unique to RN. The fact that it was a profound, overwhelming mystical or numinous experience was not lost on him because he was aware of the nature of such experiences and knew that his was an overwhelming occurrence that was unlike any other experience. If he had not been so aware of the nature of these experiences, it would have been necessary somehow to keep the discussion of the importance of the experience alive.

In further sessions, it had the consequent effect of generating anxiety that it may have been a crossover into a psychotic experience and this stirred up deeper neurosis and the possibility of a loss of control. I had failed properly to legitimise the experience as one that was not psychotic and to bring him to a more profound awareness of what had occurred.

On reflection, my fascination with RN's experience – which may have been communicated in my passive, meditative position – might have set too high a standard for him as to the importance of a new elevated goal that he was unable to maintain. This had the paradoxical effect in the fourth session after the ME of him reclaiming the analytical process by raising personal issues about payment for sessions and my not using various psychoanalytic techniques he had read about, rather than a shared, uplifting appreciation of the ME. In this sense, I corrupted the experience by collaborating with RN to make this a special event that fulfilled a higher purpose for me. Instead, it should have been a higher purpose for him alone, and that would have required me to be more active in understanding his realisation and not passive or meditative.

Jung's analytical approach

At the end of *Mysterium Coniunctionis* (Jung, 1955–1956b, para. 782), Jung offers some thoughts on how to translate an unknowable, psychic event into a metaphysical explanation. He explains in the case of numinous experiences that parallel religious or metaphysical ideas may be used (modestly) to put the experience into a framework. However, he is clear that these ideas have value in pointing to the operation of the unknowable in the psyche:

> It therefore seems to me, on the most conservative estimate, to be wiser not to drag the supreme metaphysical factor into our calculations, at all events not at once, but, more modestly, to make an unknown psychic or perhaps psychoid factor in the human realm responsible for inspirations and suchlike happenings.
>
> (Ibid., para 786)

The psychoid or unknown psychic occurrence is the proof of the non-ego in the unconscious, and metaphysical explanations reinforce this realisation. The "psychoid aura that surrounds consciousness furnishes us with better and less controversial possibilities of explanation and moreover can be investigated empirically" (ibid.). It is possible then to explain the phenomenon of a ME to a patient as belonging to a part of the unconscious that cannot be known, thus providing a bridge from the unknowable event to an intra-psychic, non-ego force. This allows a ME to be related to as a part of the unconscious rather than through the mystical and religious traditions. The images within a ME then translate into God images contained within the psychoid region that defy precision: "The realization might by this time be dawning that when we talk of God or gods we are speaking of debatable images from the psychoid realm" (ibid., para. 787).

The existence of this psychoid realm must be understood *before* any framework is formed:

> In view of this extremely uncertain situation it seems to me very much more cautious and reasonable to take cognizance of the fact that there is not only a psychic fact but also a psychoid unconscious, before presuming to pronounce metaphysical judgments which are incommensurable with human reason.
>
> (Ibid., para. 788)

In his discussion of synchronicity – the name he gives to meaningful but acausal connections between subjective experience and an external event, such as the right book falling off a shelf – Jung (1952b, para. 840) applies this term "psychoid" to that part of the psyche that is "irrepresentable." Similarly, the instinctual process is another example of that which cannot be perceived and therefore exists at some level that is *incapable* of consciousness (Jung, 1947/1954, para. 380). The measure of a process that is carried on as psychoid is that it never crosses over the "fringe" of consciousness, a term Jung (ibid.) borrows from William James. Therefore, by this explanation, the source of a ME *cannot* be brought into consciousness.

What occurs in Jung's approach is that a ME indicates that there is a recognisable, inexplicable area of the unconscious that is psychoid, making the process alien to the ego. This offers the patient a convenient "explanation" of the existence of the not-I when it is examined after the fact. The experience, in terms of the meaning for the ego, is the essence of the ontological significance of the occurrence and must have some explanation. When it is proposed that the experience itself operates at the psychoid level and is fully and utterly *inexplicable*, then no metaphysical explanations are necessary.

Bright (1997) explains how the psychoid acting in a synchronistic event may be approached and discussed in terms of meaning. This is against the backdrop of Jung's essential proposition that there is always a psychological movement towards the development of the Self, implying that the teleological significance of an experience is inherently meaningful. In the case of meaning that cannot be discerned, such as a synchronistic event or a ME, Bright (ibid., p. 617) points out that there is still a need to seek some objective meaning to avoid a magical conclusion. This attempt will necessarily result in a search for a transcendent nature of meaning, even though the emphasis should be on the intra-psychic nature of the occurrence. Jung (1952b, para. 960) suggests that such a search would require a new conceptual language because any meaningful explanation within the bounds of the knowable is impossible. However, it may be examined as a non-ego force in order to bring it to ground for its psychic significance. Bright (1997, p. 618) emphasises that any meaning always remains "subjective and provisional" as "[i]t is a work in progress, not a glimpse of absolute truth."

There is a necessary distinction between synchronicity and a ME. A ME has two parts: that which is unknowable and incapable of explanation; and that which has an effect that can lead to a change of consciousness. With synchronicity, the emphasis is on developing a meaning of the phenomenon as it has no particular effect, except wonder. With a ME, the central focus that gives the event significance is the effect on consciousness. The nature of the event of synchronicity or paranormal events also differ from a ME as they are not primarily overwhelming. Bright reminds us that Jung's mission was to point out that the rational mind stymies the individuation process, thereby directing Jung's focus to the not-I (ibid., pp. 620–621). When there is a ME, there is a particular event that makes the meaning shift to a possible effect of the not-I and away from the contents. The difference between synchronicity and a ME in terms of analysis is that the former stays in the psychoid region and cannot reach consciousness, while the latter originates in the psychoid region but can be functional and brought to consciousness. Jung (1952b, para. 840) explains the inaccessibility of aspects of the unconscious in his well-known statement about archetypes: "The archetype as such is the psychoid factor that belongs, as it were, to the invisible, ultra-violet end of the psychic spectrum. It does not appear, in itself, to be capable of reaching consciousness."

The ME is able to reach consciousness because of its overwhelming affect. Indeed, the effect is so great that it wipes away the ego, if only for a moment, and presents a different realm within the unconscious. If the conscious and unconscious dread are overcome because of the subject's receptivity, the effect of the change may be an alteration in the psychic orientation. A synchronistic event may be of that character, but it would then have to pass into the category of a ME in order to create that transit of consciousness.

Conclusions on the analytic attitude

The different arguments and ideas in respect of the analyst's role in the face of a ME are certainly understandable as the event goes beyond the normal theories and practices of psychoanalysis. There is also no one attitude that can be applied to all patients, as the example of RN with his knowledge of spiritual traditions confirms. What is most relevant for the patient is to understand that a unique event has occurred; this cannot be ignored, nor, in fact, should the experience be normalised. The unique event, in psychological terms, is in fact the energic breakthrough of a non-ego aspect of the patient's being that supplanted the ego position. This is an inescapable conclusion.

This breakthrough is, for Jung, a matter of libido energy drawing out the primordial archetype in the collective unconscious. Jung (1947/1954, para. 391) explains that the threshold that must be crossed in such an experience "presupposes a mode of observation in terms of energy, according to which consciousness of psychic contents is essentially dependent upon their intensity, that is, their energy." In other words, the energy will then break through into consciousness when it reaches the "bursting point" (ibid., para. 366).

The unique nature of the experience, its profundity, and the breakthrough of primordial material into consciousness cannot be explained in terms of the technique or stages of analysis or as occurring through an analytic approach, be it active, passive, or meditative. A patient cannot be the O; the O happens to him. The particular combination of powerful archaic archetype and achieving a dimmed consciousness through meditation practices still requires in every religious and mystical tradition an inexplicable event of enlightenment. As such, this awareness of the autonomous and profound nature of a ME will not be diminished by avoiding discussion of theory, ignoring the uniqueness of the experience, or somehow making it just another subjective phenomenon. Therefore, it must be acknowledged and legitimised as a recognisable, profound psychic event that is unique. Both the patient and the analyst must be in awe of what occurred, and it seems necessary for the analyst to articulate that it is a significant event in order to acknowledge its unique presence in the room, if that is not otherwise apparent.

The other necessary stance is that, as far as the analysis is concerned, this is a subjective event *in psyche*. There is no harm in framing it in religious or spiritual terms if it is made clear that the effect on the psyche is just as relevant. In the end, for psychoanalysis, this is only about the unconscious, as Jung (1939, para. 506) makes clear: "what in Indian philosophy is called 'higher' consciousness corresponds to what we in the West call the 'unconscious.'" For a psychoanalyst, the unconscious and its structural archetypal contents are the appropriate source of the experience and a lens through which a ME can be understood. An examination of a ME, as Jung (1939a) conducted in the case of Zen Satori, is therefore an explanation of the effect of the processes of the collective unconscious. However, there was no need for Jung (or any analyst) to characterise or define a ME *per se* other than that it is another form of possible unconscious revelation, often presaged by specific images of the Self (Jung, 1936a, para. 1331).

It is important to emphasise that there is no need to exclude the idea that this is also a religious or spiritual occurrence. The psychoanalytic numinous experience and the tradition-based ME overlap at various points. The first point is that the experience, in all cases, overwhelms the intellect; the second is that it is an event that has affect and an effect on consciousness; and the third is that the ultimate breakthrough at a specific time and place is a mystery. The difference is related to *attribution*, with the psychoanalytic requiring the unconscious and the spiritual orientation requiring the divine (or a merging with nothingness).

The appropriate analytic attitude appears to be one that gives full weight to the experience and does not allow it to remain an unformed, poorly understood phenomenon for the patient. Discussing theory or speculating about what the ME might be in order to join in with the patient in wonder about what happened is perfectly acceptable and appropriate. The profound mystery is not lost in this way because it will remain inexplicable and therefore no discussion will change its character. If anything, its treatment in this manner may lead to the event having a greater effect on consciousness as the analyst is providing affirmation that this is something unique and wondrous. A meditative or passive approach denies its power and leaves it floating for the patient, whereupon it is more likely to cause anxiety as a possible psychotic or dissociated state. In this way, if the patient is receptive, mutual recognition of the incredible event is likely to have a lasting influence on the conscious position and may encourage the patient to reflect on and consider what has occurred.

An explanation of the psychoid region and its unknowable material may be needed to bring the psychoanalytic aspect of the experience into situations where it is firmly placed within a religious or mystical tradition. Such an explanation is not contrary to those traditions, but it should be emphasised that, as far as the psyche is concerned, the source is unknowable. Continued discussion of the narrative will bring the analyst to the point of legitimising the experience, attributing it to the psyche, and making it significant. The next, critical question is whether the patient is prepared to take it further, become receptive, and open up to what effect it might have on his or her consciousness. However, it is futile to try to explain the benefits of such an enterprise to the patient. The best approach is to test whether the patient is willing to go further and begin to understand the presence of the non-ego force and what it portends. If the patient is unable to become more receptive, it is impossible to resurrect the experience.

Chapter 4

The nature of receptivity

Receptivity to a ME is not characterised for any person by a wide-open highway where there are no obstacles. Even those who are mystics reported the need to purify or perfect themselves so that they can experience the full revelation. The Sufi mystic Ibn 'Arabi refers to the process of receptivity as a step-by-step polishing of a mirror so that the divine can observe itself through the imperfect vehicle of a person. An enlightened mystic is therefore one who has no barriers and does not block the illumination of what is presented. For Jung, established mystics were a special breed: Meister Eckhart was "the greatest thinker of early medieval times" (Jung, 1921e, para. 410), while the Buddha was a "genius" (Jung, 1939c, paras. 1003–1004). To be fully receptive, according to Jung (1955–1956b, para. 782), is to have an "inspired personality."

This is not usually the patient in the consulting room or the analyst. Those patients who have such an experience must cross a vast gulf between a lifetime convinced of the infallibility of the conscious position and the emergence of a strange new phenomenon. When the experience has unfolded, receptivity is not then a simple "yes" or "no" answer but rather it appears as a tortured journey through the dense substance of the ego and the buried complexes to allow the subject to be present and interested. The conflicts are due to the tension of opposites, and each pole brings with it a grouping of outlooks that is inherently oppositional. The experience then is trapped in this matrix and cannot be fully received; it is sure to get caught. In these terms, enlightened mystics have no barriers because they have *resolved the opposites*. On meeting one of the interviewees, I casually asked, "Is everything good?" He paused for at least two minutes before replying, "There is no good or bad."

Receptivity is a vague concept because it is not a defined characteristic of the psyche as it is only suggested by a grouping of other qualities, such as an enactment of empathy or an emotional and cognitive linking favouring anticipation. Slote (2016, p. 210) has suggested that receptivity is an unrecognised "kind of virtue" implying a positive value of readiness; it carries with it, in the context of a ME, a positive predisposition to allow the intrusion of the non-ego and the possibility of change. It cannot be attributed as a male or female quality as it is not related exclusively to those attributes and embraces a wide spectrum, such as aggressive pursuit, single-mindedness, empathy, and devotion. It is, however, a summation of qualities that yield an objective, active, positive kenosis – self-emptying to allow a new direction.

James (1902/2008, Lecture 16) equates receptivity with passivity. Ancilli (1984, p. 31) suggests, "This passive character experienced by the subject is such a striking feature in the descriptions of great mystics that some philosophers saw within it the very definition of mysticism." This highlights that receptivity is both an emptying of the complexes and ideas that bind the mind, leading to a passive state, and a positive, active quality of anticipation: it is both the capacity to let go and a positive anticipation of what change might follow. The positive anticipation is a cognitive function that creates the orientation to the unknown. The two join and become fused for the mystic, leading to a readiness to receive the embrace of the mystery. It is probably for this reason that sexual images are invoked to indicate the union of the feminine qualities with the male. In Kabbalah, as a clear example, the Shekinah (the feminine aspect of God) is needed for the unity and explained as offering a sexual merging with the divine attributes.

The two aspects of receptivity – the capacity to let go and the positive anticipation – are a full explanation of what it means. If there is a positive predisposition, it can be activated only in the face of a ME when there is a capacity to suspend the conscious stream and have it replaced with unknown forces. The two work in concert because they are inextricably bound together. Because of its attraction to the mystery, the positive predisposition or anticipation might precipitate the capacity to empty in order to receive the experience. The binding occurs because of the power of the intellect to perceive what is so compelling about the mystery (Idel, 2005, pp. 184–185) and therefore this purposive, positive predisposition will predominate to achieve its ends.

Neuroscience research (van Elk and Aleman, 2017) suggests a similar dual operation through a "predictive process model," in which the brain's error monitoring function and a correction mechanism work together to create receptivity. "Error monitoring" refers to the resolution of a conflict between well-formed prior beliefs and new stimuli from the body and external inputs. When there is this conflict, it is said that a "prediction error signal" yields a correction by the natural process of the brain that struggles to rearrange the "self-model" to absorb the dissonance. Increased receptivity of experiences results when there is reduced error monitoring – less cognitive fixation – as heightened monitoring will reject occurrences. Reduced monitoring provides the brain with the capacity not to judge and therefore allows a prior belief to be more easily adjusted by the correction mechanism when faced with a ME. There is in this explanation a positive process of achieving a balance and an emptying by less cognitive fixation to achieve that goal.

Psychoanalytic receptivity

A ME is relevant for psychoanalysis if there is a *permanent* alteration of consciousness that indicates that there is a non-ego force in the psyche. If an experience is rejected, so that the alteration of consciousness is not achieved or is reversed, it fails to have psychological significance for analysis.

It is the possibility of rejection and the loss of the subject matter for analysis that require the alteration to be permanent in effect. As the experience may be rejected as it is occurring (although not during the initial onset), as it is ending, or especially thereafter when it is considered either at that time or in the future, the nature of the alteration must be one that has a lasting effect. Accordingly, if it is rejected a week or a month after the ME, the benefit of receptivity is lost because the experience cannot remain in the analysis. It is no longer a subject matter that may be discussed or that remains an object in consciousness on which one may reflect.

It is often the case with dreams, projections, or other material that are ignored or rejected that their psychological significance will arise in some other guise and at a future time, reflecting the original contents. Patience and respect for the processes of the psyche are paramount in these cases, and a rejection of any type is not conclusive. Such faith is not possible when there is a ME because it is singular and unique and carries the immediate potential for a major change in consciousness. When a rejection is followed in subsequent sessions by an outpouring of unconscious contents, it is always possible to attribute this to the breakthrough of the experience, perhaps opening a channel or a flow-on effect. However, although this seems a possibility, the source of the new material is unclear if there is no longer any reference point back to the experience in terms of its contents or the primary, emotional effect on the patient. A marked change in a patient four months after a ME has faded may appear to create a new central focus that resolved several issues. However, no direct link could be made as it is not referable to the ME.

A rejection might also have a negative effect on subsequent sessions because of transference issues. A rejected experience, as with MH, may be harmful to the analysis as it yields analytical difficulties, such as a countertransference evaluation of the patient as a hard case or a conclusion that progress will be slow. This reasoning occurs in psychoanalysis because it must be emphasised that insight is the *essence* of psychoanalysis and spiritual traditions: a person who has mystic status in the Zohar is said to be "living" even when dead (Matt, 2006, Vol. 3, p. 272, n. 77).

In terms of psychoanalytic theory, the intra-psychic failure brought on by a rejection is the loss of a symbol that holds the potential to alter consciousness. The content of the experience exposes a symbol or symbols of that greater depth, but its significance "cannot take place until the mind has dwelt long enough on the elementary facts, that is to say until the inner or outer necessities of the life-process have brought about a transformation of energy" (Jung,

1928a, para. 47). The symbolic value of a non-ego event, when rejected, ends and does not exert influence on consciousness. This is then the pivot point for the experience: whether it has been taken up or instead is rejected. James (1902/2008, p. 514) expresses it similarly: "the spiritual excitement in which the gift appears a real one will often fail to be aroused in an individual until certain particular intellectual beliefs or ideas which, as we say, come home to him, are touched."

The rejection is also a loss of connection to the archetypal primordial forces that have been propelled by accumulated libido to break through into consciousness as the thread of human development. Rejection is, however, not historically rare, because doctrinal denial of alternatives to a particular deity or experience for a requirement of a specific form of worship have been aspects of all major religions to dissuade the emergence of any other experiences. This is seen, for example, in the turning away from graven images (Yandell, 2009). In fact, the repetition of the dangers of mysticism and the admonition that it should be rejected are common features of religious traditions (Dan, 1998, p. 262). MH is a devout Catholic and his vision of the Virgin Mary would be considered an apparition that requires a "Marian" commission to assess the validity of the experience as well as the moral and mental character of the subject, as occurred with the visions in Medjugorje in Bosnia and Herzegovina. This arises because of the historical procedures for canonisation, in which proof of visions must be established (Gentilcore, 1992, p. 163). MH himself did not attribute his rejection to this religious barrier.

As mentioned, the rejection cannot happen during its initial onset. Being able to control the progress of the experience because of previous facility with the effect of the occurrence may happen for experienced mystics, but this is not applicable to Jung's examples of a numinous experience or reported instances of a ME. Jung only listed events that were immediate and sudden, giving no early opportunity for consideration of whether to be overwhelmed. He stressed that being overpowered is one of the fundamental aspects of all numinous experiences, so if there were an ability to control the gateway, the experience would not fall within his definition. This implies that a numinous experience falls upon an analysand but not necessarily on an established mystic, who may, due to past experience, recognise what is occurring. This is another reminder that Jung positions a numinous experience as an event that may occur for a patient sitting across from an analyst but it is not necessarily an explanation of the experiences of a mystic.

At any time after the overwhelming, initial onset, the ME may be rejected if there is any form of cognitive assessment. This is not a result of an intellectual examination during the experience but, as mentioned, either an intuitive, perceptive awareness that infiltrates consciousness or an unconscious process that causes rejection but never reaches conscious awareness. Jung (1904–1907/1910, para. 88, n. 36) quotes the German psychologist Munsterberg in another context: "between external excitation and conscious central excitation, there is a non-conscious state in which an association process takes place that does not reach consciousness."

It appears unlikely – or at least rare – that a rejection will be caused purely by a non-cognitive, unconscious process. Sri Aurobindo (Ghose, 1973b, p. 274) explains that intuition in a ME is involved in the receipt of a higher grade of knowledge projected into the mind but as that knowledge is being conveyed, it is "immediately caught and covered over with mental stuff" (ibid.). This mixture of intuition and cognitive awareness, he continues, opens up a "passage of communication" (ibid.) with the higher qualities. Intuition and cognitive thought therefore play significant, combined roles in the progress of a ME, and cognition will therefore, in this sense, be involved in a rejection. Jung sees intuition occurring prior to the evaluation of a symbol as the conduit for the archetype (Pilard, 2015, p. 219), which is similar to Sri Aurobindo's explanation. Jung perhaps would propose that this is entirely an unconscious process that takes place before any evaluation, but, in the case of a ME, this does not require the exclusion of cognitive, perceptual awareness when the onset is of an overwhelming experience that is accompanied by affect.

Therefore, it is unclear that the sheer, overwhelming affect will be sufficient for an experience to be received. It may suggest only a likelihood – possibly a high likelihood, but not a certainty. It may become lost as the revealed truth, although appearing as profound by the force of affect and thus initially received, is not understood, leading to confusion, amplified by thought. As Sri Aurobindo (Ghose, 1973b, p. 163) explains, what the mind grasps is only an *idea* of the infinite, not the "real spaceless infinite." Therefore, it will not necessarily be convinced of the enormity of what has occurred, and might treat the revelation, as it is occurring, as transient, unworthy, or an illusion.

The nature of a ME and Jung's numinous experience in terms of its psychoanalytic significance is that it essentially creates something new that has a particular form. It operates on the basis of the existence of a split between the subject, as having a normalised state of consciousness, and another force – the object within the unconsciousness that will break through to change that state. This does not occur merely by overwhelming the conscious state through the energic qualities of the numinous occurrence. It is clear that more is needed in terms of fixing the revelation as absolutely worthy and significant. Rejection is therefore probable between the commencement of the experience and that fixing, in whatever sequence it occurs.

The fixing of the experience – a permanence – is what is most relevant. Accordingly, the notion of communion with the divine as the highest state of a ME – either equivalent to or exceeding a numinous experience – is largely irrelevant, except as a predictor of possible embodiment. The emphasis psychologically is on the self-reflectiveness of consciousness and its ability to change its locus by the intrusion of the non-ego, autonomous psyche. This is justified as the key result as an aspect of an ideal, spontaneous unfolding of human potential, some of which occurs in a gradual manner, some suddenly by overwhelming, subjective experiences, and also by the convergence of spirit with matter by external events. To be an experience that is the subject of the dimension of analysis where it may have a role in providing insight and growth, it must create an alteration in consciousness that does not revert. This occurs when the previous conscious position gives way to the revelation of a truth, however interpreted, that *thereafter* has supremacy in the ordering function of the ego. Accordingly, this confirms the need for some indelible change that is reflected by awareness of the non-ego revelation.

Thought washes a ME down and what emerges is a form that becomes acceptable to the ego as a revelation. It is the cognitive reinterpretation of the revelation through religious and cultural ideas that shapes what can be absorbed so that what is received is only what can be understood and thus tolerated. The details or content of the actual truth that is revealed is therefore relatively unimportant as the subject must rely on the ego's recognition that there is a non-ego force and give the *attribution of that force to the unconscious*.

The psychoanalytic requirement that there must be recognition of a non-ego force in the unconscious is problematic for those who are practitioners within spiritual and religious organisations. If there is an impact on the conscious position, it is more likely to operate outside the analysis. The interviewees had MEs outside analysis and all experienced changes in their conscious position. Insights were gained, several neurotic patterns changed, and a sense of wholeness was developed in all cases to various degrees. There was no need for them to relate the experience to the operation of primordial archetypal forces or be convinced of the nature of the unconscious. For patients in analysis, a translation of the experience to a psychological explanation is necessary in the context of the therapeutic encounter. Although it does not deny the effect of a ME that arises within the context of a tradition, it is oriented to a different outcome related to the workings of the unconscious in a psychoanalytic process.

It should be emphasised that this "translation" to a psychological frame is not a destructive process where the ego is thrown into chaos and forced to abandon other points of view. As Jung (1934/1954, para. 522) explains: "Consciousness should defend its reason and protect itself, and the chaotic life of the unconscious should be given the chance of having its way too – as much of it as we can stand." The attribution of a ME to the unconscious is a shock to the ego as it is no longer in complete control but becomes "a passive observer who lacks the power to assert his will under all circumstances ... because certain considerations give it pause" (Jung, 1945/1954, para. 430). S.P. Singh (1986, pp. 153–154), in his comparison of Sri Aurobindo and Jung, explains this well:

> These considerations are the realization on its part that the unconscious contents have in a way vitalized and enriched the personality ... The

realization does not only transform the uncompromising nature of the ego but also makes the will "a disposable energy" as the latter makes itself subordinate to the [Self].

What one is rejecting by not being receptive to a ME is the possibility of a change to a conscious viewpoint and the diminution of the ego's ascendancy. This new viewpoint is critical as "the mystic seeks a new way through the world. Mystical experiences are valuable not in themselves but only as they help someone to obtain a new viewpoint on normal experience" (Yearley, 1983, p. 131). The change in viewpoint is compatible with spiritual traditions that seek gradual increases in awareness where the ME may be attributed to God or to the realisation of nothingness, but it requires a new conscious position to explain the significance of the experience and its benefits.

Morality of rejection

With all the importance and excitement surrounding a mystical or numinous experience and its capacity to change the subject's viewpoint, it might seem impossible to turn one's back on what has occurred. Symington therefore argues that "There cannot be a healthy act of refusal of the infinite. It is like speaking of 'virtuous vice'" (cited in Merkur, 2010, pp. 307–308). Merkur, who analyses Symington's work in the mystical context, concludes that the latter's thesis is that the psyche should be held accountable for a "morally culpable act of refusing the divine" (ibid.).

It may be argued that any rejection of a numinous experience indicates a tragedy, a fundamental negation, and a strong, unconscious desire to continue suffering. Singh (1986, p. 100), in examining this tragedy, quotes Sri Aurobindo that an ego not informed by non-ego forces or having awareness is only an isolated, self-existent being, and this has a profound destructive effect:

> It limits the being, limits the consciousness, limits the power of our being, limits the bliss of being; this limitation, again, produces a wrong way of existence, wrong way of consciousness, wrong way of using the power of our being and consciousness, and wrong, perverse and contrary forms of the delight of existence.
>
> (Ghose, 1973b, p. 652)

An ego structure by definition is ignorant of unconscious forces or at least their usefulness. The alteration of consciousness called for in order to evaluate a ME that is of interest to psychoanalysis may do violence to the ego position, even if it is considered dysfunctional. What appears as a beneficial revelation to the analyst and the essence of psychoanalysis is not necessarily the same gift for the patient. Clearly, however, for MH, the ME was a shock that caused a direct refusal to consider the experience. The appearance of the Virgin Mary and a moment of divine merger are miraculous and did occur, and this appeared to be the true process of the emergence of libido energy that had been constellated. The rejection of the experience as an illusion or a hallucination did have a negative moral tone, as if MH failed the basic test of awareness and the possibility of having a less neurotic life. The reasoning that follows is that the force of such a powerful image could have enabled MH to develop respect for a force that was alien to the ego, and this may have led him into a new relationship with the unconscious. The alternative attribution to his lunchtime crabstick is such an anathema to psychoanalysis that his rejection could be interpreted as a defence against becoming conscious, an inability to progress along the path of individuation, or a form of spiritual bankruptcy that then becomes a dead hand on future growth.

Jung (1955–1956b, para. 675) explains this in strong terms: "If the demand for self-knowledge is willed by fate and is refused, this negative attitude may end in real death." He is referring to a person who has this demand and is otherwise able to "strike out on some promising path" and adds: "If he refuses this then no other way is open to him ... The unconscious has a thousand ways of snuffing out a meaningless existence with surprising swiftness" (ibid.).

This judgement of moral bankruptcy arising from a rejection of a ME is inappropriate for several reasons. The first is that lack of receptivity is not a conscious choice based on a weighing of options. As an example, MH did not see his rejection as a rejection of God or an explicit turning away from the chance for growth. He made a particular form of determination that whatever was represented by the experience was a threat to his being. He did not reject it at the time of its occurrence as it was overwhelming; rather, later, but prior to mentioning it in analysis, he developed a massive defence to protect himself. For, as Jung (1921b, para. 626) explains: "the ego's efforts to detach itself from the object and get it under control become all the more violent." This is perhaps an aspect of MH's neurosis, but it also illustrates his fragility, for which he cannot be judged. At least he was in analysis and his progress was "titrated" to account for his innate sensitivity. It would be harsh to accuse him of moral failure as well as insulting the years he had devoted to trying to change. What he lacked is what Jung (1928b, para. 300) calls a "subjective aptitude": "an innate psychic structure that allows a man to have experiences of this kind."

The accusation of spiritual failure may be more appropriate to patients who accept the experience and even make a transitory change to a conscious position, but over time allow it to fade as a mere memory, treat it as a curiosity, or more likely channel it into an intellectual enquiry, so that the alteration of consciousness is impermanent. This appears to be the most common clinical experience: watching the experience gradually disappear over time until it is reduced to "that experience," with no appreciation of its magnitude.

RN's experience, described earlier, began to fade after five sessions. I found myself mentioning it in various ways, but this was of no consequence as it had already left the consulting room. Instead, it became a story around which theory and theology created an attack on the idea of the importance of the non-ego force that I was obviously expounding for the reason of resurrecting the experience. I had a sense that the resurrection was used in aid of transference issues that had been meandering their way through our work. An analyst resurrecting an experience when it has faded is most likely to be interpreted as a countertransference issue because doing so gives it importance that is counter to the patient's attribution. In order to bring it up, it is necessary for the analyst to explain why it is being discussed in terms of the non-ego forces. This is difficult as it is a concept that has been rejected, so a discussion may bog down quickly.

It may be presumed that every ME will naturally fade over time in relation to the initial affect. The fixation of a new viewpoint before it disappears is therefore implicit in Jung's concept of numinous experience evidenced by his insistence that the occurrence is overwhelming so that it is bound to present itself immediately to the conscious mind. In his conception, in order for it to alter consciousness, the initial affect must have an *immediate effect* – either at that time or very shortly thereafter. The initial effect then creates the permanent change. The initial affective aspect of the experience cannot be maintained and thus the overwhelming will, at some point, cease to be as effective. The overwhelming itself is then a single event at the time of the experience that will be eroded, so the effect must remain. The fact of the overwhelming will linger in memory even though it is no longer capable of creating a new alteration in consciousness. This is best explained by Lacan (2014, p. 14): "Affect is unfastened; it goes adrift. It can be displaced, crazy, inverted, metabolised, but not repressed."

The real problem is what the patient should do with the realisation of a non-ego force if it does not have immediate effect and so is certain to disappear or decline in significance over time. As one patient who appreciated the non-ego force operating within him explained: "I feel as if a load of lumber was dropped off on my front yard and I don't know what I am supposed to do with it." This is no different from any other insight that has arisen where there is a need to keep it alive in the analysis and let it do its own work of transformation. What is missing for a ME is a context that enables the ego to hold on to what happened. In a spiritual tradition, the insight will be kept alive by fitting it into a stage of development where it has a clear place and reflects progression. As psychoanalysis does not have the same refined declarations of the place of the insight in an overall context, the analyst can merely hope that it remains in the session as a vibrant, proactive idea that keeps open the possibility of a widening of the ego consciousness. It may remain active in the unconscious, producing a perceptible change over time, although this cannot be proven because the causal links have apparently been broken.

This distinction prompts a re-examination of the relationship of Jung's numinous experience to lesser mystical experiences. When Jung's letter about numinous experiences being the "real therapy" and his list of examples are combined, it appears that he was writing about an experience that had a curative effect on neuroses at the time of its occurrence – a permanent change, not one that merely provided insights that could be subsequently maintained. These experiences are exceptional and overwhelm the subject, so refusal is unlikely; and they have an immediate effect, so it will not fade. He could not describe such an experience as the "real therapy" if it failed to effect that permanent change in consciousness. More importantly, the "real therapy" could not include lesser experiences that are more easily eroded; it must pertain only to a major occurrence that, at the time, effected a substantive change. Therefore, the phrase cannot be used in reference to a series of minor experiences that yield insight or even to a stage in a spiritual tradition. It is used exclusively in reference to one experience that is so profound in itself that it is indelible. Accordingly, the "alteration of consciousness" suggests that the experience effects a definite, permanent change to an existing position.

There was irrefutable evidence that many interviewees had experienced an indelible ME because they had abandoned Western life either completely or in essence and referred to themselves as mystics. Yet, they had thrown themselves into a spiritual tradition that had removed the rawness of their initial, overwhelming experience and placed it within a collective narrative. Every new experience fed into the narrative and sometimes the interviewees were able to tell a good story, even though their experiences were historic and the intensity had gone. In this way, they had ultimately rejected the personal experience and replaced it with the story, but they had made it a life-altering experience at the time of the occurrence. In this context, the overwhelming effected the change but lost its power over time and was kept vibrant and effective in altering consciousness by the spiritual context.

The essence of the experience in terms of its psychological significance is therefore that the recognition of the non-ego, alien force *remains activated*. Many of the interviewees were still searching and were focused on the qualities of a force beyond their limited ego that was revealed in their experiences. They remained activated but did not understand the activation as the acceptance of a psychological fact, but as reaching a certain level of realisation that was indelible. This level is the determinant of receptivity, rather than the nature of the occurrence, its force, or the likelihood of it having an effect. It is the *continuously activated recognition of the non-ego force* so that it becomes a lens through which all phenomena are observed.

Sri Aurobindo (Ghose, 1973, p. 273) calls the activated quality that becomes a lens an "intermediate power and plane of consciousness, perhaps something more than that, something with an original creative force." In these terms, the initial event creates more than just the reception of a non-ego force into the conscious position; it effects a transformation to a plane of consciousness whereupon that force is the focal point through which all else is perceived. Abraham Maslow described what he calls the "high plateau" state during a conference on internal states:

> I found that as I got older, my peak experiences became less intense and also became less frequent ... As these poignant and emotional discharges died down in me, something else happened that has come into my consciousness, which is a very precious thing ... I can define this unitive consciousness very simply for me as the simultaneous perception of the sacred and the ordinary ... This type of consciousness has certain elements in common with peak experiences – awe, mystery, surprise, and esthetic shock. These elements are present but are constant rather than climactic ... The words I would use to describe this kind of experience would be "a high plateau" ... [T]hese plateau experiences are described quite well in many literatures. This is not the standard description of the acute mystical experience but the way the world looks if the mystic experience really takes. If your mystical experience changes your life, you go about your business as the great mystics did.
>
> (Quoted in Krippner, 1972, p. 113)

The evidence for the attainment of the intermediate power – or plateau – is the particular viewpoint of those who have had a ME. This arose for consideration in an examination of different schools of Chinese mysticism in order to show that the level of judgement is what determines the grasping of the mystical occurrence:

> What is it is also other; what is other is also it. There they say "that's it," "that's not" from one point of view. Here we say "that's it," "that's not" from another point of view. Are there really it and other? Or really no it and other?
>
> (Roth, 2000, p. 38)

The theoretical differences relating to what constitutes the elements of the intermediate power are not as relevant as the attainment of a clear view (in this tradition) of nothingness and lack of form. In this context, attainment to the numinous or the test of receptivity to a ME is the continued explanation of phenomena through the lens of the experience and not the intellect. It is not a story but rather the expression of life through the revelation of the experience.

Therefore, to enable receptivity, the ME must trigger a change of viewpoint that proceeds on the basis that the non-ego is the *primary underlying structure* of the psyche that is the central guide. This inclusion elevates the subject to another plane where the activation becomes a central, continuing focus, because once it is seen as that primary structure, all actions are related to it in some way. This is the reason why spiritual traditions channel that intimation of a primary structure into a series of well-defined steps to prevent it from dissipating or to find a means for its expression so that it reaches a plateau.

This degree of continuous activation is a level of awareness and not a static state caused by a ME. It is the platform to go forward but also, most importantly, does not allow a return – or slippage – to a prior state. The idea underlying all MEs, although not usually articulated in this way, is that the experience will somehow break through to such an extent that it will raise the subject to a higher plane of consciousness. In the *Kernel of the Kernel*, the great work of Ibn 'Arabi (n.d., pp. 20–26), it is explained that the initial stage (or "station") is a "mentation" of what might be Total Knowledge. The second stage is the reception of a teacher and the beginning of purification, but "Perplexity, remorseless distraction and intellect are at this level. Many get irrevocably lost at this stage" (ibid., p. 22). The third stage, which represents the intermediate plane, is the "station of remaining," being constantly "in a state of prayer" (ibid., p. 23).

A single ME may traverse these stages and create the state of remaining – the high plateau. As a matter of definition, for there to be no rejection of a ME by its erosion, it seems that an aspect of the revealed truth must remain as a seed, or a sense of itself, or the basis of continued self-reflection that is present in all circumstances. There is no textual proof that this is what Jung meant, but his letter to Martin suggests that, as a cure for neurosis, the experience would have to be extraordinary and not just offer a new viewpoint. It must remain an active, persistent force that invokes the plane of consciousness from which there is no slippage.

The idea that there is a plane of consciousness where there is a solid, contained state is consistent with Jung's (1951) idea that the alchemical *Lapis* is where the spirit is recognised as a concrete step in the individuation process that fulfils the notion of a new, indelible plane. Although it is not a complete state (that is reserved for the *Rotundum* – perfected roundness), it is an example of a realised station along the way. This shift to a high plateau is observable in the emergence of unconscious material, especially dreams, which show that the patient stands on solid ground. This seems to be one of the only means for psychoanalysis to reach that conclusion as it is impossible to tell by behaviour, even though it is tempting to try. One of the interviewees at the Kumbh Mela sat still in meditation for twenty-four hours, yet subsequently, when I questioned him, he became irritated and demanded food. Jung (1953, Vol. 2, p. 324) explains: "The individuated human being is just ordinary and therefore almost invisible." There is no way to tell by ordinariness, words, or behaviour that an individual has undergone a certain indelible change. The revelation of the truth is perhaps what makes for ordinariness: "the enlightened person remains what he is, and is never more than his own limited ego before the One" (Jung, 1952, para. 158). It may be revealed perhaps in conversation by the orientation of the unconscious, observed by the constant insistence on matters of the soul revealing that the relationship between the subject and the Self is of an enduring nature.

In Western society and psychoanalysis, the appearance of a higher plane is difficult to find as reported experiences rarely carry permanence of presence. In most instances, this is a consequence of the experience being lesser, with insufficient force and effect to create anything greater than a minor impact that may fade over time. This, indeed, is the nature of the experiences that are most likely to occur, because full absorption and ultimate realisation or even the planting of an activated state is not presented in the consulting room. It is as if such an experience, if it is understood in this manner, would end the analysis and render it unnecessary.

It is therefore to be expected that patients will not reach the plane of consciousness where their viewpoint is permanently changed. It is much more likely that a ME will be recognised as possibly opening the door to a view of the workings of a non-ego force, but that this recognition will fade over time. It is also possible that the opening will be a wedge in which subsequent experience may be explored in these terms as verifying the force. The question of how it will transpire may be defined, from a psychological perspective, only on the capacity of the individual to be receptive to the experience and to be a candidate for attaining the higher plane, or at least keeping the door open.

The experiences of the interviewed mystics were all of the major class suggested by Jung in his category of numinous experience and the realm of Ibn 'Arabi's third station. The alteration of consciousness for each – perhaps with the few exceptions of those who had reduced the experience to a story – was such that they thereafter labelled themselves mystics or held no doubt that they had touched a profound reality that was still alive and vibrant. These were not in the nature of insights into the psyche; rather, they represented complete *paradigm shifts* so that their new orientation was through the filter of the truth that had been revealed. As an example, when I asked a German mystic about his trip to India, he bluntly replied that he was only interested in conversations that have to do with ultimate reality. He was no longer concerned with worldly chit-chat because his eyes were focused on "another plane." I repeatedly saw that mystics had one primary conversation about the way in which the divine – or, in the case of the Buddhist monks in Cambodia, the nothingness – was manifested.

The intermediate plane is included by necessary implication in Jung's idea of a numinous experience because, although the essence of the occurrence may be lost in spiritual doctrine, the self-identification remains as a revelation to the psyche. The experience is therefore likely to be a catalyst of ongoing attraction. Jung obviously had these experiences in mind when he proposed his list of examples, but he did not clarify what he meant. This is why commentators such as Murray Stein argue that a numinous experience is not a substitute for the travails of proper analysis. This arises from a lack of clarity as to what a numinous experience may be, given that full absorption is exceedingly rare while minor experiences that are not numinous experiences are plentiful. The importance for the analytic process is not in a definition but in the crystallisation of an experience that alters consciousness so that, even if there is minor slippage or fading over time, it will still be noteworthy as it has advanced the process of individuation to a new level. If the answer truly lies in the ultimate effect on psychological growth, the notion of "subjective aptitude" is essential. Why do some patients and not others reject or abandon these experiences that could have led to further development? And might anything be done during analysis to solidify or make more manifest the experience?

Keeping the experience alive or activated may not be easy. After such an experience, many patients relate it back to spiritual traditions, such as Buddhism or a Hinduism-based group with a guru. This may be helpful for analysis, even though the immediacy of the affective experience may be reduced. A spiritual tradition, through its elaborate categorisation of what occurred in a wider context, facilitates the development of faith and the reification of the experience because the markers of development along the path are clarified. A lesser experience may fit within one of the stages of the path so that a patient's struggle, say with a Zen Koan, may lead them to lesser insights but these are still validated as developmental stages in the tradition. In the "Five Ranks of Tozan" of the Soto-Zen school, for example, the realisation of *any* sense of emptiness is the first stage and a pointer to a larger truth. Hence, the tradition can keep the experience alive and increase the likelihood that it will reorient the subject so as to make an alteration in consciousness indelible. This process requires elaborate support mechanisms and constant reinforcement of the overarching doctrines as applicable to worldly problems that ensue.

Psychoanalysis alone may not have the necessary tools to fortify a ME as it returns constantly to pathology or the shadow elements as its essence; and it does not, by the way it is practised, provide reinforcement of a ME as proof of individuation. It is accordingly likely that the experience will be eroded over time because of analysis's inability to provide a context for the experience or because of a lack of interest on the part of the analyst. The rejection may take place as the experience is not reinvigorated as subsequent sessions bring up other matters for attention. Psychoanalysis, however, does have an important role to play because of its ability to recognise the psychological effect of the experience on the conscious mind by being witness to the occurrence of an unconscious breakthrough. This witnessing at least gives faith that there is communication from the unconscious that allows a psychological readjustment to the presence of the organising, beneficial forces in the psyche.

Jung advances the possibility that the experience itself is what alters consciousness, not the subsequent spiritual tradition or psychoanalytic understanding. However, this proposition ignores the fact that for a lesser ME, a substantial revelation can occur when there is cognitive assessment of what happened by the ego relating to the occurrence. The ego needs to reorient to the experience, provide itself with an explanation, and not remain confused by an affective, overwhelming event. Every ME, even if seen as purely subjective, at some point ceases to provide direct insight and then requires a context, especially if it goes on to alter consciousness and remain activated. The interviewees found that context in different spiritual traditions that were most congruent with the qualities and dimensions of what occurred. Their experiences were so profound that they began the reorientation as a result, but they became indelible only when the mystics were able to integrate them into their ego structure as the central focus of their life journey.

The key to treating rejection of a ME is not to blame it on the weakness of the overwhelming, the lack of recurrence, or even its failure to reveal a profound truth. It is instead that a new viewpoint is only obtained and maintained because the subject is *receptive* to its meaning and able to separate the experience from normal occurrences and be convinced of what it has declared. The truth that must be faced and made lasting is a movement away from an exclusive individuality to "some indirect and constructive idea of these hidden activities" (Ghose, 1973a, p. 734) of the non-ego. Sri Aurobindo explains that making the transition to acceptance and a new plane cannot be accomplished by the "surface mind," as it is too weak for this task. Instead, he assigns that task to the "subliminal consciousness," which is not hampered by limitations and must break through the ego consciousness. This corresponds to Jung's notion of necessity for the unconscious force but, as Sri Aurbindo (ibid., p. 1027) explains, it is a "difficult task to lay upon the normal consciousness of the human being, yet there is no other way of self-finding." The task may be carried out only by those who have a particular receptivity that maintains the process despite obstacles and dread.

The dread

The potential for rejection is contained within the overwhelming experience; a ME always has an element of fear. As the *Book of Psalms* (25:14) states, the secret of God is only for those who fear Him. In the context of a ME, this may mean that it is necessary to be as nothing before the boundless enormity of the mystery. This is the origin of Otto's "creature feeling," which occurs because there is no equal relationship where the ME is merely a product of mutuality. The purpose of it being overwhelming is not just that it overrides the conscious position but also, and more importantly, that it *shocks* the ego, requiring the latter's humility in the face of the full, vast reality that has been revealed.

Rejection based on fear, to create a protective barrier that prevents the experience from occurring, is unlikely to take place at the moment of initial onset or as the ME is beginning to overwhelm the subject. No matter what level of scepticism a person holds about MEs, or even if there is a complete denial that they exist, such experiences are invariably sudden, unbidden, and uncontrollable. This raises the question of whether it is ever possible – because of a religious, dogmatic viewpoint or a deep fear of the unknown and losing control – actively to prevent a ME from occurring. In terms of psychoanalysis, if this were feasible, it would suggest a subject with no openness to material from the unconscious, which would create a closed loop where the constant rejection would never allow the build-up of libido. In describing receptivity to the unconscious in words that are similar to the operation of a ME, Jung (1928b, para. 254; emphasis added) explains:

> But once the unconscious contents break through into consciousness, filling it with the uncanny power of conviction, the question arises of how the individual will react. Will he be overpowered by these contents? Will he credulously accept them? Or will he reject them? (I am disregarding the ideal reaction, namely critical understanding.) The first case signifies paranoia or schizophrenia; the second may either become an eccentric with a taste for prophecy, or he may revert to an infantile attitude and be cut off from human society; the third signifies the *regressive restoration of the persona*.

Here, Jung is referring to a rejection of unconscious material arising from *within* the unconscious that results in rejection. In addition to psychosis or eccentricity, a rejection because of a "regressive restoration of the persona" is a lack of awareness brought about by a return to an "early phase of his personality" (ibid.) in order to function. Jung is applying this concept to a person who "owes a critical failure of his life to his own inflatedness" (ibid., para. 263) and reverts back to an immature state. The consequence of this regression is the creation of that closed loop that would diminish the possibility of the experience altering consciousness. Each time the material arises from the unconscious, enters consciousness, and is rejected, the subject returns to the starting point caused by the regression.

It is common in analysis to have patients who maintain a position against the unconscious for many years and do not necessarily make any progress measured by observable changes of viewpoint or behaviour. It is thus easy to subscribe to the idea that the closed loop created by regression will block the possibility of a breakthrough of the unconscious. MH was just such a patient as he had a very wary approach to the unconscious, turning every insight into a logical puzzle that he had previously failed to solve. Yet, he had a forceful ME. As Jung suggests, the breakthrough occurs – it cannot be stopped because the psyche is autonomous – but the patient might then have an immature (psychological) attitude and the revelation has no effect because it is blocked soon after the initial onset, when there is some evaluation, or after the fact of the ME.

The absence of a closed loop – a regressive restoration of the persona – does not mean that the ME will necessarily be received in a manner that will alter consciousness. Many patients have an open door to the unconscious, but a ME does not take them to the "high plateau" – or intermediate level – where it will have a long-term effect on the conscious position. The ME is an invitation that is not necessarily accepted because it is a bizarre occurrence that portends the existence of another psychic dimension that is against all logic and ego understanding. Fear of the unconscious and fear of a ME are thus similar, and the fear of a ME may be especially pronounced due to the overwhelming power of the event.

The fear that leads to rejection of a ME arises immediately after the experience commences. There is a momentary shift after the onset that what is occurring is not rational, even before the full overpowering is felt. Most interviewees explained that there was a post-onset instant when it was perceived that *something* unusual was occurring. In some cases, this was so rapid that it blended into the overwhelming. In others, it was sufficiently gradual to be noted. In both cases, what seems to happen is the creation of a hypnogogic state where ego consciousness diminishes in terms of rational thought. At this time, fear may emerge, but a rejection would be difficult as the state is not a cause of panic or dread as it emulates a familiar, sleep-like state or dizziness.

The fear is, in fact, most prominent just after the onset as the subject is being overwhelmed and the force of the event cannot be easily curtailed as it is extraneous to the ego, although those who have had a previous ME and recognise its imposition might be able to push it away. One mystic who "shook off" an experience as she was going through airport security described it as flowing towards her after she had perceived it, like a wave heading to the shore, so she was able to stop it having evaluated that she could not function in that state. For her, the overwhelming conformed to a recognised pattern resulting from many previous MEs.

This parsing of the experience does not really convey the enormity of the struggle for acceptance that is presented by the power and significance of a ME. It is necessary to come to grips with a strange psychic occurrence that *always* leads to a question of what is happening to mental functioning. At this stage, in the barest of evaluations after the initial onset, the strangeness of the ME may attract any underlying personal issues or touch upon previous trauma or psychotic episodes. One of the New York interviewees, who had suffered two drug-induced psychotic incidents, described his experience as starting with what felt like a new psychotic episode in which he was in the depths of a fiery hell and pinned down like Gulliver, but it then turned into a mosaic of colours and a feeling of warmth and connection with God, which rescued him from the depths. This experience came upon him with an intuition that he was going to be delivered to a higher place, so he remained a passive observer in the process, which softened his fear. An Indian mystic interviewed at the Kumbh Mela felt panic as Lord Shiva burst out of his chest, stood in front of him, and began to explain the mystery the mystic was seeking. Jung (1938/

1954a, para. 86) relates the intense vision of Zosimos, the third-century alchemist and Gnostic:

> For there came one in haste at early morning, who overpowered me, and pierced me through with a sword, and dismembered me in accordance with the rule of harmony. And he drew off the skin of my head with the sword, which he wielded with strength, and mingled the bone with the pieces of flesh, and caused them to be burned upon the fire of the art, till I perceived by the transformation of the body that I had become spirit.

In defining "numinous experience," Jung explains that it comprises a conversion, emotional shock, and blows of fate that force a loss of control as the experience overwhelms the subject. The Zosimos vision is probably closer to this definition than a feeling of oneness with nature or even a benevolent connection with God. The reality of Zosimos's experience is that it is a psychic explosion in which one feels "dismembered," necessarily invoking dread. According to Jung, only some unknown force, such as the "caelum" of alchemy or that unknowable aspect of Mercurius, can help the subject to get through the experience and overcome the dread. In the Tantra tradition, it is said, "Now, at every crisis or critical position the aspirant or *sadhaka* requires and often gets what we may call ultra-ego-centric 'help,' or 'extra-scheduled' power" (Pratyagatmananda, 2002, p. 82).

The struggle to overcome the dread always occurs, to a greater or lesser extent, because every overwhelming numinous experience or ME disturbs the mind, causing a conscious reaction of at least some degree of confusion, fear, and awe. It is a momentary *observation* by the ego consciousness of an event, but not at that time a rational *evaluation* of what it might be. After the critical moment, following the peak experience, an evaluation of what has occurred certainly does take place. Functionally, therefore, there are two occasions for the experience to be disturbing and resisted: during the experience itself (immediately after the onset or prior to the peak); and on later examination of the experience through reflection.

The importance of receptivity to a ME is predicated on the fact that the subject has a choice and also that there is a sufficient interstice during the experience to decide to open (or close) to the numinosity. The enormity of the experience is not subject to choice as it first occurs until there is some cognitive or perceptual awareness; it is only that which opens a sufficient gap. Rejection at either of the two possible points – during an evaluation as the experience unfolds or after the fact – is therefore a *natural* reaction because, as Jung (1942/1948, para. 222) declares, there is a "holy dread" of the numinous, which indicates that there is a choice to suppress, discount, or ignore what is occurring or has occurred so that it does not result in an alteration of consciousness.

The dread is cumulative and originates at the unconscious level from a primordial fear of the unknown. Jung (1921d, para. 488) reveals a quote by

Tibbullus that: "the first thing God made in the world was fear." This is what Kierkegaard (1957, p. 45) calls the "immediate determinant": the inherent dread in all individuals that prevents a possibility passing over to an actuality. This occurs because of what he calls the "alarming possibility of being able" to attain freedom (ibid., p. 40), which makes dread a form of "dizziness" to which freedom succumbs. This philosophical explanation accords with the psychological position of fear that is apparent in the deep unconscious incest taboo and manifested in the mother complex arising, as Jung (1927/1931a, para. 59) suggests, from a "phylogenetic relic."

Jung (1921d, para. 489) determines that the result of any fear is the creation of an "abstraction" or a withdrawing from a connection that arises from a negative projection on the object. This means that the initial reaction arising from fear is always initially unconscious (by projection), followed by a conscious decision, leading to neutralising of the object "that renders it inoperative" (ibid., para. 491). In this analysis, Jung is commenting on art, but his words accord with the appearance of the not-I as an object in consciousness. The negative projection on the new object that appears to consciousness arises from a pre-existing unconscious fear, stirred by the powerful affect.

Marie-Louise von Franz (1995, pp. 71–72) offers two reasons, one related to fear, as to why an experience may be rejected. The first is that the "elastic open-mindedness," as she calls it, to receive a revelation is blocked by religious and scientific dogmatism or the formation of a fixed and certain view, so that an alternative is threatening. This postulates an otherwise receptive subject that has lost open-mindedness because of immersion in dogma. Dogmatism certainly could be a reason for rejection of a ME: the possibility of an otherwise receptive person has been channelled. The second is that the communication from the collective unconscious does not cross the threshold into consciousness "without suffering certain changes" (ibid., p. 81). This occurs because consciousness is structured in a temporal and spatial order but the material that crosses does not partake of any order and presents all its attributes simultaneously. This reflects Lacan's idea that the unconscious has a different structural language so that what it presents is not the Real or the absolute truth. Von Franz (ibid., p. 84) applies this idea to a ME of Jacob Boehme, who experienced great revelations but was unable to articulate his insights successfully: "The qualitative difference between things in the unconscious and the same things after they come over the threshold of consciousness probably creates the threshold difficulties" (ibid., p. 84). The importance of this observation is that there is never a direct transmission of the experience because it is scrambled spatially and temporally, then reinterpreted. It is therefore subject to continuous reflection and, as von Franz records for Boehme, that one second of ME may need to be interpreted over a lifetime (ibid.). In the gap of the experience and its translation, there is an open door for confusion and dread.

Von Franz did not conflate the difficulty of translation from unconscious material to consciousness with fear. As Lacan (2014, p. 158) explains, "It will be said that fear, of its nature, is adequate to, corresponds to, *entsprechend* [German: in accordance with] the object from which danger stems." The fear in the case of a ME therefore arises from "something that has the character of being referred to the unknown aspect of what is making itself felt" (ibid., p. 159). In this form of expression, the difficulty of translation suggests an unknown aspect that will be responsible for fear arising, because it is confusing and unknown. Perhaps Bion's (1962/2014, p. 362) phrase – "nameless dread" – most accurately describes the consequence of this unconscious fear.

Whatever the multiple causes of dread, the fear is both at a primary, unconscious level and at a cognitive level, due to the intrusion of the unknown. In the case of a ME, it is therefore experienced from the moment after its onset as appearing from outside the ego. That fear, when triggered at this stage, needs to be quelled or else it will be taken up and increased by cognitive consideration. Quelling the fear, then, seems essential to the maintenance of the insight and its effect on consciousness.

Fear cannot be quelled by a solitary act of belief or faith; rather it needs some spiritual or psychoanalytic setting before it is too late. Without that setting, it rapidly increases in its otherness and may be rejected as not being a recognised part of ego consciousness. However, there is always a gap between the experience and a chance to put it into a context so that the critical issue is the *innate receptivity* to the experience – the aptitude of the subject. Dread is not a conscious choice but rather arises from primordial roots and the alien nature of the experience, prompting self-preservation. It may be met by innate receptivity, which is the *only* counterbalancing force; hope is insufficient.

The limited research into this subject (Russ and Elliott, 2017) indicates that a previous crisis or stress may be a predictor of the degree of dread and resultant rejection. On a conscious level, when the experience comes to be evaluated, the rejection is therefore particularly natural for a subject who has had a psychotic episode or holds a negative prediction, perhaps because they have witnessed unpleasant effects in others due to ecstatic experiences. In this situation, dread is not a moral failure but an understandable response to the impact from what is unknown in relation to a sensitivity.

It is clear that for most people conditioned by a roadmap of civilised living, the aberration of a mystical event is inherently objectionable. Jung (1942/1948, para. 274) explains how these limitations caused by societal dread lead to denial, misunderstanding, or a discounting of what is being experienced:

> Modern man has hopelessly muddled ideas about anything "mystical," or else such a rationalistic fear of it, that, if ever a mystical experience should befall him, he is sure to misunderstand its true character and will deny or repress its numinosity. It will then be evaluated as an inexplicable, irrational, and even pathological phenomenon.

Here, Jung refers to evaluation of the experience after the fact due to a "rationalistic fear." The dread, in his terms, arises from the *tremendum* and the corresponding inability of the intellect to address the irrational directly as it is occurring, because, as Otto (1923, p. 5) explains, the numinous "eludes apprehension in terms of concepts." Sri Aurobindo (Ghose, 1973b, p. 770) elaborates:

> The sense mind, this intelligence, this reason, however inadequate, are the instruments in which he has learned to put his trust and he has erected by their means certain foundations which he is not over-willing to disturb and has traced limits outside of which he feels all to be confusion, uncertainty and a perilous adventure.

It would follow from this statement that if a subject is engaged in a spiritual tradition, the "limits" of what is tolerable will be extended as MEs are the essence of spirituality, thereby suggesting increased receptivity beyond that which is innate and a reduced amount of dread. In many instances, unfortunately, joining a tradition is a means to protect against the uncertainty of a random world and a *defence* against the fear of an overwhelming experience. This establishes a reference point for an occurrence that suggests the possibility that it might lose some of its raw force, mystery, and ambiguity as that fear is still present. It is common in clinical practice for patients to join a spiritual group that adds to their neurotic patterns, especially if there is a failure to carry out the required goals or practices.

Contrary to these ideas of indwelling fear, the interviewees suggested that receptivity to the mystical is outside any teaching and in the hands of a higher power, or, most importantly, innate because of inter-generational issues, and that this is merely confirmed by the tradition. This acknowledges that the likelihood of receptivity during the experience is not necessarily granted by being part of a tradition because the event arises outside any ego position, including one derived from previous MEs. It indicates, however, that, by having a context, it will be more likely to be received in terms of its significance within a tradition.

The drift of Eastern philosophy and practice into the West may not have increased receptivity because teachings that are translated through a teacher and writings may be diluted for Western ears. Whether this is the case need not be debated here. The interviewees suggested that the necessary refinement for increased receptivity by embracing Eastern teachings is immersion in the culture that is the source of the tradition because it is then ever present and not reduced by a Western, neoliberal approach to living. For them, as their MEs occurred during their involvement with certain traditions, the conclusion that a cultural context is necessary is understandable. It is, however, more likely that emulating the culture outside its country of origin creates conflicts for a Western subject as they follow a path where they do not understand the real ethos or origins of the practice. In this realm, psychoanalysis has the capacity to remove the need for cultural association and to bring the experience back into an understandable event for the ego.

Jung also exposes another, perhaps more compelling and obvious reason for the dread: a numinous experience always carries a taint of psychopathology. As he writes, "Naturally modern ignorance of and prejudice against intimate psychic experiences dismiss them as psychic anomalies and put them in psychiatric pigeon-holes without making the least attempt to understand them" (Jung, 1955–1956b, para. 780). This taint is obvious in psychology and psychoanalysis, affecting the analytical attitude and the manner in which the experience is in the analysis. It is also present in the general population, which is dominated by a diagnostic, medical model of all mental illness.

The reasons for a specific marginalising of MEs are complex, but summarily attributed to the "secularisation" of religion and the weakness of Western, New Age spirituality (Main, 2008). This causal theory, however analysed, is not as important in dismissing MEs as the telling, evidentiary facts of a historical trend of denial of mysticism and its relegation in psychoanalysis and psychiatry to non-scientific speculation. This is borne out, for example, in Merkur's comment on Bion that his mysticism is taken as "an idiosyncrasy that can be ignored by analysts who value his contributions to their secular practices of psychoanalysis" (Merkur, 2010, p. 228). There is the reality in this taint that would make a patient tentative (and rejecting) in the telling of a ME because of a concern, created by the tone and methodology of the process, that it may amount to potential pathology.

It is often overlooked that rejection is a legitimate stance not because of a taint of pathology but because MEs may be horrifying as they are not always interesting or beneficial; they can, as Jung (1947/1954, para. 405; emphasis added) suggests, be "healing *or destructive*." The vision of Zosimos ended with a beneficial outcome, but the appearance of a Gorgon, for example, or the *tremendum* of an experience revealing the antimonial power of God may cause an individual consciously to reject MEs then and perhaps for the rest of their life. The destructive experience may be an immediate source of rejection, or a ME could alternate between curative and destructive, creating later rejection or later openness. In the case of one mystic interviewed in India, the initial experience was positive, but this was followed by a long period of depression and then a negative ME. The negative experience of a sense of being overpowered by a deity (Kali) ultimately became positive again as feelings of inadequacy revitalised the need for a stronger ego. This created greater longing and suggests, in this single instance, that the negative was in pursuit of a positive outcome and the subject was then more impressed with the corrective power of unconscious forces.

When it is touched by the taint of pathology, feelings of anxiety, as Merkur (2006, p. 212) explains, trigger unconscious resistance to the experience in the form of dissociation. This dims consciousness, preventing the event from having any impact. A pre-existing dissociative pattern would especially add to the diminution of the experience and loss of receptivity as there would be no structure within which the result could be manifested and maintained.

The effect of a crisis or trauma, even though it may bring on pathology, seems to be linked to the possibility of a weakening of the ego structure that opens the door for a possible ME, rather than being a cause of rejection. Four of the interviewees situated their primary ME as occurring after crises in health, relationships, or financial stability. Their explanations were similar, and well articulated by one woman who identifies as a mystic:

> I had a series of disasters. I was living in Berlin and was notified that my father in LA had been murdered. I turned to my partner for support but he chose that moment to tell me he was leaving. I had relied on him for support in Berlin as I did not have permission to work. My entire world – my work as an artist, my dear father, my most important relationship – just collapsed. I sat under that Stonehenge-like structure in Britzer Garten and cried my eyes out. I then closed my eyes and sat quietly and was overwhelmed by what felt like a hand on my shoulder. It felt like my deceased mother's hand and then I sensed it was a goddess. I then felt her embrace me, easing my heart, soothing my mind, and when I opened my eyes everything around me felt connected. Within a week I had moved to India and I've been living here for ten years.

This conscious position was weakened prior to the experience by a disruption in the ego's expectations and a profound awareness of its limitations. In this instance, the need for a solution was answered by a life-changing experience. Of course, this is not always the case, but it illustrates that a ME can serve a soothing, healing function, and therefore it is likely to be received in these circumstances.

The fear of pathology from a ME is significant. Neumann (1948/1969, p. 397) explains that the experience should not be taken lightly as it can result in "catastrophe [which] can take the form of death in ecstasy, mystical death, but also sickness, psychosis, or serous neurosis." If a patient has had a psychotic break, as mentioned, there may be a well-defended line and a rigid ego boundary that stave off the feeling of the abyss or the unknown just after the onset. There is nothing in the initial onset of the experience that would allow a distinction to be made at that time that this is offering a beneficent new insight rather than a descent into a dissociated or psychotic state. The border between numinous and psychosis has always been treated as blurred when either comes upon the subject spontaneously. There are many instances of this blending, such as the well-examined phenomenon of meditation-induced psychosis (Kuijpers et al., 2007) and of MEs having psychotic features. However, it is possible that the experience after the outset can immediately trigger a lapse into a psychotic interlude and this could account for immediate rejection of the experience prior to the peak. This pattern of rejection is more likely to be a rejection after the fact because the post-onset and the peak may come too rapidly to allow withdrawal.

The rejection of a mystical or numinous experience may be as much conscious during the periods of cognitive assessment of the experience as it is unconscious where forces in the psyche react to defend a position just after it has commenced. The idea of an unconscious rejection is akin to Freud's (1900, p. 517) notion that there is an unconscious dream censor that protects the dreamer's sleep by supressing a dream. The main reason is to maintain the critical need for sleep, but this could also apply to the need to maintain an intact ego. Freud's (1915a, p. 173) suggestion is that this is an unconscious process as the censor may reject the dream content before it reaches the pre-conscious, keeping it in the unconscious. This indicates that there may be an unconscious – perhaps primal – dread of the numinous, which is unrelated to the discounting of the experience through conscious fear after the onset that arises by equating the experience with psychosis.

Nine of the mystics who were interviewed reported a disturbing initial experience, but in all cases, it was not rejected. One stated that he had an image of being forced to have sex with a powerful male god who was instilling knowledge in him as they were joined together. Another had the feeling, reported by Otto, of a humiliating nothingness when witnessing the divine and the mystery of creation that caused her to cry and bury her head in her hands. The significance of these experiences is that they were not rejected or diminished because they were negative or fear-inducing; the destructiveness was overcome and redirected to a positive reaction to the revelation of a truth.

There are many barriers to the reception of a ME, both from consciously held views and from unconscious resistance. Dread permeates our culture and it makes the rejection or lack of receptivity understandable. Even the endless literature on all aspects of mysticism and religious practice that espouses a particular path to the numinous serves to reduce openness to the unknowable. That reasoned path of information and minor experiences is built up and becomes what Trungpa (1973) calls "spiritual materialism," where ideas are accumulated like goods to keep the apparent as a substitute for the real. This materialism and usurping of Eastern knowledge may be causing greater harm than is apparent in patients who are involved with traditions by blocking openness and receptivity to what is truly unknown. The opposite alternative is the doctrinal position of St John of the Cross: that there should be a rejection of all visions and illuminations – the negative way – as these foreclose the truth of God's mystery. On this interpretation, "every mystical grace sent by God becomes a problem, not to say a stumbling block" (Werblowsky, 1966, p. 181). This is the sound proposition that the mystery is already within us, buried in the unconscious, and that it will be revealed when it is ready, making all of the spiritual and religious traditions useless as they are merely concepts and stories.

A tradition cannot defeat the occurrence of a ME, even if there is an accumulation of spiritual materialism. Among the interviewed mystics, the experiences were largely consistent with their respective traditions and the explanations that followed conformed to doctrines, but none of them stated that their tradition was the source of their ME. For instance, a Western sadhu interviewed at the Kumbh Mela described his experiences traditionally as the merging of the Atman with the Brahman, and in other terms that reflected classic Vedanta philosophy. However, in this and other cases, the doctrine was a convenient means to explain the unitive experience rather than a barrier to opening up to the experience. There is, then, a fine line of a tradition becoming an aid to fortifying the ego against the mystery and providing a useful context to keep alive the effect on consciousness.

From a psychoanalytic perspective, resistance brought on by dread appears to arise in uncomplicated terms because the strong affect of the experience may shock the ego, as it is diminished as the centre of psyche. Neumann (1948/1969, p. 381) explains that this shock occurs when the ego "falls or is wrenched out of its shell of consciousness and can return 'to itself' only in changed form." Thus, there is "an upheaval of the total personality and not only of consciousness" (ibid.). The shock and upheaval yield a reluctance to receive the experience at the time or after the fact because, as Jung (1942/1948, para. 275) explains: "it goes against not only our pride, but the deep-rooted fear that consciousness may perhaps lose its ascendency." This is consistent with his aphorism: "the experience of the self is always a defeat for the ego" (Jung, 1955–1956b, para. 778).

The ego and receptivity

For a ME to be received as conveying a psychological fact, it must enter into a relationship with the ego as "nothing can be conscious without an ego to which it refers" (Jung, 1935a, para. 18). The ego must recognise it as an unconscious force and thus ego consciousness is expanded by a wider view of psyche. This is essential to the role of a ME in psychoanalysis but contrary to the nature of what is experienced. The mystical field of the presence of a divine essence or the existence of links between all things is not related to the subject and is not its object; it exists on its own plane as "pure immanence" (Deleuze, 2004). It is therefore complete within itself and the true source of life as it is constantly creating and recreating. This is a deep ontological truth that cannot be swept aside by bending it to fit the needs of the ego in psychoanalysis. What has occurred in a ME is the presence of the complete other that is not an object and not an alter-ego but rather beyond the subject and object (Derrida, 1967, p. 156).

The idea of the ego structure being expanded by the revelation of this non-ego force and therefore creating an alteration of consciousness may be an entirely material idea based on a drive for the acquisition of knowledge and goal-setting. It is a materialistic view of mysticism as an object of accretion employed for the betterment of the individual. Outside the formulation used for psychoanalysis, the ME does not augment an ego by creating a wider perspective; it is viewed as the existence of a mystery for which there is ultimately no perspective. This is the apophatic explanation of the existence of that which cannot be said, leading first to a humbling and then to an abandonment of the supremacy of the ego. That loss of ego is the goal of all spiritual and religious traditions. What was most revealing about many (but not all) of the interviewees was their loss of social ego by withdrawal from a Western community and a movement away from material life brought about by their connection with a deeper truth. Their MEs led to a quiet communion with that truth and a diminution of ego strength, viewed in the classic sense. They neither inflated the ego nor created a stronger ego for the purpose of navigating material society.

In psychoanalysis, the plane of pure immanence during the peak experience or the ineffable sense of unity that must be converted into a psychological object is *utilitarian* in seeking a modification of the ego for its own purpose – individuation or psychological growth. This is required because of the importance given to these experiences as the "real therapy" and the character of pure immanence is thereby lost. In this approach, psychoanalysis denies the potential harm done to the occurrence and its subject by corralling it and translating it for the ego's purpose. The process of objectification essentially requires making a non-object into an object for the express goal of delivering it to the ego. The contents of the experience and what is revealed as a truth are too amorphous to form a single or coherent object. How do you make an object from a sense of merger with a higher power? Psychoanalysis insists on creating the experience as a benefit to the ego, which makes the content irrelevant, reducing the importance of what transpired. Consequently, as can be seen in Jung's list of examples, profound MEs and non-immanent events, such as blows of fate, are grouped together as numinous experiences because they are all capable of expanding the ego by altering the conscious position.

When a ME is directed to its relationship with the ego, its purpose is to change the ego's sole identification with its normal primary object – ego consciousness. This is accomplished by the appearance of the derived object of the non-ego nature of the ME. The ego identification that must be changed is, of course, not fixed; rather, it is a "complex of ideas" (Jung, 1921, para. 706) and the position it holds in order to benefit from a ME is that it has previously lacked the viewpoint that is presented by the new experience. It is not holding a fixed position as to what it believes about God or nothingness; rather, it has a viewpoint that is deficient because of a narrow view of psyche. Accordingly, psychoanalysis is concerned with the effect on the ego of bringing it face to face with a previously unknown revelation so that it may obtain a wider view. However, at no point, from the psychoanalytic perspective, is the state of pure immanence that is derived from a ME dissolved in the ego;

rather, it remains apart and provides new information that changes the conscious position because it is a novel object to the ego.

The relationship of the ego to the objectified experience suggests that it will take the subject away from the revelation, not bring them closer. According to Meister Eckhart (Forman, 1990, p. 112), this ego involvement in a ME is not the right approach if the subject is pursuing the ultimate goal because it is then seeking God for "outward wealth or inner consolation." It is critical then, if a real connection with the mystery is sought, not to make the ME a personal enhancement because this will require the ego to develop a structure to fit the narrative into the existing worldview. Psychoanalysis is therefore culpable in degrading MEs because the relationship is focused on the ego's point of view, so that the ego must form a new, complicated structure to understand the mystical content through a derived object of the non-ego. The irony, according to Eckhart, is that only "he who seeks God without structure apprehends him as he is in himself," and this *loss of structure* is necessary because "When discoursing on God I often shudder at how totally detached the intellective soul must be to attain that identity [in God]" (quoted in Kelley, 2009, p. 239).

In the course of analysis, a ME is inevitably added to the ongoing analytic evaluation of early conditioning, complexes, and inter-generational beliefs, all of which have been building to create the existing viewpoint and to define the width and depth of the psyche. These considerations come together with the non-ego quality of the psyche to form the lattice of intersections that create the new structure. The psychological background of the subject may not be pronounced as the basis for understanding a ME, but it is ever present in terms of the existing viewpoint and thus how the ME narrative is received by both subject and analyst. Once this new structure that includes the ME is formed, it will gradually replace the complexity of the actual revelation. This is because a mixture of wide and unrelated associations will yield a new point of view as the original experience is reinterpreted as the structure is formed. This is likely to limit or restrict the experience so that the structural view of the patient is entirely different from the understanding of the analyst or what might be a more fulsome understanding of the event. This may seem capable of avoidance by careful development of a structure, but it is inevitable, as Jung (1921c, para. 850) explains:

> the author of the concept can produce only just such a concept as corresponds to the psychic process he is endeavouring to explain; but it will correspond only when the process to be explained coincides with the process occurring in the author himself.

This occurs because the experience, even though it takes place outside the realm of ego consciousness on a plane of immanence, will, in any event, be processed thereafter by the ego through the four orienting functions of consciousness (Jung, 1935a, paras. 20ff): thinking providing the cognitive understanding of the experience; feeling enforcing its worth; intuition recognising at a non-cognitive level that what has occurred is significant; and sensation, when it is experienced directly due to the qualities of an external object. The processing, assuming that there is no object in which sensation is relevant, is a mixture of thinking and feeling of an experience that has been conveyed by intuition as part of its occurrence.

It may be that the derived object of the revelation is so amorphous (or so minor) that it cannot be reduced to one that can be brought to aid as the basis for a non-ego force. It is interesting that experiences reported by others, such as the list prepared by Merkur (2010, pp. 18–28), or even the examples given by James (1902/2008) throughout his work, all reveal instances of lesser experiences with similar themes: a transient sense of peace or happiness; a momentary communion with nature; dropping some attachments; heart opening; insights that all people and matter are as one; and an intimation that all is as it should be. However, it may be difficult to create an object and a wider view of the psyche out of that content when it lacks the overwhelming quality of an entirely new perspective.

A new revelation is presented through the images and intensity of the experience, and it is this that makes it unique in delivering a perspective for the ego. The images will be a new way of representing the truth of the non-ego that is of sufficient intensity to drive home what has occurred to the ego. The mixture of images and intensity is always variable, permitting different revelations, even though the overall themes may be the same. One interviewee, as mentioned, reported an experience of the feeling that there was a divine hand on her shoulder, conveying a feeling of bliss and peace. A subsequent experience was observing that the landscape around her was one fabric held together by a powerful presence that provided her with further peace and the ability to drop attachments. The second experience (there were others) created a new perspective on what had been understood by the use of different images and a more intense engagement with the mystical revelation, even though the second ME was enhancing the first.

The experience, in any event, is eventually absorbed into a well-defined cognitive framework by after-the-fact analysis. It reaches a point where it becomes circumscribed by the intellect and no longer provides new insights because it has been absorbed into the story of the ego. It may be used then as a reflection for other experiences in that it can augment a belief in a non-ego force, but the scope and dimension of the previous experience eventually become fixed and unable to deliver more to consciousness. The need for greater or higher-level experiences in spiritual traditions may in fact be *caused* by a lack of receptivity and the necessity to reframe the experience to give it greater meaning.

If there is a new orientation due to the acceptance of a wider dimension of the psyche, there will be a quality in the individual to remain open to further revelation. This was a common theme among the interviewees, sometimes explicitly stated, often not: they now had what they wanted, yet wanted more. Even if the experience has reached the intermediate plane where recognition of the not-I is solidified, repeated experiences are considered as necessary to progress to greater insights and further development. No one saw an end point.

The requirement of a relationship with the ego means that the critical time for achieving the alteration of consciousness is primarily after the experience, not when it is occurring, as the cognitive involvement at that time is not as expansive. There may be rejection during the event after the onset, but the cognitive, intellectual function at that stage is not yet subject to the full panoply of implications and integration, so it is unlikely to have that effect (unless, of course, it is a numinous experience). James (1902/2008, p. 77) explains this in relation to a ME:

> The fact is that the mystical feeling of enlargement, union, or emancipation has no specific intellectual content whatever of its own. It is capable of forming matrimonial alliances with material furnished by the most diverse philosophies and theologies, provided only they can find a place in their framework for its peculiar emotional mood.

This line of reasoning assumes that there is a sufficiently strong ego to relate to an overwhelming experience after the fact, rather than either shrink in its presence or reject it. Murray Stein (2017) has presented an investigation of the strong versus weak ego in analysing the difference between the multiplicity of ego states in Japan. These states lack the "heroic ego" of Western cultures and suggest a difference between the Western sharp divisions of ego compared to the Eastern lack of separation and closer ties to the unconscious. He adds, "The West has dealt itself (and suffered) a radical psychic cut, with the result that its ego construct is more profoundly separated from its source in the self than is the ego of the East" (ibid., p. 72). His conclusion, which seems both hopeful and acceptable, is that the process of individuation is expressed in different forms by East and West, but there is a common pattern of development that is not reliant on the nature of the ego structure.

A strong ego structure may, however, be relevant to receptivity. If there has been no detachment from the primacy of intellect and reason because of an "heroic ego," there will be greater confusion about the occurrence of a ME and a possible decrease in the power of the event. Sri Aurobindo (Ghose, 1973b, p. 120) states: "So long as we work only through our mentality governed by appearance, this something beyond and behind and yet always immanent can only be an inference or a presence vaguely felt." When a ME occurs for a powerful, reasoning mind, the truth that is revealed may be compressed into the appearance of a merely non-logical inference and dissipated. For there to be greater influence, the subject must have a logical structure that is permeable and capable of regarding the truth of the experience directly by perception and not through reason alone. This is the finding of neuroscience reflecting the dual action of a positive regard and a reduction of reason.

For there to be receptivity, the ego must have sufficient faith in itself to risk going beyond appearances. This suggests a different definition of a strong ego for a ME: not one that will cling on to reason desperately for its own protection, but one that has the courage to explore at its boundaries. This is the "positive anticipation" suggested by neurological process theory that is a quality that is indeed courageous and indicates sufficient longing to push beyond the threshold. As Bion (1978/2014, p. 172) suggests, "one does not know whether the patient is strong enough to hear the truth."

The ego structure must be able to extend itself to the boundaries of consciousness, but also able to relate to the truth that arises as a revelation in a ME. It has a dual role to allow itself to be permeated but also to be sufficiently interested to enter into a relationship with the non-ego. This is both a weak ego in the heroic sense, because the ego structure may be disrupted, and a strong ego in that it is flexible and able to cope with overwhelming affect. In receptivity terms, there must be strong anticipation and longing: a willingness to go beyond the gates of consciousness *and* the capacity to be comfortable with emptying the intellect.

Attainment needs receptivity

There is no straight line from the ME to an alteration of consciousness. Many factors intervene to reshape the experience, diminish it, allow for doubt, and ultimately it may be twisted beyond recognition. For it to survive and have an effect on consciousness, there must be a subject who is receptive, regardless of its convoluted journey to recognition. There is no attainment without receptivity.

The first complicating step *after* an experience is for the ego to evaluate what has occurred through the thinking, intellectual function. This requires that the subject is able to find a framework in which to examine the content and the initial affect, or else there will be no alteration in the ego's position as the experience will be rendered meaningless. This is more difficult than it appears, as Jung (1952, para. 735) explains in relation to an object imbued with spiritual or religious qualities:

> It is altogether amazing how little most people reflect on numinous objects and attempt to come to terms with them, ... and how laborious such an undertaking is once we have embarked upon it. The numinosity of the object makes it difficult to handle intellectually, since our affectivity is always involved.

To come to terms with an experience requires the laborious undertaking of finding a placeholder for the event within an *available* framework. For most

Westerners, there will be an established religious framework that seeks to fit the mystical into its own confining doctrines, thereby reducing its potential or even denying its existence. The visions of the Prophet Isaiah (Isaiah 1:1, 6:1–8) and the ecstatic experiences of St Paul (II Corinthians 12:2) are largely seen as historical pointers to a time of more direct revelation of God that is no longer an aspect of New Testament analysis (Johnson, 1998).

A new viewpoint is the adoption of a previously unknown or not yet understood framework. This adoption requires that the framework fits the narrative of the ME so it can be discussed by the patient and the analyst. The more congruence there is between the framework and the experience, the greater is the clarity as to what occurred. Jung (1947/1954, para. 405) states that a numinous experience will be received and have an effect "provided of course that it has attained a certain degree of clarity." This is consistent with his approach that requires clear, cognitive understanding of archetypal material for it to become conscious: "the only question is whether it is perceived by the conscious mind or not" (Jung, 1937, para. 329). He affirms this in a discussion of images produced by archetypes: "When there is only an image, it is merely a word-picture, like a corpuscle with no electric charge. It is then of little consequence, just a word and nothing more" (Jung, 1935a, para. 289). In commenting on numinous revelations in a dream, he states that they represent "a new climax of insight and understanding" *because* the dreamer has noted it was a powerful experience (Jung, 1936, para. 294).

The insistence on a framework that brings clarity to the experience suggests that the revelation of a truth from a ME is insufficient in itself. The truth that is revealed does not arrive as a pure, direct knowing because it is already mixed with cognitive assessment, both prior to the peak and, more importantly, after the peak but before ending. Hence, what is being revealed and how to make sense of it are not always clear. Therefore, some framework is necessary because, for psychoanalysis, a ME is delivering a new viewpoint through a narrative and that must be placed in some context for the ego in order for it to be in a relationship with the occurrence.

The phrase "*attain* to the numinous experience," as used by Jung in his letter to P.W. Martin, implies even more than that the recipient achieves a clear understanding through an existing religious or spiritual framework for the ego to relate to what has occurred. "Attaining" to the numinous also requires a psychological understanding that the phenomenon has come from a *non-ego force within the unconscious*. This attainment of a numinous experience is in addition to the religious or spiritual framework and requires the shifting of those frameworks into the psychological matrix.

The psychological framework for attainment is not just that it is a non-ego force that exists in the psyche but also that this force is ultimately more essential than the ego, or at least the guide for the ego's journey. The significance is not merely that there is an aspect of the psyche that is more than ego consciousness, but that it is the fundamental orienting principle. This arises from Jung's (1955–1956b, para. 777) statement that the alteration of consciousness occurs "only if the centre experienced proves to be the *spiritus rector* of daily life." This reference to the *spiritus rector* is made in the context of the realisation of the Self, the sense of wholeness in the psyche. It may be that the revealed truth is of the existence of this organising psychic principle. However, because a ME must be structured by cognition in order to be understood, it is more likely that it will initially have a religious or spiritual form. The analyst must then assist in a conversion or translation of the framework into psychic content. This is a weak link in the impact of a ME in psychoanalysis.

This difficulty of translation is the reason why Bion suggests that the goal is for the patient to become "O" rather than to provide a gradual transformation brought about by using interpretation. The idea that there must be a conversion from the actual experience to the non-ego force as the essential guide and controller of life suffers from the requirement that it must be subject to discussion and speculation during the translation. The process of the analyst being the passive, mystical container, the alternative that Bion suggests, may, however, allow a ME to dissipate or mean that it is insufficiently evaluated to form a framework and become a psychic object.

The process of conceptualising the revealed truth into a psychic object requires reconstructing the image from its original form to one that leads to an alteration of consciousness. It then changes what Lacan calls the "Real" into a symbolic revelation by use of a different language and context. This may, however, be necessary for the patient, as Jung (1955–1956b, para. 787) suggests: "it is uncommonly difficult for our consciousness to construct intellectual models which would give a graphic description of the reality we are perceiving." Some translation is therefore required, and one that includes the existence of a non-ego force in the unconscious is appropriate, congruent, and necessary, as it does not dilute the revelation in the experience but merely gives it a psychological source. Fink (1995, p. 27) has suggested that the gaps that form in the creation of the symbolic "Real" during the translation open up an understanding of the not-I because the act of reconstructing highlights the importance of the original. In this sense, the revelation contained within the experience retains force and effect.

The experience of the truth as suggesting a guiding principle is such a high bar that it would require a profound psychological formulation created jointly by the patient and the analyst that the patient's particular experience was of such profundity that it was a revelation of the central source of being. Any lesser experience, such as a sense of oneness with nature or a feeling that we are all connected, would not constitute the material for the necessary psychic revolution as it would, because of its lack of force, not survive the translation. This is consistent, as previously explained, with the idea of Jung's numinous experience being of such an extraordinary quality that it is sufficient, in itself, to accomplish the goals of the individuation process. The realisation of the psychic object as the guiding force brings the realisation of the *spiritus rector* into a realm approaching that of the alchemical Lapis or Philosopher's Stone, where the spirit or spiritual qualities are perceived in all things, even though there is no final completion. It is therefore accurate to say that the numinous experience, as expressed by Jung, *equals* the Lapis. It is related to a very high form of mystical or religious experience that could include a unitive experience or one that has sufficient power of revelation so that rejection is incomprehensible.

A ME, when resisted, will not be sufficiently overpowering to reach the level of having "attainment" in Jung's terms, so resistance in any form will prevent a numinous experience. In discussing receptivity to images, Jung (1955–1956b, para. 754) explains that a patient "frequently stops short at the mere observation of his images" and "If he cannot seize on the power of the image arising from the unconscious, it is 'far from easy.'"

The need for a reflecting ego and a psychological framework suggests a paradox that a person who has reached a state where there is a complete merging of the ego with the divine (or nothingness) is *not* having a numinous experience, as there is no observing ego. This is a situation that barely needs to be mentioned as there will never be a patient who is in this state. It has been suggested that Jung did not even admit the possibility that there may be a unitive experience or a winking out of the ego:

> However, his great concern for the maintenance of ego consciousness … leads him, at times, to draw back from the possibility that the ego and its faculties might undergo a moment of total oblivion in the unconscious portrayed by the very mystics he presents so vividly.
>
> (Dourley, 2010, p. 211)

It seems more accurate to say that Jung accepts that there are moments of this form of union but that the cognitive aspect of the ego always remains an observer in the experience. In his foreword to the *Spiritual Teachings of Ramana Maharshi*, Jung (1972, p. xii) mentions that the goal of Eastern practices is the same as Western mysticism: for the "I" to disappear in the Self "and the man in God." Sri Ramana teaches that the purpose of spiritual practice is the dissolution of the "I." Jung (1944a, para. 958) contrasts this viewpoint with the position of Ramakrishna – that the "I" cannot be destroyed – and consequently insists that Sri Ramana's position is "certainly more radical." Ramakrishna felt that it is almost impossible for the ego to disappear as it always returns. This is consistent with the idea that there is always some form of perception during the peak experience of a ME.

On the basis of their own experiences, all of the interviewees agreed that it is impossible to achieve a complete union when there is no trace of ego. Perhaps they did not reach the highest unitive experience. In any event, they believed that such a state is irrelevant and that moments of *samadhi* – or complete union – are less important than the experiences that altered their consciousness. One of the mystics made the critical observation that the change in viewpoint is extremely difficult to achieve, so it cannot be obtained via a continuous series of unitive MEs, only via a single ME that occurs for a receptive subject. This combination is all that is necessary; hence, much of the traditional spiritual path involves preparing a subject to be receptive while they wait for a unitive ME to occur. *There is an alteration of consciousness only when a ME meets a receptive subject.* It is not the overwhelming that does it, or the application of cognitive processing, or the nature of the truth that is revealed, or a possible non-ego unitive experience, or a framework that provides understanding, but rather the "spiritual aptitude" of the person who has the experience. The distinction between unitive and not unitive is therefore irrelevant, and what creates the alteration is a hand-in-glove ME.

Hence, it is probably more accurate to use the phrase "effective numinous experience" to imbue it with its psychological purpose rather than its religious, mystical, or metaphysical perspective. A numinous experience or a ME, after all, has no psychoanalytic value if it does not alter consciousness and provide new possibilities for the psyche, or if it fails to meet the ongoing process of individuation. As a ME is always considered by the conscious mind, either at the time of its occurrence or afterwards, the psychological viewpoint is that what is critical is that it provides a new orientation. This change in viewpoint occurs only in a subject who is receptive as so much of the original ME is lost due to processing, dread, the difficulty of translating the unconscious irruption, and turning a mystical event into a psychological object.

The ultimate state – equating individuation with MEs – is the recognition that the non-ego force is in all things: it is not only in our unconscious but in others and in matter. On a practical level, it may be hoped that patients (and analysts) will start to recognise the power and vastness of the unconscious and reach an understanding that the vicissitudes of the ego are less important than the mystery that lies within us and is working towards our refinement. A *samadhi* – or unitive experience – may enhance that purpose, depending on the subject's receptivity, and it may provide recognition of the non-ego force, but it is not an end in itself. The true gift of recognition of that force is its effect: a loosening of attachment, a quieting of the mind, and the peace that results from reconciling the opposites. This requires receptivity to the force of the event.

God as the psychological object

The attribution of an experience to the divine offers an immediate and convenient framework that is complicated by alterative religious doctrines and can channel the impact of what has occurred. Hence Meister Eckhart's (1981, p. 202) cry, "I pray God to make me free of God." The likely result is that the framework and narrative of a ME are changed to accord with the gift of the divine.

The standard psychoanalytic position, as Corbett (1996, p. 8) suggests, is that MEs arise from "an autonomous level of the psyche that is either the source of, or the medium for, the transmission of religious experience." Identifying the unconscious as the true source of religious experience and religion does not allow it to stand alone as a clear psychological fact, as it is impossible to understand the true source in the context of a ME. In fact, Jung (1959a, para. 864) suggests that numinous experiences are an "aspect of God" and that they arise from the unconscious as "God's actions springs from one's inner being" (Jung, 1921e, para. 413).

This "inner being" is found in the depths of the unconscious in what the late John Dourley (2018, p. 36) suggests is a "dimension of psyche beyond the archetypal as the source of all definition and formality, infinite in its creativity." In a penetrating analysis, he argues that this is the divine, which is the "ever present structural dimension of the deeper unconscious, the undermining yet sustaining abyss beneath the light of day and its easy but superficial assurances" (ibid., pp. 36–37). There is no doubt that every interviewee and indeed every person who has ever had a ME would agree.

Psychoanalysis, however, prefers to stand outside religion as a secular form of self-examination based on a theoretical platform of the operation of the psyche. Religious and spiritual traditions do not turn to psychoanalysis for explanations of the working of God through the unconscious as a source. The unconscious may be seen as the progenitor of religious feelings, thereby claiming a higher position, but must eventually give way to the existence of a transcendent being as the experience is made the subject of after-the-fact examination. This occurs precisely because psychoanalysis has a weak and inconsistent view of the unconscious that does not have deep historical roots, while the experience of transcendence has an ancient archetypal power that flows through most (but not all) societies.

The leap from the direct experience of overwhelming affect to initial insight of what has occurred and then subsequent, more complex processing that brings in a mystical or spiritual tradition occurs because of the search for meaning within *available* sources, as Jung (1955–1956b, para. 781) explains:

> Nor is it astonishing that in every attempt to gain an adequate understanding of the numinous experience use must be made of certain parallel religions or metaphysical ideas which have not only been associated with it from ancient times but are constantly used to formulate and elucidate it.

This statement, consistent with that of James, affirms that the affective, dramatic nature of a ME brings the experience only to the edge of consciousness, not to receptivity. Receptivity – or the attainment of a new plane of consciousness – requires the cognitive assessment that embeds it as a new viewpoint. At the time of the experience, before and especially after a peak moment, the revelation of that truth can create an indelible alteration in the viewpoint of the subject because there is an active cognitive component at work. Indeed, several of the interviewees who identified themselves as mystics spoke of an immediate, raw power that made them understand that there was a previously hidden secret relating to the relationship between an individual and a higher power. However, it is more common for the ME not to cause an immediate alteration in viewpoint; rather, it is made explicable through a tradition or notions of a transcendent presence when it is processed after the event. As such traditions are aware of the need to make the structure firm and conclusive, the reference point of God is essential as it binds the ideas, especially if they are expressed as emanating from those who have come close to absorption in the divine.

Transcendence becomes so integral because an ME "leaves a strong impression of having encountered a reality different from and, in some crucial sense, higher than the reality of everyday experience" (Wuff, 2000, p. 397). "Higher" is always translated as transcendence as it goes beyond human understanding. There are two consequences of this intermingling of God (or, in Theravada Buddhism and Zen, nothingness) and the unconscious. The first is that analysis cannot proceed in translating a ME into a psychological fact with an exclusion of the religious or mystical. The second is that the mixing of the two opens up new dangers brought about by an inflation.

In Eastern-based traditions, the ego starts in a diminished position. As it is expressed for India (although, with some modifications, the same may be said of the Western position):

> There is evident here a total disjunction of the phenomenal self (the naively conscious personality, which together with its forms will in time be dissolved) from that other, profoundly hidden, essential yet forgotten, transcendental Self (atman), which when recollected roars out with its thrilling, world-annihilating, "Wonderful am I!"
>
> (Zimmer, 1969, p. 11)

God is more important than the ego of the individual and it is impossible to exclude a transcendent presence when the ego relates to the experience. The difficulty with the idea that the ME is a gift from God or a merging with the divine, when viewed through a heroic ego, is that, as Jung (1958, para. 721) recognises, the mystical, religious, or metaphysical explanations lead to an inflation, or become abstracted (Jung, 1955–1956b, para. 781). God – or the ME itself – is abrogated by the ego, which adds to its accomplishments and then associates itself with the higher power. Inflation has the effect of reducing the experience to an achievement of the ego. In any event, this may be inevitable to some degree because, as it is the ego that has processed the event, it has already convinced itself of a wider stance, and its previous static quality has been enlivened. Invariably, to some extent, a ME, the attribution of it to a transcendent being, or even the glimpse of a previously hidden revelation, will make the subject feel inflated.

The practical effect of inflation is that the point of view of the religious or the mystical becomes fixed and is maintained by a coherent narrative that allows it to be explained to others. God is then embedded in the narrative, and the subject deepens the story around the experience through reading and greater immersion in a tradition. Consequently, they may form a more solid structure that is less permeable to a new ME. This structure becomes even more rigid if there are no subsequent MEs because the historical experience remains as a fixed viewpoint. When this has occurred, patients tend to insist on this viewpoint because it has weathered a long period of reinforcement and is now interwoven with the ego. This makes it more difficult to translate the experience into a phenomenon occurring in the psyche.

It appears that the most important factor is not that the ME is fully understood at the time of or after its occurrence and placed in a mystical, psychological, or religious framework, but that the depth of the experience offers a sustaining insight that the ME arose from a non-ego power, be it the psyche, God, or nothingness. Such an insight has a transformative effect as it presents an *intimation* of what it might portend for the ego: that there is an "other" that is not of the ego. In this sense, a complete overhaul of the conscious position is unnecessary; rather, the ego is simply aware that it is not the sole resident of the psyche. This is consistent with Otto's (1923, p. 8) statement:

> The holy cannot be defined, taught, handed down, or described. [A person] must be guided and led on by consideration and discussion of the matter through the ways of his own mind, until he reach the point at which "the numinous" in him perforce to stir, to start into life and into consciousness.

The intimation or awareness of a non-ego force – seen as God, nothingness, or the unconscious – provides the ego with the possibility that the "other" may then be *valued* and pursued in the future. In this interpretation, the other does not need to be seen as the *spiritus rector*; rather, it is simply acknowledged as of value. Neumann (1948/1969, p. 382) suggests:

> The epiphany of that which had hitherto been hidden requires not only an ego to which it can manifest itself, but, to an even greater degree, calls for an act of attention and devotion on the part of the ego, an aptitude for being "moved," a willingness to see what wants to appear.

The concept of having an "aptitude" for being moved therefore seems to be the critical element, so it is *unnecessary to bend the ME into a psychological explanation*. This is an attitude as well as an aptitude, and it is this attitude that equates with receptivity.

This leads to several conclusions. The first is that there are different degrees of receptivity – some in which there is an intimation and others in which a change is indelible, making a life's journey one of consecration of the non-ego force. This is not necessarily a result of the type of ME, the attribution to a non-ego force in the unconscious, God, or nothingness, but rather one of an attitude brought about by an aptitude.

The emphasis in psychoanalysis on the ego having a relationship with the ME may be misplaced. The ego alone, operating through cognitive assessment, does not account for receptivity, which comprises unconscious factors that are unrelated to the complex of ideas that form the ego structure. This is instead a super-ordinate quality that dictates *how* the ego will react to the experience and is not dependent on a prior state of the ego.

The relationship with a ME that raises it to a higher level of insight and effect is therefore an unconscious reaction to unconscious forces. The ego is always given priority in this and other encounters with the unconscious because consciousness is privileged in psychoanalysis and its enlargement is the overall goal of the process. The deeper question is whether the individual will, upon the appearance of a previously hidden revelation, be sufficiently influenced so that the psychic structure is widened. What occurs may not just be the expansion of ego consciousness but a relationship of the unconscious with its objects so that it creates a feeling or a sense of presence that is not cognitive but reorientating and ultimately curative.

This is not to deny the power of psychoanalysis and the extraordinary possibility of a ME breaking down the strictures of a bound ego and revealing another, more compelling, aspect of the psyche. Discussion of ego strength in receipt of the experience or the recognition of a non-ego force – or God – does not, however, seem particularly relevant to the real operation of the occurrence.

Clinical implications of rejection

Consequences arise when there is a rejection of a ME. Jung (1945/1954, para. 437) explains that the content of the experience does not disappear if it is not received: "It possesses a certain autonomy, and when it is regressed or systematically ignored it reappears in another place in a negative and destructive guise." Perhaps it has a negative effect because of the impact of the experience on the deeper layers of the unconscious. Marie-Louise von Franz (1980, p. 31) writes:

> An experience of the Divine is often of an overwhelming power beyond one's comprehension, which is dangerous, but which one has to adapt, as one has to adapt to a manifestation in nature such as the explosion of a volcano.

This suggests that a ME's stirring of the unconscious is not a transient phenomenon that can be ignored. Rather, it is responsible for the psyche gathering further libido because of the impact of the event, meaning that it can erupt in another form in the analysis. As the unconscious is not presenting itself in a logical, structured manner, it is possible that a series of eruptions will become evident if a ME is not explored. Indeed, this outcome is borne out by clinical experience. In this context, rejection of a ME becomes important.

Where there is rejection – or even fading – it is necessary to be prepared for a redirection of accumulated libido that will need to break through in some other way and express itself. The rejection or fading is unlikely to result in a new ME, but it may lead to major disruptions in the psyche in some other form. The subsequent sessions are then a carry-over from a ME and do not offer the same opportunity to develop an awareness of a non-ego force within the psyche, although they will become the conduits through which a new breakthrough in some other form may occur.

There is no predicting how that spill over effect will present itself, although two clinical vignettes present two possibilities. In the first, a sixty-five-year-old patient had a clear ME, saw it as very healing, and felt at peace in consequence. It was a profound session in which we were both moved by his revelation and an apparent alteration in his consciousness. In the next session, the ME was not mentioned; instead, he brought up a life situation and was acutely annoyed, in a way I had not seen before, with the behaviour of a colleague. After two more sessions when the ME was again not mentioned, he attacked me for misunderstanding his take on the experience and suggested an alternative approach that made no sense. As I struggled to understand, he used my incomprehension to get angry and then started yelling that I was too rigid and uncaring. The transference became very negative. After two and a half years of working together, this was aberrant and, I suspected, brought up a father complex of never being heard. This became the subject matter of further sessions and revealed, for the first time, previous psychotic episodes.

In the second instance, a thirty-year-old woman with early trauma had a lesser ME of a feeling of connection with nature while visiting her father in the country. In the telling, it was clear that this gave her great peace. She did not discuss it during the next few sessions and then said she felt very alone, that no one understood her, she had left her boyfriend, and had spent a week in bed. All of this was unexpected.

In both instances, there was a dramatic change several weeks after the ME, with the faded experience giving way to a strong, atypical reaction. These reactions had pathological elements: uncharacteristic, disjointed aspects of the psyche that caused great suffering for the patients and those around them. In both, they accentuated previously recognised pathological elements: the man had previous psychotic episodes and the woman, as mentioned, had suffered early trauma.

The idea of a repressed or ignored experience sitting in the background of the psyche, waiting to erupt, has clinical significance. Jung (1955–1956b, para. 782) warns that the unconscious contents "break through into consciousness and overwhelm it in the same way in pathological cases accessible to psychiatric observation." MEs, whether positive or negative, therefore have clinical relevance as they may yield pathology when rejected or allowed to fade. Early writing by Leuba (1925) on the psychological aspects of MEs considers that they are caused by an ego regression of degraded and diminished mental activity, meaning they exist pathologically in any event and, if not channelled, may erupt. On the same theme, Greeley (1974, p. 81) suggests that these experiences arise from "badly disoriented personalities."

A ME is usually contained within a recognised discourse so that it can be differentiated from pathological symptoms when there is rejection or it fades. It has been suggested that this differentiation should be based on: a lack of suffering; a lack of impairment to ego functioning; a spontaneous occurrence for a short duration; maintenance of a critical attitude to the objective reality of the ME so it may be critically assessed; the absence of comorbidities; possible compatibility with a cultural background; some measure of control over the experience; it promotes personal growth; and it is directed towards others (de Menezes Júnior and Moreira-Almeida, 2009; Moreira-Almeida, 2012). There are clear indicators derived for those who are at high risk of psychosis (Morrison, 2006) and it may be possible to create a connection between a ME and those indicators in particular patients. However, for patients in a psychoanalytical setting with no dysfunctional pathology, it may be possible to observe these deeper psychotic elements in retrospect, after the material in subsequent sessions indicates that the experience has been harmful if the rejection has caused a deep disturbance, or if the material that is stirred is not tolerated because it cannot be held within a cognitive framework.

Some of these distinctions between a ME and psychosis are inaccurate and reflect a conundrum in diagnosis: there is always a lack of control over the experience and there is no socially directed aspect. However, the comparison offers an important reminder that the analyst must be alert to the cultural and personal significance of these experiences in order to reduce the iatrogenic harm from a misdiagnosis (Lukoff, 1992; Kemp, 2000) following rejection. In a study of four Jewish mystics who manifested psychoses, it was found that the symptoms were consistent with the result of established mystical practices; it was therefore difficult to determine when the ecstatic experiences left the cultural framework and crossed over into psychosis (Greenberg, Witztum, and Buchbinder, 1992). This cultural significance must also be expanded to spiritual and mystical traditions. The extreme practices of Tanta or the self-abnegation of the body in Hinduism are understood only in context and not in any known Western framework.

When a patient has had previous psychopathology, but it is being worked through in analysis, there is a tendency to normalise it and patiently work through the messages from the unconscious. However, in the case of serious pathology, the contents and then the rejection of a ME may accentuate psychopathological symptoms and cause harm. For example, a patient with OCD may reject an experience because the images are frightening, but they might then become an object of obsession because of their affect. A patient who has a schizoid personality disorder may immediately discount the emotionality of the ME and may be too detached to have a cognitive reaction to what is so powerful, making the contrast more obvious and the cause of a retreat into isolation.

It must be assumed that, in terms of the sequence of the analysis, the experience is likely to accentuate underlying pathology, if it exists, making it evident in subsequent sessions that the unconscious is in an upheaval following a rejection. The presenting issue then becomes more apparent and there will be a crystallisation of the primary conflict. This is understandable and should be taken as part of the normal clinical effect of a faded or rejected ME. The breakthrough could then be psyche's way of intensifying the conflict because it needs expression or resolution. This may not be a short-term eruption but the beginning of a more intense direction for the analysis based on the invasion of unconscious material.

This examination of the distinction suggests that the determination of a pathological quality for a ME takes place only some time after the rejection, when the effect can be observed. An earlier signal to be noted could be the fact of the rejection itself, the rapid fading of the experience after it occurs, the presence of a core issue in the next session after it was disclosed, or a change in intensity of issues following its disappearance. Any of these might indicate that the experience has indeed had an effect on consciousness but not the sort of positive impact that is associated with MEs.

Comments on clinical practice for rejection

Upon hearing the contents of a ME, it is impossible to observe that it has pathological elements that are responsible for its rejection or later fading. Nothing may be considered alien to the presentation of the original experience, even if it is filled with monstrous or destructive images. It is not similar to a dream, where any element – and especially a shadow element – may be interpreted as a symbol. The breakthrough of constellated libido filtered through dread and fear is not a simple communication from the unconscious but reaches back to primordial, collective archetypes for a unique presentation to the psyche. There is no marker along the path of the creation of a ME that could indicate it is infiltrated by a pathological element.

The content of the ME in terms of images and feelings that arise may appear to be helpful in understanding the subsequent rejection or whether it is mixed with pathology. However, the images are not from the personal dimension of the psyche but primarily from the collective unconscious – the primordial archetypes of the nature of existence that have broken through due to the build-up of libido. As Jung (1945/1954, para. 353) points out: "In consequence of the collective nature of the image it is often impossible to establish its full range of meaning from the associated material of a single individual." In the case of a ME, as opposed to collective images arising in dreams, it derives its significance from its invocation of these original primordial archetypes of God, the devil, nothingness, or emptiness. These "are as much feelings as thoughts; indeed, they lead their own independent life" (Jung, 1917/1926/1953, para. 104). There is therefore no link between the personal material of the patient and the primordial archetype that may be used to understand the rejection. To do so would be to create a bridge across a vast canyon, with the personal material on one side and the fundamental "'thought forms' of humanity" (ibid.) on the other.

This leads to the conclusion that the rejection may be caused by collective images that are, by their nature, too overwhelming to be accepted. The rejection then would be more than just a cognitive fear or dread; rather, a primitive, unconscious response, reflecting the earliest upheaval of dark and light forces. Jung (1921, para. 749) reminds us that the primordial image is related to the continually operative natural processes that are the basis of psychic life and thus a "condensation of the living process." He explains that these primordial images free energy, which leads to "sheer uncomprehended perception," and direct the "mind back to nature and canalizing sheer instinct into mental forms" (ibid.). If this is the case, then it may be that the power of the ME will cause a response that will not be rational but rather will operate unconsciously, below the level of cognitive evaluation.

The after-the-fact examination of the experience does raise the possibility of an intellectual, abstracted reaction to what occured. This is instead a deeply felt reaction to a highly evocative personal, past event that may invoke a genuine fear that emerges when the enormity of the event is analysed. The mix of the primal effect of the experience with the personal dread is likely to cause a hint or a sign that some personal complex has been activated. A strong need for control in an out-of-control experience, a reminder of the precipice of a past psychotic interlude, or the liturgy's dismissal of outlier thinking may add to a personal level of what has been accumulated at the conscious and unconscious levels as a reason for rejection.

It is therefore inevitable that the rejection of the experience must be considered in the context of the patient's background. This appears to be correct because there is a cognitive interpretation, which is personal in all cases, that may give rise to rejection or fading. An analyst is then bound to consider the developmental background and the revealed structure of the psyche to place the experience in its appropriate context in order to determine if the occurrence is aberrant or within a range of possibilities that may be expected. In the context of psychoanalysis, the result is that rejection or fading of a ME will be considered as part of the analytical process rather than a reaction to a separate, incongruous event arising from the deepest archaic history of humankind. Accordingly, the proper approach would be to observe how a ME has been reimagined by the conscious mind according to its effect on consciousness, thus revealing the reasons for rejection or fading.

If the ME has been rejected after it is presented, or if it fades from view, this in itself is not evidence of pathology, even in cases where the patient has previously exhibited pathological symptoms. In fact, it may be that the rejection of the ME signals that it is serving a function of protecting the patient from an unbearable intrusion on a fragile ego. As mentioned, MH's rejection of a ME could have been fear of the process of verifying Virgin Mary visions or a genuine intrusion into an ego that needed to stay intact to function during intense life situations.

As there can be a concern as to whether a rejection is a sign of pathology, it is necessary to place the experience in a context that explains this result. The context is how the personal unconscious has interacted with the revelations of the primordial material within the collective unconscious. This enquiry is divided into three distinct issues that will better explain this context. The first is the relationship the patient has had with the unconscious and to identify, if possible, the factors that have been responsible for a poor connection thus far. It is then necessary to determine if the rejection is consistent with those factors. If it is, this establishes a line of sight between a poor relationship with the unconscious and a rejection of an event originating in the unconscious. In such a situation, it is unlikely that the rejection or fading should be examined further for pathology.

The second issue, if not completely answered by the first, is to assess whether the ME and its rejection have created a problem with mental functioning that is unaccounted for in a cultural context. The cultural factor relates to whether the patient is in a spiritual or religious tradition where the rejection of the ME is consistent with the tradition's teaching or a strongly held belief. One of the Indian mystics interviewed at the Kumbh Mela explained that he had an image of Lord Shiva eating a human liver. He was an adherent of the Agora sect who drink from human skulls and are known to eat anything, including their own faeces, to show their awareness of death and the existence of God in matter. If a patient had this as a reason for rejection, it might be a warning sign of some deeper disturbance as it has no cultural container. This is an extreme case, but it illustrates that the ME or its rejection must be considered as an aspect of the patient's history, not outside it.

The third issue, where the rejection is not inconsistent with the cultural tradition, is to consider whether there are developmental characteristics or an attitude towards the unconscious that may make a patient receptive to processing an ME, in which case rejection would be incongruent. This, then, is the issue of receptivity, which is the essential characteristic of the impact of a ME on consciousness – the profound issue of aptitude. If a person is likely to be receptive, rejection may signal the emergence of an incongruent issue. On the other hand, if they are unlikely to be receptive, rejection is to be expected.

The result better explains the manner of working with a person who is not suffering pathology but nevertheless lacks receptivity. The degree of receptivity indicates appropriate forms of intervention, such as the use of active imagination, development of fantasy thinking, a particular approach to the interpretation of dreams, as well as understanding the nature of the counter-transference. A person who is not receptive to a ME and has accordingly rejected it may not benefit from the use of certain imaginal methods, so it may be better to continue with concrete methods, even though a ME indicates that more is stirring than is obvious. In turn, the identification of developmental markers or an open attitude that indicates receptivity may encourage the patient's use of symbolic thinking. This suggests that even in the case of rejection, a ME must be considered in conjunction with all of the revealed aspects of the psyche that are responsible for receptivity. It is through this examination of receptivity that misdiagnosis may be minimised.

The reality of the situation will appear over subsequent sessions but it must be understood in the context of the patient's background and proclivities. Foremost among these is the question of whether the subject has a *developmental structure* that would suggest that the ME and its receptivity is consistent with the intra-psychic patterns and vectors of psyche. The developmental background shapes the psychic structure in which receptivity is considered.

Chapter 5

The capacity for receptivity

Longing, in its widest sense, impels the receptivity; it is not a character-istic of either a strong or a weak ego. Freud (1915, p. 165) explains that longings must be allowed to persist in a patient "in order that they may serve as forces impelling her to do work and make changes." The anatomy of longing is that it is a generalised desire that is a characteristic of the particular individual that arises developmentally or by some other cir-cumstance. In the case of the interviewees, the ego strength was irrelevant, but the longing was paramount and did not end with a single experience; rather, it opened up a road that could lead to more. In an analysis of the Lacanian idea of objectless desire, Fink (1997, p. 51) has observed: "Desire thus does not seek satisfaction, rather it pursues its own continuance and furtherance."

The longing for a ME may have greater force than objectless desire. It is directed at seeking the revelation of a particular truth because the ego wants answers to the confusion of the mind. The subject of the longing is inevitably the ego itself, seeking its expansion and dominance by providing answers to complete its purpose of discrimination and establishing order and predict-ability. Jung (1912/1952, para. 417) explains Faust's longing as that of the ego-hero "yearning for the mystery of rebirth, for immortality." Sri Aurobindo explains that there is an "inherent, intrinsic, self-existent consciousness which knows itself by the mere fact of being" (Ghose, 1973a, p. 855), and it is that which seeks to discover itself further.

Expressed in this manner, the longing arises from an individual, but it can also be described as a response to a beckoning. That beckoning is, in psy-chological terms, a call from the Self or the unconscious archetype of whole-ness that seeks its own unfolding. It has, contrary to Lacan, an object in the form of a sense of wholeness that beckons the psyche to elevate it to the guiding principle. It is activated because we live in duality and there is a natural orientation towards unity. It is a formative, substrate of the psyche that can be traced back to the essential presence of opposites, especially as to the split between spirit and matter, both as the primordial separation but offering the possibility of a fundamental oneness.

The longing itself creates a split between a present state and an idealised object, which is a fantasy of some form of freedom or wholeness. This brings with it methods, rules, and explanations derived from traditions, teachers, and literature that lead from that state to the fantasised state. All of this results in suffering as the goal is not reached because its nature is not subject to demands placed upon it by the longing. Even in those traditions where the goal is considered God's grace, or even in the Advaita Vedanta tradition of non-duality where the soul and the divine are one and the same, the longing remains.

The longing is insufficient, in itself, to account for receptivity, but it is its basis, contained within a coherent ego that is able to absorb a ME. Neumann (1948/1969, p. 400) proposes that when there is a pathological, fragmentary, or unstable ego, the individual is overpowered, and the experience manifests in seizure, ecstasy, inflation, depression, or psychosis. The ego must therefore make room for the longing by enlarging itself to reach a greater consciousness: "only by enlarging consciousness and the personality can ego make possible a larger manifestation of the nonego and the world. It is through the ego and its heroic resolve that the creative numinous attains vaster and vaster manifestations" (ibid., p. 402). The capacity for receptivity is therefore the congruence of the experience with the degree of longing contained within a coherent ego. If it is consistent with the ongoing longing, it will find open pathways and explanations that respond to that receptivity. If the longing is not present or has been diminished, it will lack energic value, no matter how overwhelming or revelatory the experience.

There may be developmental markers that can account for longing. Neumann (2014, p. 17) suggests a starting point that longing is a return to the lure of uroboric incest and self-dissolution. In *Longing for Paradise*, Jacoby (2006, pp. 25–26) argues that the infant does not have any knowledge of these states – referring particularly to the uroboric, paradisiacal state – and therefore cannot form a desire to return. The psychological explanation, suggests Jacoby (ibid., p. 26), is that a unitary reality may be developed not by the child alone but as between the mother and the infant, because the mother is not yet perceived as a differentiated, independent entity: "She is an integral component of primal infant experience, is simply 'there,' symbiotically woven into the infant's fabric of needs" (ibid., p. 27). Winnecott (quoted in Merkur, 2010, p. 174) suggests that God becomes a "good object" by transferring the goodness of the mother at an early developmental phase. The idea that the longing consists of a return to a previous developmental state does have cogency, leading Lacan (1992, p. 118) to conclude that the object of desire is "by nature a refound object."

Longing as a psychological concept is slippery because it is a description of an aggregation of developmental states and resultant complexes that combine to create a vector of desire. Early longing for attachment, as an example, may form a complex when unfulfilled, adding to other complexes that have formed to create a generalised longing that has no specific orientation or object. The longing for God or a ME is thus buried in the unconscious from the cross-currents and interactions of the various developmental contacts and complexes.

The longing that leads to a ME may have a particular quality because what is being sought directly or indirectly is not only a salve for neurosis but that which is at the depths of the collective unconscious. It is here that the idea of seeking that personal "refound object" may be inaccurate. If great longing were enough, many individuals would be receptive to a ME and would over-come doubt and dread to pursue that longing to its possible end. Instead, in most instances, no ME is forthcoming; and even if it is, it is rarely of suffi-cient impetus to arrive at full absorption. It is more likely that a strong longing is the precursor to receptivity but insufficient as a general proposition to account for the reception of a ME and its alteration of consciousness.

If longing is strong, it is more likely to be channelled into one of the societal modes for its manifestation, such as the accumulation of wealth or power. For it not to be diverted, it requires a particular, unique orientation that is concerned primarily with that which is inexplicable. In the face of the liturgy or a tradition that professes to incorporate a clear answer to the inex-plicable, the longing must be so great that it is not thereby tethered. The offer of an answer is everywhere and that could easily quell the inconvenient power of the longing so that the dominance of the day-to-day prevails. To remain open to a ME and to have it change the conscious position therefore requires a form of longing that is not generalised and is characterised by a willingness to turn away from doctrine and hold a hot coal of desire to experience unity with the primordial mysteries.

The unity is, in part, a sense of wholeness from an infantile solipsistic or infant interactive merging with the mother as a memory that lasts beyond infancy. "In part" because the intimation of unity as an infant is insufficient to keep the longing alive through the obstacles or have it do more than land only a few steps from where it started. As the sudden alteration of con-sciousness is rare (as Jung specifically reminds us in relation to a numinous experience), there must be a greater congruence with that which already exists that is incorporated into the structure of the emerged personality.

Who may be receptive

For Lacan, a patient has an unconscious sense of the void and wishes to fill the lack. He considers this emptiness, deprivation, and loss – the lack – as the cause of desire. He uses the term *"object a"* for that which is substituted to fill the lack so that it becomes the cause of desire. The desire is main-tained and manifested by seeking *object a* in the Other: a person or an ordered structure. Having a relationship with *object a* is a "Fantasy" that supports and reinforces the desire (Lacan, 1979, p. 185). The Lacanian Fantasy may be a search for a ME or a spiritual tradition that fulfils *object a*.

If this is the case, a ME is the presence of *object a*, supposedly in the possession of the Other, but which is a substitution for the initial, primal sense of unity. The "lack" of a ME being delivered in a traditional religion – its lack of *object a* – allows the subject to achieve "Separation" or an awareness that *object a* is not in the Other. For mystics, as reported by the interviewees, the illumination comes from *outside* the tradition.

Expressed in this way, a ME is just a form of desire channelled through a tradition. It never quells a pre-existing longing and therefore it will not necessarily be assuaged by a sudden, inexplicable unitive state. Mysticism, as a tradition, implies a linear progression along a path that is definable, suggesting an answer to the endless longing through a structure for what is unstructured and allowing rewards for insights along the way as a means of offering possible fulfilment. No doubt this is the reason why Eckhart eschewed obtaining spiritual objects and therefore criticises those who "want something definite, some experience of higher things" (quoted in Tobin, 1986, p. 124).

The longing required to be receptive to a ME can be said to require that there is no rest: "one should not halt at any particular state or outcome of the mystical quest, but rather maintain a constant movement toward the inner source of these states" (Garb, 2004, p. 303). This implies moving away from the pleasure of mystical feelings and an orientation to the longing itself. If the longing survives a ME and is not channelled into a tradition or a ready-made answer, it will be the characteristic that most describes receptivity. This is because the ME is not then likely to fade over time; nor will it be rejected after it occurs, because the longing is the characteristic of the seeker's psyche.

Although the occurrence of a ME in varying forms may be commonplace, a longing that is of such generative power that it may resist the intellectual confusion caused by the presence of a non-ego power in the unconscious is extremely rare. In discussing his No. 2 personality as receptive to fantasy thinking, Jung (1998, p. 62) explains: "In my life No. 2 has been of prime importance, and I have always tried to make room for anything that wanted to come to me from within. He is a typical figure, but he is perceived only by the very few."

Ascribing limited receptivity to the numinous is consistent with the views of Rudolf Otto. He accepts the innate capacity of all individuals to have numinous experiences, which he calls "divination," but states that a "numinous person" (Otto, 1923, p. 152) or a seer who has "more highly endowed natures" (ibid., p. 177) is required for the experience to be fully kindled. This requirement conforms to the idea that most people who experience a ME need some context. In distinguishing between the majority who need that other person and a seer with "more highly endowed natures," Otto implies that the endowment is an inherent quality or innate ability.

Neither Jung nor Otto offers any opinion as to the characteristics of a person who may be included within the "very few" who are receptive to the numinous, might be numinous themselves, or have a "more highly endowed" nature. Jung (1946, para. 361) mentions only that receptivity to numinous experiences arises according to a "man's temperament." He uses the word "temperament" more generally in the context of psychological types in reference to either extroverted or introverted attitudes (Jung, 1935, para. 77), but, as it relates to the numinous, he does not employ the extroverted/introverted distinction; instead, "there are some people whose attitude is essentially spiritual and others whose attitude is essentially materialistic" (ibid., para. 79). He draws no other relevant distinctions and clearly declares that he will avoid all presuppositions "about what a patient can and ought to do" (ibid., para. 81). Neumann (1948/1969, p. 394) echoes this sentiment: "the scope of the revelation in which the numen can manifest itself is contingent on the scope of the personality which receives the revelation."

There are statements throughout the *Collected Works* that illustrate Jung's reluctance to be specific about the capacity of an individual to be receptive to and digest experiences. In his commentary on *The Secret of the Golden Flower*, in reference to some patients that can "outgrow" a problem that destroys others, he suggests that this capacity has nothing to do with their desire: "In no case was it conjured into existence intentionally or by conscious willing, but rather seemed to be borne along on the stream of time" (Jung, 1929, para. 18). Jung asks, "What did these people do?" and answers, "As far as I can see they did nothing ... but let things happen" (ibid.). Accordingly, the desire for numinous experiences is not an act of will: there is nothing that can be done to guarantee they will arise. Rather, in the "stream of time" such an experience *may* occur because a person is able to let things happen: they are receptive.

When Jung states that some people "let things happen," he does not speculate as to the character of a person who is receptive to that happening. The phrase does express a particular quality or ability of the passive acceptance of the non-ego. The nature of the personality that is receptive to a ME and capable of having this passive quality yet also maintains an active longing is therefore a question that is often raised but remains a matter of speculation. In reference to Martin Buber's "I–Thou" relationship with God, Progoff (1966, p. 107) asks: "[W]hat is necessary psychologically in order to bring about the quality of consciousness that makes an I–Thou relationship possible[?] This is a major question that needs to be approached in as large a perspective as possible." Progroff suggests that there are two unique personality types that will allow an individual to break through the strictures of childhood developmental issues and attain that revelatory consciousness (ibid., pp. 134ff). He calls the first a "cogni-type," identified as a person with an innate capacity for insight, and the second a "dynatype," which is best explained as someone who is possessed of an archetype known for its inherent potential, such as a prophet or a hero. Those possessing a dynatype contain within them a "seed-image ... that indicates a process of growth whose source is hidden in the depths, this is to say, in the potentialities of the seed of the person" (ibid., p. 136). Jung's No. 2 personality is given as an example of a dynatype (ibid., p. 138).

In *Perennial Philosophy*, Huxley (2009) suggests that body types better explain receptivity than an innate psychological type. The ectomorph is the type that is receptive because his body structure suggests "cerebrotonia": a predominance of the intellectual accompanied by sensitivity, introversion, and shyness; an internalised, subjective world (ibid., p. 158). James (1907/1995, pp. 4–6) proposes that there are "tough minded" and "tender minded" types, and only the latter are interested in religious possibilities.

In the vast literature on mysticism, there are many theories about factors that are surprisingly formative for a mystic, such as low self-esteem, high stress (Hood, 1977), fear of isolation, need for moral support, affection, or peace (Leuba, 1925, pp. 116ff), or a quality called "transliminality": a high degree of accessibility to subliminal consciousness (Wuff, 2000, p. 409).

In psychology, a few attempts have been made to characterise the nature of the person who pursues and has a ME. In one study, the literature is analysed to suggest that "pre-experience dissatisfactions with life associate with general positive features of the mystical experience" (Spilka, Brown, and Cassidy, 1992, p. 253). Among the significant qualities that appear to be positive for receptivity are a religious background and not being overtly negative to a ME. The authors conclude that further study is needed to "determine the paths that lead to these situations" and that "[t]he shaky nature of establishing the kind of lives experiencers lived prior to their experience cannot be dismissed lightly" (ibid., p. 255). In another study (Lehtsaar, 2002), the author explores the lives of 121 individuals who professed spirituality, including Barth, Darwin, and Schweitzer, as well as others who might be said to have enunciated a spiritual ground for their theories without recording a ME. Lehtsaar concludes that the shared characteristics were previous religious learning, a recollection of the past as God's work, achievement of a new religious understanding through intellectual struggles, some degree of emotional tension, and conflict that demanded a religious solution.

There have been attempts to find a genetic, biological substrate of spirituality (Seybold, 2010), as well as neurobiological indicators (Schjoedt, 2009). Neurobiology's findings in relation to the operation of a ME are not consistent in terms of the activity of the brain regions, but they suggest that there are varying forms of cognition that are relevant to religion and religious experiences, so different regions of the brain are associated with aspects of the experience, including belief and non-belief (Smith, 2014, ch. 6). To some extent, this research confirms that an ME will be cognitively mediated (Azari, Missimer, and Rudiger, 2009), a conclusion that corresponds with the interviewees' experience.

In all instances, the authors of neurological studies as to religion or MEs do not relate their findings to the developmental phases of a child and how brain patterns are created or changed. Instead, they refer to fixed characteristics or innate tendencies that are structurally predetermined. These neurobiological markers may indeed relate to the proclivity of an individual to be receptive to numinous experiences. However, the research does not establish why, how, or by what neural pathways a person is more or less likely to be receptive to a ME. The ME embraces so many qualities, including affect, absorption, perceptual intensity, and cognitive transcendence, that the research is probably suggesting a model that is multi-dimensional, examining the interplay between different dimensions rather than determining a single, causal model.

In Jungian terms, psyche consists of complexes, so it is important to consider if any constellation of complexes also suggests a proclivity to be receptive. As Jung (1931, paras. 925–926) explains, a complex is not only an obstacle for an individual but exists "also as a stimulus to greater effort, and so, perhaps, as an opening to new possibilities ... The complex is a valuable symptom which helps us to diagnose an individual disposition."

This particular Jungian approach of cleaving towards the complex is only one way to examine a patient's developmental characteristics. In addition, other psychological theorists have focused more attention on an infant's psychosomatic realm of instinctual drives and intense emotions. The search for any development factors that may create a proclivity for receptivity to a ME must be general because they remain unconscious. As Jung (1947/1954, para. 380; emphasis added) states: "Where instinct predominates, *psychoid* processes set in which pertain to the sphere of the unconscious as elements incapable of consciousness." The complexes that form are the only signs capable of entering consciousness that crystallise the instinctual, psychoid elements and therefore point to the best indicators for examining the innate tendencies of receptivity to a ME.

Developmental factors as a prelude to a ME

For Freud, MEs have their origins in a solipsistic, neonatal state. In *Civilization and its Discontents*, he ascribes a ME in adulthood as derived from an "oceanic feeling" brought about by regression to that neonatal feeling occurring in the primary narcissism phase, independent of the mother (Freud, 1930, pp. 66–68).

Merkur (2010, ch. 1) traces contemporary Freudian thought regarding the oceanic feeling. He explains that after the breakthrough of clinical observations of the importance of mother–child interactions, commentators now doubt the theory of neonatal solipsism as the source of the oceanic feeling. Rather, it is believed that it is obtained in the interactive relationship between mother and child. Although not discarding Freud's theory, others suggest that mother–child interactions augment the solipsistic feeling. Edith Jacobson (1964), for example, suggests that MEs arise because of a toddler's fantasies of an early, mother–child merger. The French Freudian analyst and philosopher Julia Kristeva (2009) squarely places parent–child interactions as the source of what she calls a "religious feeling."

An analysis of Freud's concept of the oceanic feeling (Parsons, 1999, p. 40) points out that, as such a feeling exists in many, it could be better understood as a developmental influence on the personal unconscious rather than a deep, innate connection that manifests in a religious feeling. Parsons suggests that Freud "stressed its statelike character over its 'subterranean' origins and thus mitigated any attempt to interpret it with respect to the unconscious" (ibid., p. 39).

In developmental terms, placing the oceanic feeling at an infant, instinct-driven age means that it is imprinted in a manner that is formative in the structure of the psyche, as consciousness then organises around this memory. It creates what Anna Freud (1981) terms "developmental lines" arising over time from early id–ego–superego–environmental influences. She postulates:

> Long before a personality is sufficiently aware of environmental demands, or sufficiently divided within itself to suffer from internal strife, normal progress can already be threatened and harmed by any of the developmental disharmonies arising from any of the qualitative, quantitative, or temporal reasons.
>
> (Ibid., p. 134)

In another work, she explains that, to understand these lines, "it is essential to accompany the child uninterruptedly through at least the first dozen years of his growth" (Freud, 1983, p. 113). This creates the possibility that the oceanic feeling may achieve greater or lesser significance because of development disharmonies that may differ from normal developmental patterns at least until the age of twelve.

Jung's contributions to understanding early childhood development, elaborated by Neumann and Fordham (see Samuels, 1985), do not mention numinous or mystical experiences in relation to childhood development. However, this connection is apparent elsewhere in Jung's exposition of the parental archetypes. The parental archetypes of a father and a mother are the essence of childhood development and therefore have a role in the formation of all complexes. As Jung (1927/1931a, para. 65) explains, "The archetype of the mother is the most immediate one for the child. But with the development of consciousness the father also enters his field of vision, and activates an archetype." The father and mother archetypes are the "mightiest archetypes of all" and the "supreme regulating principles of religious and political life" (Jung, 1927/1931, para. 336). He explains that the ideal image of the archaic, historical archetype is unconsciously projected, so when the parents die, "it goes on working as though it were a spirit existing on its own" (Jung, 1928b, para. 294).

When a parental complex is created through a disturbance caused by the actions of the personal parents and difficulties in the child's adaptation, the parental archetype gives the complex its force and effect. For example, Jung (1909/1949, para. 744) states: "The fateful power of the father complex comes from the archetype." The nature of the mother and father archetypes is that they are the source of the child's divinities, and, when a complex is reacti-vated later in life, as Jung (1921c, para. 201) explains, "The fantasies pro-duced by this reactivation gives rise to the birth of father and mother divinities, as well as awakening the childhood relations with God and the corresponding childlike feelings." Accordingly, the activation of a parental complex has the capacity to create a symbolic substitution for these divine entities and can lead to the numinous appearance of the substituted image of God, the *Imago Dei*, which Jung identifies as a "progression" in the psyche, not a regression (ibid.).

This far-reaching connection between the parental archetypes and their inherent divinity suggests that every child has a pre-existing, innate structure of a religious feeling arising from the presence of the archetypes. For this reason, Jung (1935a, para. 220) suggests that there is no difference between archetypal forms and mystical forms. The consequence is that the mystical is innately present through deep archetypes, so it may be said that the mother and father are the living embodiments of the mystical core.

The archetypes remain dormant in the unconscious and need to be brought into the light of consciousness in order to have a mystical effect. The reacti-vation of the "father and mother divinities" arises by the triggering of the complex due to a "retardation of affective development," thus causing the libido to become introverted (Jung, 1913, para. 304). This introversion "invests to a greater or lesser degree large areas of memory, with the result that these reminiscences acquire a vitality that no longer properly belongs to them" (ibid.). The parental complexes therefore account for the strong, inward movement of libido and the consequent awakening of a religious orientation:

> [T]he aim of the great religions is expressed in the injunction "not of this world," and this implies the inward movement of the libido into the unconscious. Its withdrawal and introversion create in the unconscious a concentration of libido which is symbolized as the "treasure" as in the parables of the "pearl of great price" and the "treasure in the field."
>
> (Jung, 1921e, para. 423)

Religious, premonitory feelings therefore arise when parental memories are reawakened, connecting the child to the divine, archetypal source: "The regressive reactivation of the father and mother-imagos plays an important role in religion ... [because] religious feelings are rooted in the unconscious memories of certain tender emotions in early infancy" (Jung, 1912/1952e, para. 134). Jung calls these feelings "archetypal intuitions" (ibid.).

The parental complexes are thus the *prima materia* for a ME as they activate the divine aspects of the parental archetypes. For this to occur, the parental complexes must be the subject of what Esther Harding (1973) calls "willed introversion": deliberate and continued introversion arising from considering or analysing the complexes. This is a cumulative process, as she explains, because "ever and anon a further instalment of libido becomes accessible to the process by which it can be transformed" (ibid., pp. 466–467).

In this manner, analysis appears useful in the continued introversion of libido in that a regression will assist in its accumulation, allowing a possible breakthrough to consciousness. This is also seen through meditation, where the continued inward focus draws energy within. Drawing from alchemy, Jung (1955–1956b, para. 707) refers to meditation as "internal talk" to a deity, or oneself. This has important implications for the depth psychology of the ME as it implies, contrary to Freud, that the seeds of a ME are pre-existing in the collective unconscious and remain there until a complex becomes reactivated and the archetypes burst through again. This does not detract from the metaphysical or spiritual tradition view of a ME as it describes the process in the psyche that brings the revelation into being.

As precondition for the Pleromic archetypes

Jung (1938/1954, para. 164) suggests that a mother complex is a source of receptivity for a son: "Often he is endowed with a wealth of religious feelings which help to bring the *ecclesia spiritualis* into reality, and a spiritual receptivity which makes him responsive to revelation." This assertion forms part of a list of positive mother-complex effects, such as good taste, an aesthetic sense, a gifted teacher, a feeling for history, and a "finely differentiated Eros instead of, or in addition to, homosexuality" (ibid.). This depicts an individual who has "psychic relatedness" (Jung, 1927, para. 255), evidenced by feeling that is "strongly accentuated emotionally" (Jung, 1934, para. 201). It amounts to a softening of the personality to enable receptivity. It does not, however, include the active longing and positive apprehension that are necessary for a ME, and it is only one aspect of receptivity. In addition, the use of the word "often" in the quote indicates that not every mother complex will yield receptivity – a realisation that is confirmed by clinical practice. Jung (1938/1954, p. 87, n. 3) clarifies this issue in respect of the mother complex of a daughter that it "is comprised of a series of different 'types' of mother complexes ... The types are ideal instances, or pictures of average run of experience with which no single individual can be identified."

There are varying types of mother complex that may be categorised by the well-understood attachment theory relating to different mother–child bindings. In any event, the types of mother complexes are probably, as Jung (1931, para. 937) states, "a relatively small number of typical primary forms." This lack of specificity in describing the type of mother complex that will yield receptivity is consistent with Jung's repeated refusal to draw out the "developmental lines" to see how a particular complex traces through to adulthood. In outlining his proposal for explaining psychological types, he gives the reason as: "The existence of a parental complex therefore tells us little or nothing about the particular constitution of the individual" (ibid., para. 928). He asserts that the "crux" of a parental complex is "the special way in which the complex works itself out in the individual's life," and "each of them reacts to it in a totally different way" (ibid.).

The importance of the environmental factors and developmental changes recognised by Anna Freud from early childhood disturbances emphasises that, if any single form of parental complex presents itself, there is no clear line of sight that might indicate what effect it will have on the capacity of an individual to be receptive to the numinous in the future. The parental complexes indeed relate to the divine aspects of the mother and father archetypes, but it does not follow that a numinous experience will occur *in every instance*.

The interviews with the mystics give rise to a theory as to the quality and depth of receptivity. Two specific parental complexes, *working in concert*, provide preconditions for the breakthrough of Pleromic archetypal forces that are sources of the numinous and contain such affect that they are more likely to be received. Rather than suggest a certain "type" or innate quality for receptivity, the proposition is that these two complexes combine to amass sufficient psychic energy to prompt the release of what Jung (1947/1954, paras. 388–389) calls a *scintilla* – a spark of primal archetypal forces – which will bring about an overwhelming affect that takes such an experience beyond the edge of consciousness, where it is most likely to be received.

The prompting of the archetypal forces does not derive solely from the mother complex (or indeed any other complex), but rather from a combination of complexes. This is the essential basis for receptivity because psychoanalysis points to personal complexes as the means for the release of the forces in the collective unconscious through engagement with the archetypes. The personal complexes are therefore the engine for the accumulated force of the Pleromic archetypes to deliver a ME that is likely to be received.

In "The Psychological Foundation of Belief in Spirits," Jung (1920/1948, para. 582) speaks of "autonomous complexes" arising from the personal as well as the archetypes of the collective unconscious that are not in contact with the ego complex. He gives an example, which is germane, of an unexplained longing arising from the collective unconscious that goes beyond a personal, mother complex (Jung, 1928, para. 711). When linked together, the personal and collective are therefore felt as "strange, uncanny, and at the same time fascinating" (Jung 1920/1948, para. 590) and "beyond the reach of the conscious will" (Jung, 1928, para. 710). Jung adds that they are a source of religious expression (ibid., para. 712) and, thus, the numinous.

This strictly psychological explanation of the origins of a ME has a logical consistency as it relies on the existence of the Jungian constructs of complexes and archetypes. These terms are a convenient language with which to analyse a ME, but they are certainly not the only means to explain the phenomenon. It is outside the scope of this work to examine alternative, non-Jungian categorisations of developmental issues that may yield the same result. The idea that there is an early childhood rupture because of the failure of the child to meet the idealised form of a mother does not require any terminology. In addition, the concept that there is an inherited, global creation story that imbues the mother and father with divine qualities is universal and not reliant on Plato's forms or Jung's archetypes. Bion (1961/2014, p. 177) confirms that he perceives there is a realm of primordial vestiges that "exist in the unconscious as undifferentiated symbols," calling them "proto-mental memories." These primal memory fragments include the transcendent, divine unknowable realm (Reiner, 2012, p. 6).

The importance of these constructs for a ME is that they link the personal complexes with the primal core that contains these archetypes or proto-mental memories. In his foreword to Jolande Jacobi's *Complex, Archetype, Symbol in the Psychology of C.G. Jung*, Jung (1959, p. x) indicates that the complexes arising in the personal unconscious and the archetypes emanating from the collective unconscious are linked. Accordingly, the archetypes behind the parental complexes merge with the Pleromic archaic archetypes.

"Pleroma" is a Gnostic concept that describes the dual aspect of the ineffable divine, consisting of both the fullness of God's presence and the absolute nothingness of God *before creation* (Stein, 2015). There is nothing before the Pleroma; hence, it is the primordial essence. Neumann (1948/1969, p. 394) calls these powerful Pleromic archetypes the "archetypal firmament of the collective unconscious." , Neumann explains that the "ego penetrates the archetypal heaven and attains the pleromatic, uroboros sphere of being" when a ME occurs (ibid., p. 395). He describes this as the godhead "or else the creative nucleus of nothingness at the center of man" (ibid.). These primordial archetypes, however described, have their place at the core of the collective unconscious. It is for this reason that Jung (1935a, para. 219) defines mystics as "people who have a particularly vivid experience of the processes of the collective unconscious. Mystical experience is experience of the archetypes."

The Pleromic archetypes, when they break through, overwhelm the ego and push past all resistance, perhaps because they are the ground of our existence and provide a revelation that is numinous and has the capacity to alter consciousness. It is this archetypal foundation of the collective unconscious that is the force that creates the "fundamental upheaval." The likelihood of it breaking through and becoming a fundamental upheaval is aided, if not created, by the massing of psychic energy accumulated through the inward movement of the libido initiated by the personal complexes.

When the personal, parental complex and the primordial archetypal core are aligned, the possibility of a ME breakthrough increases. Jung (1947/1954, para. 413) summarises the process as the excitation of an energy concentrated by working through the personal complex that evokes the archetype:

> [This] represents the climax of a concentrated spiritual and psychic effort, in so far as this is understood consciously and of set purpose. That is to say, the synthesis can also be prepared in advance and brought to a

certain point – James's "bursting point" – unconsciously, whereupon it irrupts into consciousness of its own volition and confronts the latter with a formidable task of assimilating the contents that have burst in upon it, yet without damaging the viability of the two systems, i.e., of ego consciousness on the one hand and the irrupted complex on the other.

Jaffe (1959, p. 26) states that the personal complex is always the visible layer, which, when exposed, reveals the collective: "If the complex embedded in the material of the personal unconscious seems to stand in inexorable conflict with consciousness, its 'nucleus,' once laid bare, may prove to be a content of the collective unconscious." Dieckmann (1999, p. 44) also suggests that the collective archetypes stand behind the personal:

> It is here that we trace a direct connection between the complex that expresses itself in the personal unconscious as an acquisition in the life of an individual and a deeper basis that is anchored in the archetypes of the collective unconscious.

As the two are linked, there are consequences of their closeness or separation. When the personal complex is far from consciousness and not the subject of examination, the archetype of the complex is closer to the Pleromic archetypes. Jacobi (1959, p. 11) explains that the "complexes take on in the unconscious an archaic-mythological character and an increasing numinosity through enrichment of their contents" when the distance is great. The enrichment then comes from the co-immersion of the contents of the complex with the ancient archetypes in the unconscious. With respect to receptivity of a ME, this means that the work of accumulation of the libido and preparation occurs not only by bringing the complex to consciousness with the accompanying internal reflection, but also by it autonomously developing over time while it still remains unconscious.

Material in the unconscious that is not brought into awareness is always active and ever changing as it combines and recombines with aspects of both the personal and the collective unconscious. Jacobi's notion that the two aspects are closest when the complex is not in consciousness means that, when it *is* finally in conscious awareness, it may be further from the collective and its primordial archetypes, and will become instead a subject that is caught up in the ego's realm. It then loses the raw power of the archetype in the unconscious.

Sri Aurobindo (Ghose, 1973a, p. 937) suggests that the process directed to a ME requires the activity within the unconscious as well as bringing the subject matter into consciousness:

> These higher powers work already in the human unspiritualized mind, but indirectly and in a fragmentary and diminished action; they are

changed into substance and power of mind before they can work, and that substance and power are illuminated and intensified in their vibration, exalted and ecstasised in some movements by their entry, but not transformed.

This confirms that the archetypes in the unconscious are ever present and always working. However, they must be changed into the substance of the mind – ego consciousness – where there will be a gradual acceptance of what Sri Aurobindo calls the "higher dynamics." These dynamics – the archetypes working in the unconscious and then being brought into consciousness through the personal complexes – constitute the higher dynamics at work and "this progression continues until some complete and mature action of them is possible" (ibid.).

The essential link is the connection between the personal complexes that are formative because they carry the projection of divinity by the child, and the collective underlay of the archaic forms of the Pleroma of existence. Therefore, there must be a point in the unconscious where they come together and draw upon the fuel of the accumulated libido to provide a breakthrough of the archetypes. The progression to which Sri Aurobindo refers is the continued, conscious revelation of the divine aspects that begin to open, perhaps in imperceptible ways, consciousness to the higher powers that exist in the unconscious. The two sources of divinity – the divinity of the parental archetypes and the divinity contained within the Pleromic archetypes – fuse to create the source of energy that facilitates the breakthrough.

It seems that nothing may be said or done in analysis to prompt the divine quality of the parental complexes to fuse with the collective archetypes, aside from providing a space where it *might* occur. This is a critical use of analysis as it is the retort in which the material accumulates and fuses. Much is therefore made in Tibetan Buddhism (Jinpa, 2008, pp. 418–423) of "spiritualising" the environment by consecrating the area, with, among other things, a ceiling that is white, the east wall yellow, the south white, the west blue, the north green, and the ground white.

Examined in this way, when a person has receptivity, there is a mixing of the divine aspects of the personal unconscious material with that which is in the deep unconscious as a collective archetype. Theoretically, this could offer a clearer reason for the variation in MEs as it is a trajectory of the collective filtering through the contents of the personal, thus altering the images for different subjects. This is perhaps a better idea than the notion that it is the presence of cognitive assessment early in the ME that shapes the images. This clearer reason draws its force from the power of the collective, archaic archetypes to seek expression and avail themselves of the personal impressions arising from the manifestation of the complex.

If the emphasis is placed on the power of the archetype, it is relevant to repeat Dieckmann's (1999) concern that the autonomous nature of the collective unconscious – because of its overwhelming archetypal character – may break through in a destructive manner, as the Pleromic archetypes include nothingness and the devil. However, this did not seem to be the case for any of the interviewees, who reported only positive experiences. The ME is more likely to be positive because the unconscious is prospective, seeking its own expression and expansion so that, as Dieckmann recognises, the Pleromic archetypes contain "the mythological symbols of the beginnings of and possibilities for the fundamental transformation of consciousness" (ibid., p. 44). Moreover, the positive character of the breakthrough relates to consciousness being the harbinger of evolution. According to Sri Aurobindo (Ghose, 1973a, p. 924), the duty of an individual in evolutionary terms requires achievement of the intermediate plane so that one may become "a conscious partner, agent, instrument of the Cosmic Spirit in the working of the universal Energy."

An intersection of the psychic energy resulting from immersion in the personal complexes and the energic emergence of the collective, archetypal core is essential because, as Jung (1920/1948, para. 582; emphasis added) explains, the "fundamental upheaval" occurs only when preceded by "*a long period of incubation.*" This critical phase of incubation is when the archetype gathers strength in the unconscious and the personal complex gathers libido through its activation to create a powerful energy source to activate the inchoate, numinous potential of the archetypal core. The parental complex, long held and considered, is therefore an indicator of incubation and the possible future activation of the collective, primordial archetypal substrate.

In discussing the "incubation" that is necessary for the emergence of the deep archetypes, Jung (ibid.) employs what he calls the "excellent and well-known" example of the conversion of St Paul, who had his vision on the road to Damascus only after his "preparation [was] complete," which meant he was "ripe for conversion." Paul's preparation was a long-standing Christ complex arising from his resistance to Christianity, which was disconnected from his ego complex and therefore unconscious. This preparation, by long personal exposure and immersion in that complex, was necessary before the archetypal core could break through and cause a fundamental upheaval: his vision (ibid.). It is particularly appropriate to Paul as he is regarded as a "hero of the introspective conscience" (Stendahl, 1963, p. 199), and the Pauline letters indicate his process of engaging with a complex by regression with the consequent accumulation of libido.

Expressed in psychological terms, the preparation must occur in sufficient intensity before the ME will have any significance and so, most importantly, it will not be rejected. Sri Aurobindo (Ghose, 1973a, p. 929) explains, "A long, difficult state of constant effort, energism, austerity of the personal will, *tapasya* [physical austerities], has ordinarily to be traversed before a more decisive stage can be reached." The result of insufficient incubation is not a total absence of MEs – as lesser forms may still break through – but rather a likelihood that any experience will be rejected or will fade over time. The preparation is primarily the inward-directed, regressive interaction with the parental complexes, resulting in sufficient gathering of the entire range of emotion and cognition that these complexes carry. In spiritual traditions, this can take place through the processes of internal conflict, meditation, and striving without success for long periods of time.

In this light, a ME that is not derived from incubation is only a sign or a pointer to the role of the non-ego force in the psyche. A single ME or a series with no preparation might be effective in altering consciousness, but it is much less likely to hold and not fade or be rejected than one that has resulted from accumulated intensity brought about by immersion in a parental complex or in some deep practice that requires an inward turning of life energy. The reason for this critical distinction is that the ME *must be adapted to the ego*: "The intermediate planes of consciousness ... adapt the divine knowledge and force into terms that can have impact on the mind and life in the body ... [It] spiritualizes the mind" (Krinsky, 2017, ch. 13). A ME that is a numinous experience or a sudden overwhelming that changes consciousness with no preparation is feasible, but inconsistent with the idea of the importance of preparation, the build-up of libido, and the possibility of a permanent change.

There is no measurement for the nature or degree of the build-up that is necessary for the collective, primordial archetypes to be released and travel to consciousness. Lesser MEs may actually begin the process of activation and bring it to the tipping point. This is because each of them creates an unanswerable puzzle that offers the possibility of great reflection. When there is an ME, "potentials belonging to the body unconscious and the instinctual archetypal unconscious are reactivated and begin expressing themselves within consciousness" (Washburn, 1995, p. 166).

The emergence of the primal archetypes after incubation is likely to have a profound effect on the subject for two reasons. First, they have arrived from psychic, libido energy and therefore have innate force: "if the image is charged with numinosity, that is, with psychic energy, then it becomes dynamic and will produce consequences" (Jung, 1961, para. 589). The energic quality is derived from the continuum of psychic energy that has led to the breakthrough; therefore, by that force alone, it overwhelms the subject because it "has a characteristically numinous effect, so that the subject is gripped by it as though by an instinct" (Jung, 1920/1948, para. 225). According to Jung, the grip is at the unconscious level, as it would be by an instinct. Second, the Pleromic archetypes arrive "at the same time as emotions" (Jung, 1961, para. 590). This is *caused* by the overwhelming of the subject, who accordingly has a corresponding reaction.

The overwhelming affect is due to the occurrence of something extraordinary but also to the subject's memory of the presence of the subject matter of the divine aspects of the parental complexes that have led to the build-up and breakthrough. There is a crucial link between the personal parental complexes and an archetypal core so that the emotions travel through as remembrance, in addition to the overwhelming experience. The emotions become even more powerful when there is a cognitive evaluation after the fact of the images by way of parental metaphors because "metaphoric words, even when deeply appropriated, must carry with them historical traces, the vestiges of presences, events, affective exchanges, and perceptual discovery" (Rizzuto, 2001, p. 555).

The distinctions between affects and emotions are complex (see Aguillaume, 2008), but with respect to a ME suggest that the overwhelming affect is an unconscious, instinctual, or body-based reaction that occurs with the infiltration of the ME into consciousness. It is a non-evaluative reaction to what is occurring and fits into the many descriptions given of the onset of a mystical event. The emotional states that thereafter follow, such as anxiety, fear, or interest, arise from the cognitive assessment at the post-onset stage of the ME or its later evaluation. In terms of the parental archetypes, there is no recognition of the concordance between the images that break through and the actual parents. However, the fact that there has been a build-up of regressed libido means that emotions that are later manifested may be contained within or relate to the parental subject matter.

However expressed, the personal ego complex and the non-ego collective archetype are two parts of a single structure. When this alignment occurs, *the nature of the personal complex becomes relevant* in predicting the potential impact of the collective Pleromic archetypes. Dieckmann (1999, p. 45) affirms this view that personal complexes may be predictive of a possible outcome when viewed as part of a complex structure that includes the collective archetypes:

> But they can be hypothetically included with a degree of probability bordering on certainty either on the basis of specific early experiences (for example, the very early birth of a younger sibling or a hospitalization) or according to the character of the parents.

Parental complexes and trauma

For many reasons, personal parental complexes may result in childhood trauma. As two examples, abuse from a violent parent or a developmental illness will create a different childhood experience of the archetype. It is difficult to determine if childhood trauma increases or decreases the possibility of receptivity to a ME.

The Jungian psychoanalytic viewpoint is that the build-up of libido is the catalyst for the breakthrough of the Pleromic archetypes. This is the manner in which the effect of trauma may be examined to see its effect. "Psychic energy" or libido is the energy that belongs to the deep instincts and the archetypes of the unconscious (Jung, 1912/1952e, para. 130). Jung attributes an inherent, internal force that is akin to physical energy to psyche. It may be observed in the movement of the psyche through "instinct, wishing, willing, affect, attention, capacity for work, etc" (Jung, 1928a, para. 26). As such, it has intensity in terms of its build-up and therefore a quantity, so it may increase. The principle of "equivalence" suggests that the depletion of psychic energy in the unconscious will find a place for its expression in consciousness as the amount of energy is always the same.

In normal circumstances, psychic energy "applies itself wholly to the complex at the expense of other psychic material" (Jung, 1907, para. 103). Expressed in another way, the libido is drawn up with the unconscious complex that then has priority over other issues. This amounts to a damming of the libido, "which transforms the kinetic energy of the flow into the potential energy of a reservoir" (Jung, 1928a, para. 29). When there is a regression, a critical source of libido accumulation, "parts of the psyche that have been repressed and cut off from the total personality are restored, and their energy is released for creative living in the present" (Harding, 1973, p. 292).

The parental complexes are the key touchstones for the damming of energy and the most likely candidates for the introversion and regression that yield the build-up of libido. In themselves, these complexes are not responsible for the evocation of the Pleromic archetypes, but they serve as the critical subject matter for the accumulation and subsequent release of psychic energy. These parental archetypes create a complex that is unconscious, and a link survives with the actual parents so that the complex is later capable of reflection and integration.

Some have discounted the concept of psychic energy (Zepf, 2010). However, it does provide a theory to explain the movements in psyche based on parallels with physical or bio-chemical energy. In this theory, childhood trauma dams up libido and, more importantly, de-integrates consciousness, resulting in depersonalisation and dissociation. The child then has an "inability to create [an] integrated experience of the self" (Bob and Laker, 2016, p. 9). The trauma thus causes a blockage and engenders intense inner opposites, creating a psychic split. Kalshed (2013, p. 132) explains that the hyper-sensitive nature of a child combined with "unavoidable, insensitive, or punitive parental care can lead to trauma." The consequences, he suggests, are a defensive, persecutory structure and a humiliated, wounded child-self (ibid.). According to Jung (1910/1946, para. 13, n. 4), the obstacle creates introversion, but this has an effect on the manner in which libido is directed and accumulated:

> When life comes up against an obstacle, so that no adaptation can be achieved and transference of libido to reality is suspended, then an introversion takes place. This is to say, instead of the libido working towards reality, there is an increased fantasy activity ... [T]his may in time lead to a practical solution.

The libido in the case of an obstacle such as trauma flows *away* from its normal direction and is diverted in efforts to find a solution. The normal direction is the building up of concepts that makes it "capable of further development, so that its continued, active realization is assured" (ibid., p. 5). Jung (ibid) suggests that this is how infantile conflicts are resolved. Therefore, it may be that a traumatised child's relationship to a parental complex does not build up the essential concepts of divinity that can then be remembered as a source to link the archetypal contents.

Trauma is often suggested as a basis for a spiritual search. After a traumatic adult event, there is a particular focus on the relationship between what has occurred and pre-existing religious faith, and a consequent struggle. This "spiritual struggle," as it is commonly called, naturally arises by external events that threaten a person's ego stability, such as car accidents or random violence. At this point, a person seeks meaning and hope and must reconcile a potential loss of faith. In this sense, "Trauma acts to increase spiritual development if that development is defined as an increase in the search for purpose and meaning" and is a necessary result of the presence of trauma (Decker, 1993, p. 34). Accordingly, the presence of a ME will create, as Maslow (1964, Appendix G) puts it, a "death before rebirth."

The process that leads a ME to occur in such a manner that it will create an alteration of consciousness requires a context for the ego to relate to the experience. Relating to an experience that has occurred evolves within a framework, which may exist only a long time after childhood trauma:

> Older individuals have had greater opportunity (i.e. a longer period of experience) to construct a framework of meaning (and thus have the most 'metaphysical momentum' in the sense of the longest period of building up behaviors and beliefs to substantiate and support core belief systems), or are more rooted in the social conventions of meaning (including religion) and possess cognitive skills that enhance their ability to meet the challenge of trauma to meaning successfully. Davidson and Smith (1990) report that when faced with potentially traumatic experiences, children under the age of 10 are three times more likely than teenagers and adults to respond with post-traumatic stress disorder (PTSD)...
>
> (Garbarino and Bedard, 1996, p. 471)

There is no doubt that adults who have not suffered childhood trauma can still have a ME (von Gontard, 2017, p. 104); hence, trauma is not a specific requirement for receptivity. Indeed, it may even *reduce* the likelihood of a ME if de-integration is extensive and, rather than aiding the build-up of libido, the trauma seeks another path of rectification. This is speculative, of course, but it is interesting that only a few of the mystics interviewed indicated a traumatic childhood experience or, if it was objectively traumatic, such as the loss of a parent, did not approach that as a basis for the ME. For adults with trauma, it is clear that a traumatic event increases self-reflection to discover meaning (Bob and Laker, 2016, p. 9). This search for meaning may invoke great longing, which may be an incentive for the deep introversion that itself builds libido. However, once again, it could be that the longing is for a corrective idea and does not rely on the process of a connection between the parental archetypes and those of the collective.

Chapter 6

The father archetype and orthodoxy

The father archetype that underlies a father complex is the *primum movens* of religious feeling: it is the "creative wind-breath – the spirit, pneuma, *atman*" (Jung, 1927/1931a, para. 65) and thus contains the seeds of all MEs. It is at the heart of the collective, Pleromic archetypal core that is responsible for numinosity because the father archetype, at its highest, is synonymous with God, and conversely "in God we honour the energy of the archetype" (Jung, 1912/1952e, para. 135).

Religious feeling and interest arise from the father archetype for at least two reasons. The first is that it appears as both the deity and the devil, which Jung (1909/1949, p. 321, n. 22) explains yields the "roots of the first religious sublimations." The second is that, as Jung (ibid., para. 739) explains in a difficult sentence, the parental archetype "resists conscious criticism with the force of an instinct, for which the soul (*anima*) may fittingly be described a *naturaliter religiosa*." Here, Jung suggests that the father archetype is an example of a primordial, powerful influence, making that archetype parallel the *anima nautraliter religiosa*, or the natural religious instinct of psyche.

Although the father archetype is an underlying ground for a ME, it cleaves towards the authority of established religion so that the nascent religious feelings it engenders are diverted to orthodox doctrine. Dieckmann (1985, pp. 216–217) asserts that this is less a function of the father archetype than a separate "archetype of authority," which he describes as an instinctual drive that seeks a societal structure and stands behind the power of father archetype:

> [W]e can assert that authority is a principle which is inherent in nature with the instinctual force of structure and order ... From this point of view, the personal father is neither the creator nor the first authority, but only the projection screen of an impersonal principle.

The father mediates this authority principle, according to Dieckmann, and therefore is not the prototype of that authority, merely a copy (ibid., p. 218). However, as this authority principle is most often perceived as paternal, the principle is conveyed and carried by the father archetype. Among the consequent structural roles of the father that convey this authority are, according to Jung (1936, para. 159), the "transmitter of traditional wisdom," he who contains the realm of "moral commandments," and the purveyor of the rational spirit (ibid., para. 59). The father archetype is therefore the representation of the authority of religious orthodoxy in its structures and liturgy, as well as the ground of religious feeling.

For Freudians, as Lacan (1996, p. 66) puts it, the personal father in a marriage relationship introduces the child to the structuralist, symbolic order of society. In Freud's (1923, ch. 3) analysis of the Oedipus Complex, the personal father requires the child to internalise authority: the superego. Accordingly, Freud (1912–1913, pp. 156–157) states: "the beginnings of all religions, morals, society and art converge in the Oedipus Complex." The association Freud makes with religion is noteworthy as he too suggests that the personal father is the patriarchal God, who stands "hidden behind every divine figure" (Freud, 1927, p. 19).

Freedom from the father complex and the orthodoxy of religion in adulthood can arise only through an individual's conscious realisation of his or her own individuality, not subsumed within the father. Jung (1942/1948, para. 271) explains that "Legitimate detachment consists in conscious differentiation from the father and from the habitus represented by him." However, detachments are "not everyday occurrences" (ibid., para. 274) because differentiation from the father "brings a sharpening of opposites in particular of the moral opposites" (ibid., para. 272) and runs counter to the instincts (ibid., para. 273). These psychoid instincts or archetypes are involved because "The fateful power of the father complex comes from the archetype, and this is the real reason why the *consensus genitum* puts a divine or daemonic in place of the father" (Jung, 1909/1949, para. 744).

This dual aspect of the father as consisting of both a divine and a demonic aspect is not only the underlying archetype of the complex but also the source of the complex: "A typical neurotic situation arises: he (the child) wants (the father) yet does not want: saying yes and no at the same time" (ibid., para. 740). The neurotic struggle with an inevitable father complex ultimately will not free the individual from the fundamental power of the complex; at most, it may "summon up enough honest self-criticism admixed with humility to see where he (still behaves as a child) – irrationality, and with unreflecting receptivity" (Jung, 1942/1948, para. 273).

The unavailable father complex

The predicament of an inevitable father complex that is difficult to overcome is immensely complicated where there is an absent father or a father whom the child discounts as weak and ineffectual. Absence includes being unavailable either emotionally or for any regular period of time, so it has been suggested that actual absence and the unavailability of the father *for any reason* should be treated in the same way as a "father *experienced* as unavailable" (Seligman, 1985, p. 72; original emphasis).

Psychological research reports the practical consequences that arise from an absent father, such as a child's rejection of authority, increased verbal skills but lower cognitive performance, and less interest in both aggression and dominance striving (Draper and Harpending, 1982). An unavailable father suggests a father complex that questions or rejects authority, a passivity, and also a never-ending, primal longing for that father: "The quest for the father is an ancient and archetypal theme, which symbolically tells both society and the individual that a father is an always continuing effort that never reaches a definitive end" (Zola, 2001, pp. 281–282).

The dramatic effect of this absent father complex has been recognised by contemporary psychoanalysis. The absent father is becoming more common with changing family structures and results in what Herzog (2001) calls "father hunger" – a pressing, continuous ache to connect with the father, so well illustrated in *Hamlet* (Erlich, 1977) – which is a quest for both the personal father and the order and structure of authority that are inherent in the archetype. With reference to Telemachus waiting for Ulysses, Zola (2001, p. 282) explains that the "quest contains an unconscious residue of phylogenetic memory."

Father hunger will influence the development of a religious orientation and the search for alternative authority substitutes. D.T. Suzuki (2014, p. 203), who introduced Zen to the West, is explicit that meaning in his life through Zen was derived from an endless search for his father, who died when he was six. Bishop (2014, p. 27) reports that Jung's lack of respect for his father led him to seek "a symbolic father in the figure of Sigmund Freud."

Father hunger is a "transformer" of libido because the continuing, painful reflection causes an introversion that is powerful as it both "carries conviction and at the same time expresses the content of the conviction" (Jung, 1912/ 1952, para. 344). Therefore, crucially, it will mediate an individual's relationship to authority. A positive father complex "produces a certain credulity with regard to authority and a distinct willingness to bow down before all spiritual dogmas" (Jung, 1945/1948, para. 398). When there is an unavailable, negative father complex, there is a concomitant rejection of authority and a powerful, unceasing longing for the structural and predictable order he could not offer. As the need for authority is perhaps instinctive, as Dieckmann suggests, there is simultaneously a rejection of established religion and a longing for some alternative form.

It is the longing and the unavailability of the father that engender a search for some external or internal authority that holds the principles needed for a relationship with society and God. If the external orthodoxy is rejected, the longing continues and may seek a substitute outside the organised, doctrinal structure. This is well explained in the story of King Saul and the Witch of Endor.

King Saul and the Witch of Endor

Saul is unaware of his future role as king and is searching for the asses of his father, Kish (I Samuel 9); he is serving the authority of his father. In search of a wise man who might help him find the missing animals, he encounters Samuel, a man of God and the ultimate human father and authority. Samuel has a writ from God to find a king, and he anoints Saul as such (I Samuel 10:1). However, Saul does not accept that he should be king, and when the tribes of Israel come to him, he hides among the baggage (I Samuel 10:22). He remains under the complete authority of his own father and there is as yet no father substitute or need for him to control his own destiny or accept an authoritative role. His inability to accept or exert authority is clearly expressed.

Although Saul becomes king, it is Samuel who is in control and gradually becomes the father substitute for Kish. Wiesel (1981, p. 78) points out that "Saul maintains a kind of sovereignty but cannot ignore Samuel's towering figure that stands behind him, as though to watch him, guide him and supervise him." In this sense, Kish's father imago is overpowered by the father archetype, but Samuel's interference and control annoy Saul, creating a complex.

Samuel maintains the position as the central father figure even though Saul carries out his royal duties. This is logical as there must always be a father archetype that is the locus of control as there is a need in all individuals for a *numen* as the guiding or organising principle (Perry, 1991, p. 20). After appointing Saul, Samuel requires him to wait on the battlefield for seven days until he can come and proffer a burnt offering (I Samuel 10:8). Saul does as instructed, but as Samuel does not arrive on schedule, Saul becomes impatient and carries out the burnt offering himself (I Samuel 13:9). Samuel then arrives and berates Saul for not waiting, warning him, "now thy kingdom shall not continue" (I Samuel 13:14). The relationship between the father archetype and the child, and the consequent complex, is intensified. The reason for Samuel's overreaction is unclear, although Sandford (1985, p. 17) speculates that he did not face his shadow and projected it onto Saul.

Samuel then tells Saul that God has instructed him to kill all of the Amaleks: "you shall not have pity on [any Amalek]; you shall slay both man and woman, infant and suckling, oxen, sheep, camel and ass" (I Samuel 15:3). Saul defeats the Amaleks but spares their king's life and keeps the best sheep and cattle as booty, thereby disobeying the word of God. It is suggested that Saul does this because he recognises that the Amaleks represent archetypal evil, so they cannot be destroyed completely (Gubitz, 1977). However, Samuel castigates him once again: "For rebellion *is as* the sin of witchcraft, and stubbornness *is as* iniquity and idolatry. Because thou has rejected the word of the Lord, he also rejected thee from *being* king" (I Samuel 15:23; original emphasis). The reference to witchcraft and sin is perhaps a warning not to abandon orthodoxy.

The archetype of God is above the archetype of Samuel, just as Samuel is above Kish. The Old Testament provides a gradation of archetypal figures. Dieckmann (1999, p. 47, Figure 5.1) illustrates this gradation for the father archetype as a series of descending quaternities – from higher forms to lower forms. The father complex arising in Saul because of Samuel's control and emotional distance is exacerbated by his lack of protection from the wrath of God. In this sense, Samuel is the unavailable father, unable to fulfil the archetypal role of protector. Samuel, rather than God, is the "unavailable father" because the father archetype in its highest form cannot be assailed, as it is the primogenitor. However, as such, any rejection by the highest form of the father archetype – God – causes unbearable trauma, and neurosis must follow: "[A]n evil spirit from the Lord troubled him" (I Samuel 16:14). Saul falls into a great depression as well as mania, and attempts to kill David, his successor (I Samuel 18:10–11). It has been suggested that Saul therefore had a bipolar disorder (Stein, 2011) or some other DSM-categorised mental disorder (Ben-Noun, 2003).

When Samuel dies (I Samuel 24:1), Saul turns to God, who does not answer him in any manner; not even through a message in his dreams (I Samuel 28:6). The supreme archetype is unavailable and absent, so Saul's longing becomes immense. In desperation, he disguises himself, visits the Witch of Endor, and asks her to summon the spirit of Samuel, which she does. She is the authority of the pagan – the forbidden alternative to orthodoxy.

Samuel appears from the invocation and explains that Saul has lost the "face of God" (I Samuel 28:16). The complete loss of authority and the activation of the merged complex cause Saul to faint, apparently from hunger, which is perhaps the father hunger. He is compelled to eat a feast prepared by the Witch. She is the necromancer, the pagan, yet becomes the cause of his survival and his recognition of what has occurred. Thereafter, Saul falls on his sword: the ultimate act of self-denial arising from the loss of the spirit contained in the father archetype.

The Witch offers another form of authority that Saul initially embraces but that is not sustaining and is shunned in the Old Testament. The Witch explains that Samuel has banned all witches, so acceding to Saul's request will put her life at risk; nevertheless she will help him. Sandford (1985, p. 113) suggests that "Samuel was wrong after all. Saul wasn't entirely cut off from God; for God acted through this woman to restore Saul to himself." In this interpretation, Saul has been given an alternative structure. Although it has been argued that her helping of Saul was merely the Witch's survival strategy (Reis, 1997), it is an acceptance of the healing power of an alternative, pagan religion. In fact, the Witch of Endor's goodness was cited as a reason for repealing the statute banning witches in the seventeenth century (Oates, 1736). In the end, despite Saul's father hunger, failure to follow the structure of orthodoxy leads in the Old Testament to disorientation, madness, and death.

Chapter 7

The mother archetype and the abyss

The archetypal feminine is the *prima materia* (Jung, 1955–1956a, para. 14), the *anima mundi* (Jung, 1912/1952c, para. 550), and the "world soul" (Jung, 1912/1952b, para. 198). The mother archetype is the generative, creative, numinous aspect of psyche. The view of Jung that creates God as a masculine archetype is no longer universally accepted. Young-Eisendrath (1997), for example, sees the feminine archetype as primarily a construct of the patriarchy. It is not necessary to examine how the feminine archetype came into existence as either *a priori* or *an sich*, free from content and developed by our constructs. In any event, the feminine as God enhances the power of the mother complex as creating a profound longing by its withdrawal.

Kuras (2006) argues convincingly that fantasy thinking, essential to the cognitive recognition of the numinous, is associated with the feminine. As evidence, he presents Jung's work with Miss Miller (the "weak woman," as Jung calls her), which seems to have been the cause of Jung accepting that form of thinking in himself. In fact, Jung (1935b, para. 45), states, "I have no small opinion of fantasy. To me, it is the maternally creative side of the masculine mind." This attribution of fantasy thinking to the maternal relates to the characterisation of the entirety of the unconscious as feminine (Jung, 1912/1952c, para. 508). As Neumann (1972, p. 292) points out, the feminine is therefore the archetypal "Mother Vessel," the womb wherein spiritual transformation can take place, leading always to a longing to return. In examining the tale of Hiawatha, Jung (1912/1952) explains Hiawatha's longing for the abyss of the mothers: "his own inner longing for the stillness and profound peace of all-knowing non-existence, the all-seeing sleep in the ocean of coming-to-be and passing away" (ibid., para. 553), "for whoever sunders himself from the mother longs to get back to the mother" (ibid., para. 352). As Faust reminds us, no journey to awakening can take place without immersion in the realm of the mothers.

The uroboric connection within the Mother Vessel is the primary source of spiritual renewal. In the Zohar, the sacred text of Jewish mysticism, the feminine aspect of God – the Shekinah – is a nursing mother with nurturing qualities (Haskell, 2012, pp. 68–69). In a classic study of the mother as the origin of spirituality, she is recognised as the inner source of the numinous, even though the external God may be perceived as masculine: "The Feminine has been shown to be the cause and power. The Masculine is form and shape" (Bjeragaard, 1913, p. 2). Jung (1912/1952c, para. 508) explains that in the depths of the unconscious lies the capacity for birth of the "divine child," which is beyond duality and preconfigures full conscious realisation. Therefore, the mother archetype as the womb and the abyss of "all-knowing non existence" (ibid., para. 553) offers the possibility that the numinous it contains may be born.

The Epode mother complex

"Epode" is, among other things, a dirge used in magic to summon a spirit from the land of the dead (Cole, 2010, pp. 23–24, 30). It is used here as convenient shorthand to describe a complex that develops when a child is *entwined* with a mother who subsequently becomes absent, leading to a great longing for her return and revival.

Jung (1912/1952, para. 367) explains, "The motif of entwining is a mother-symbol." The entwining by the mother's over-involvement is the negative side of the archetype as the devouring or terrible mother that is synonymous with the dark, vortex aspects of the abyss and the world of the dead, which seduces and is inescapable (Jung, 1938/1954, para. 158). The complex arises when the personal mother is overvalued by the child because of a "consuming passion," resulting in an inability to break away from the entwining for fear of losing connection with the world (Jung, 1912/1952c, para. 552). The entwining manifests in many forms, such as the mother controlling and monitoring the child or inappropriately making the child a confidant. The positive side of the archetype is that the mother paying full attention to the child may foster a secure attachment. Entwining therefore yields what Jung (1938/1954, para. 158) calls "the loving and terrible mother."

The "Epode complex" is crystallised by the mother's entwining and then there being a continuous or intermittent absence, which creates a profound longing to bring the absent mother back to life. The possibility or presence of a secure attachment is lost by the absence, leaving confusion and a search for what is missing. The longing, which emerges from that complex, is for a "return to the womb," expressed in the Bible as a return to Jerusalem – the centre – because, as Jung (1912/1952, para. 315) explains, the "regression of the libido reactivates the ways and habits of childhood, and above all the relation to the mother." This personal Epode complex aligns directly with the collective aspect of the mother archetype and, as Jung (1928b, para. 260) explains, there is a profound longing to "wed oneself to the abyss and blot out all memory in its embrace … [which] is innate in all better men as the 'longing for the mother,' the nostalgia for the source from which we came."

Kernberg (1985, p. 219) explains the consequence of having, then losing a parent: it creates a "subjective experience of emptiness" because of the temporary or permanent loss of a self-object. The child caught in this Epode mother complex is subject to the force of the personal complex *and* its archetypal power, suggesting it will have a great impact and produce an overwhelming longing for a return to the peace of the womb.

The goose girl

The fairy tale of the goose girl echoes the force of the Epode mother complex, the longing it leaves, and its link to the numinous. The queen loves her beautiful daughter and sends her off to marry a prince, accompanied by a maid and a talking horse called Falada. Before the party leaves, the queen cuts her finger and gives her daughter a white napkin spotted with three drops of blood. She tells the daughter to keep the napkin near.

The horse is a mother symbol (Jung, 1912/1952, para. 373) as well as nascent, unrevealed sexuality (ibid., para. 370); the blood on the napkin symbolises the spirit of the mother (Jung, 1955–1956, para. 401); and the cloth's white colour is virginal (ibid., p. 302, n. 182) as well as the primary stage of the alchemical opus. In her absence, the mother still intends to dominate and control the daughter and her development, and the latter will find it difficult to evade this entwining.

On the journey, the daughter is thirsty but the maid refuses to help, so the princess dismounts in order to drink. Her dryness and quenching her thirst are explicable as a pair of opposites that are the representations of an emerging libido (Jung, 1910, para. 1078). The drops of blood speak: "Ah, if your mother knew this, her heart would break." The emotional control, shame, guilt, and fear are all employed by the entwined mother through her agencies to prevent the child from gaining autonomy.

On another occasion, the princess leans over a stream and the napkin floats away, causing her to become weak and vulnerable. The removal of her mother's spirit initially causes a regression, and the maid, sensing the weakness, dons the princess's clothes and assumes her identity. The maid is the earthy, sublunary aspect of the mother as she participates in both the spirit and the material world (Jung, 1955–1956, para. 452). In the fairy tale, her function is to bring the material world – a world that is subject to betrayal – to the daughter.

When they arrive at their destination, the princess is assigned to look after geese with a boy named Conrad, who is actually, unknown to her, the king's son. In order for the maid (who is still pretending to be the princess) to overcome the mother's influence, she convinces Conrad to kill Falada. However, the daughter does not let go of the idea of the horse and has its head nailed to an arched door. Thereafter, she speaks to the head every day. The longing for the absent mother is strong and causes the wind to blow. Wind generates the pneuma (Jung, 1938/1954a, p. 87, n. 111) and is associated with the horse's instinctive energy (Jung, 1912/1952a, para. 422) as the archetypal force that represents conception (Jung, 1936b, para. 95). It is the Pleromic archetypal form of the mother that has emerged from the parental complex as spirit to create the numinous.

At a hearth – the alchemical womb for the journey of individuation – the princess relates her story to the king, thereby engaging with the Self and reaching another level of consciousness by her acceptance and recognition by the king as the true princess. Her longing for the mother has emerged from the pain and betrayal arising from the personal complex and the spirit is transformed by the experience of the archetype of the wind to be connected to the Self. It was the entwining of the mother that, when gone, was the impetus to move along the path of consciousness. The Epode complex accelerated the longing to the point where the unconscious libido was released as the wind that created the situation where the princess could tell her story to and enter into a relationship with the king – the Self.

Connections within the parental complexes

The unavailable father complex increases the effect of the Epode mother complex. Dieckmann (1999, p. 61) maintains that "there is an extensive confluence of the mother and father archetypes" at a deep level of the unconscious, and this supports a comment that "The 'absent father' syndrome encourages a mutually collusive 'embrace' with the mother, nourishing a shared illusion of 'oneness'" (Seligman, 1985, p. 81). The touch of the abyss of the mother and the deep connection with the Pleromic archetype are made more apparent as the psychic energy shifts from the absent father to intensify the mother relationship.

As the father mediates authority, his absence not only increases the Epode complex but creates a "hunger" for him and a search for an alternative form of order. The mother offers the sense of the abyss or the primal source of life, but when this is cut off, her absence also creates a deep longing to return to her embrace. Spielrein (1994, p. 165) states: "Because activation (of complexes) does not destroy these (parental) images, they remain in the psyche as an intense longing for a return to the source, specifically a merging with the parents (which remains obscured)." The Pleromic archetypes rise through the accumulated libido of the intensity of the personal complexes to manifest the numinous, which provides the solution to the longing. This is illustrated in Figure 7.1.

Using the Gnostic exposition, the archetypal level is the primordial nothingness or void as well as the fullness of God. Without the longing for both the father and the mother emerging from the complexes, there would be no psychic energy to allow the Pleromic archetypes of the collective unconscious to emerge. The longing creates a need and it is a need that makes the

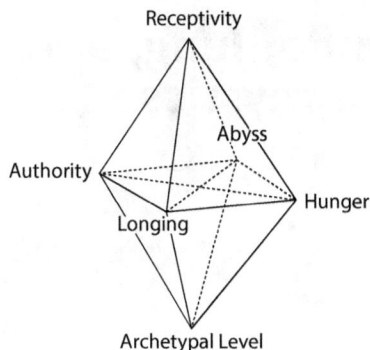

Figure 7.1 The quaternity of spiritual receptivity

archetype activate. As Rumi says: "New organs of perception are born as a result of necessity. Consequently, O man increase your need, so you can increase your perception" (quoted in Shah, 1993, p. 197). This need or longing moves the energy and creates what Sri Aurobindo (Ghose, 1970a, p. 604) calls a "passion of pursuit."

The two complexes, when apparent in a patient, will present a *marked proclivity* for receptivity to the numinous. The power of these two complexes, working together, is created from the immense longing as well as an openness created by a loosening of orthodoxy. Patients may manifest this longing in many ways, such as creativity or fantasy, but when sufficient attention is paid to the complexes, there is a strong possibility that a ME will be received and given room to develop. This ME, by its revelation, will answer some of the longing that is otherwise insatiable.

Chapter 8

Sri Aurobindo, Jung, and the interviewed mystics

Both Sri Aurobindo and Jung express a process for the fulfilment of a life that requires the development of consciousness and thus offers a reason for giving importance to a ME. They were both receptive to the numinous and grounded their ideas on promptings from unseen forces. "[T]he major events in the lives of both of them were guided not by conscious considerations but by dreams in the case of Jung and visions and voices in the case of Sri Aurobindo" (Singh, 1986, p. 14). A significant juncture where they meet is that there must be an ego to understand a ME for it to enhance the development of consciousness. To both Jung and Sri Aurobindo, "what is of utmost importance is the spiritual transformation of consciousness and not experiences that are ultimately unrelated to consciousness, regardless of how exalted they may be" (Johnston, 2016, p. 201).

The early childhood of the two men provides some possible insight into the interplay of the parental archetypes in their particular personal complexes as a basis for their receptivity. Although close in age, the biographical data for Jung is more complete than that for Sri Aurobindo, and every attempt has been made not to make the material on the latter work too hard to fit the hypothesis.

Sri Aurobindo Ghose

Sri Aurobindo Ghose is rare in the array of Eastern mystical figures because he was also an intellectual and a political revolutionary. Other well-known mystics, such as Ramana Marashi, Papaji, Sri Ramakrishna, and Ajahn Chah, were not from an intellectual background that included degrees from Cambridge and nominations for Nobel Prizes in peace and literature.

The writings of Sri Aurobindo are not derived from faith or from following a particular strain of Hinduism but from experience. He perceived that what he witnessed as the Light from above was contained or "involuted" in all things, including matter, but that humans are incapable of reaching the fullness of that Light, requiring an evolution of the species. The sophistication of his mystical understanding and his different approach to psychoanalysis are ironically best illustrated in his comments about Jung. In a letter he wrote to one of his disciples (Ghose, 1988, p. 1608), he explained:

> It is difficult to take Jung and the psycho-analysts at all seriously when they try to examine spirituality by the flicker of their torchlights ... half-knowledge is a powerful thing and can be a great obstacle to the coming in front of the true Truth ... They look from down up and explain the higher limits by the lower obscurities; but the foundation of these things is above and not below.

In his thirty-seven-volume complete works, he writes of nothing other than the numinous as the highest experience of a life. The great poet Rabindranath Tagore said about him: "At the very first sight I could realise that he had been seeking for the soul and had gained it" (quoted in Heehs, 2008, p. 360).

As with any person born almost 150 years ago, the exact details of his relationship with his mother are imprecise. The details that exist are drawn from letters that his father wrote to friends that explained that his mother, Swarnalotta, suffered from a recognisable emotional disturbance of some kind from when Sri Aurobindo was six months old. It is suggested by his biographer that these disturbances may have been only temporary, albeit recurring when he was five years old (ibid., p. 8). At that time, his father wrote to an acquaintance that Swarnalotta had entered a "new stage." Thus, there is nothing to suggest that the mothering of Aurobindo was either inappropriate or deficient between his birth and five, but the loss of her attention seems to have been clear thereafter. His brother describes her actions when florid as:

> Storms of rage and storms of joy came alternately to the madwoman ... During her happy moods she would laugh and laugh to herself and babble uncontrollably. In her rage she would pace around the room like a caged tigress roaring at someone.
>
> (Quoted in Heehs, 2008, p. 31)

One of Sri Aurobindo's biographers gathered comments from psychiatrists that suggest that his mother was bipolar or, according to a Jungian analyst who corresponded with the biographer, had schizo-affective disorder of the hebephrenic type (Heehs,1997). Schizo-affective disorder of the bipolar type is certainly a modern ICD-10 diagnostic category and suggests a detachment from nurturing and neglect of a child. When Aurobindo was sixteen years old, his brother wrote a letter to a friend that described his own relationship with his mother: "how I strove to snatch a fearful love, but only succeeded in hating and loathing, and at last becoming cold. Crying for bread, was given a stone" (Heehs, 2008, p. 8). According to Heehs, this "seems a bit exaggerated" (ibid.), as Swarnalotta was comparatively normal during much of her time in Rangpur. She was there for the first five years of Aurobindo's childhood, when it appears that she was able to host her husband's friends and could look after her sons.

However, Sri Aurobindo was sent to Darjeeling at the age of five, possibly to keep him away from his mother (ibid., p. 9). He reported a dream that he had as a young boy (although he did not specify his age) in which he saw "a great darkness" rushing into him and enveloping him and the "whole universe." Later, he interpreted this as a darkness that came over him from the "alien atmosphere" of Darjeeling, where he lived until the age of seven, and then England, and reported that it lifted only when he returned to India at the age of twenty (Mitra, 1976, p. 17). The reference to the "whole universe" suggests an all-embracing developmental complex activated by Aurobindo's separation from his mother. His biographer points out that "mother" was ever present in his writings and prose (Heehs, 2017), and he named his greatest devotee, Mirra Alfassa, "The Mother."

Sri Aurobindo is recognised as bringing the feminine principle into play in masculine-dominated Hinduism by seeing the divine as mother (Radhakrishnan and Moore, 1957, pp. 575–609). In his epic poem *Savitri*, it is She – the divine mother – who has the power to confront death. These connections are, of course, speculative, but it is difficult to ignore some congruence with this idea in this passage from *Savitri*:

> The sorrowing women they saw not within.
> No change was in her beautiful motions seen.
> A worshipped empress all once vied to serve
> She made herself the diligent serf of all, ...
> In her acts a strange divinity shone:
> Into the simplest moment she could bring
> A oneness with the earth's glowing robe of light,
> A lifting up of common acts of love.
> All-love was hers and its one heavenly cord
> Bound all to all with her as golden tie.
> (Ghose, 1970a pp. 470–471)

During his early years, Aurobindo was with his mother and witnessed her feeling alternatively joyful and enraged. A study of twenty mothers with mental illness (Montgomery *et al.*, 2006) found that they often try to hide their illness from their children in an attempt to imitate mothering ideals. This entails keeping the children *especially close* to affirm their motherhood. A meta-analysis of twenty-three similar studies concluded that effective motherhood is the central issue for women with severe mental illness, which leads them to overcompensate the relationship with the child because of guilt and in an effort to protect the child from the stigma of the illness (Dolman, Jones, and Howard, 2013).

The concept of "entwining" in Jungian thought arises from Osiris being physically entwined in branches. Jung (1912/1952, para. 367) equates this with a mother symbol as trees are birth-giving mothers in many mythologies. He explains that "devouring" and entwining are closely connected, with the former entailing embracing and entwining, leading to fear but also "tender interest" (ibid., para. 365). In the first few years of Sri Aurobindo's life, it may be said that he experienced devouring and entwining as well as fear as he witnessed his mother beating his brother (Heehs, 2008, p. 8), but also her tender interest during her joyful moods. The entwining gave him the touch of the void, as expressed in his dream, but this was snatched away when the illness was florid and he left her to live in Darjeeling.

This reasoning has wider implications for receptivity to the numinous for children of bipolar mothers. It may be that entwining is a feature of that illness, which may account, on the positive side, for a child obtaining affection, as research suggests that it is impossible to conclude that the children are at risk emotionally because of the mother's disorder (Doucette et al., 2013). Moreover, one neurological study of the children of bipolar mothers indicates that those who have no illness themselves are more likely to be creative (Kim et al., 2016).

Sri Aurobindo's brother points out that their father, as a district physician, spent much of his time administering to his one million patients, so his sons "never saw much of him" (quoted in Heehs, 2008, p. 8). Of course, this was even more the case when Aurobindo was sent away to boarding school in Darjeeling. Then, when he was seven, his father put him in the care of a Congregationalist minister in Manchester in an effort to minimise his exposure to Indian culture. The minister was also instructed not to raise Aurobindo as a Christian, as his father was an atheist. Aurobindo remained agnostic until the age of seventeen, when he started studying the Upanishads at King's College, Cambridge, and became activated by the idea of a Self or Atman (Ulrich, 2010, p. 126). Then he had his first ME: "I felt the One only as true; it was an experience absolutely Shankarite in its sense. It lasted only for a short time" (quoted in Purani, 1959/1982, p. 378). "Shankarite" refers to a form of non-dualism in which the subject is not separated from the divine. Aurobindo describes this and later MEs as numinous and not emerging from any spiritual practice (Sadhana): "But these were inner experiences, coming of themselves and with a sudden unexpectedness, not part of a Sadhana" (Ghose, 1972, p. 50). He later describes his MEs as "A thing I knew nothing about, never bargained for, didn't understand either" (ibid., p. 81). It is clear that he placed these experiences within the existing context of non-dualism, which he then expanded. This is consistent with the idea that the ME needs to be grounded in some structure for the ego to connect to it and reconcile what has occurred. He suggests that *some* may be able to receive the force of the divine and then must be able to "work out what the Force puts through him" if he has "responsiveness, capacity, etc." If not, he "does it imperfectly or frustrates it" (ibid., p. 204).

The life of Sri Aurobindo explains, through the lens of the absent father complex and the Epode mother complex, a possible early proclivity for rapidly increasing numinous experiences that were of such force that they caused a particular alteration in his consciousness. Both complexes are evident in his autobiography, but they do not diminish the greatness of the man in any way. From a psychological perspective, the "Force," as he calls it, worked through him.

C.G. Jung

Jung's receptivity to the numinous is self-evident in *The Red Book*, where he overcomes powerful, threatening numinous fantasies that, according to Bishop (2014, p. 121), destroyed both Nietzsche and the Romantic poet Hölderlin. Faced with these forces, Jung cast aside the dread and uttered the profound statement: "I let myself drop" (Jung, 1998, p. 202).

Perhaps his capacity was evident in an early dream, in which he holds a tiny light that he must keep burning against a strong wind and dense fog (ibid., p. 108). His proclivity for the numinous, Bishop (2012, p. 337) suggests, was a product of or enhanced by his philosophical education. However, the two complexes – unavailable father and Epode Mother – are there and may have had a role in his capacity for receptivity.

Jung's comments about his mother show insight regarding her entwining. He states that "early on [she] made me her confidant and confided her troubles in me" (Jung, 1998, p. 52). "By day she was a loving mother, but at night she seemed uncanny" and had a "natural mind" (ibid., p. 50), which appears to be a reference to being open to the numinous. Sherry (2012, p. 19) concludes: "She was a demanding woman, unhappy in her marriage who manifested her affections and ambitions in her son."

Jung's mother's participation in séances and her involvement in the spirit world apparently caused him to have what Bair (2003, p. 20) calls "nebulous apprehension." He was entwined with his mother not only as her confidant but also in sharing the irrational, No. 2 thinking. Hence, he was linked to her unconsciously, as witnessed in his underground phallus dream in which she points out that primordial energy.

The conscious and unconscious entwining with his mother was interrupted by her frequent absences when she resided in a rest home in Basel, perhaps due to her failing marriage. Bishop (2014, p. 26) suggests that this was why Jung associated the mother with innate unreliability (Jung, 1998, pp. 28, 30). He was sent to live with his aunt, and Bair (2003, p. 21) suggests that he remained anxious that further separations would occur.

The entwining and the absence fit the Epode mother complex. The enmeshed mother provided exposure to the creative mystery of being. She was enmeshed consciously through making Jung a confidant and unconsciously by drawing him into the non-rational experience of the spirit. She then withdrew, leaving him with anxiety, mistrust, and longing.

According to Bishop (2014, p. 25), Jung's father, Paul, "cuts a sad figure ... [Jung] came to realize that his father, the local pastor, had, in reality, lost his religious faith." Bair (2003, p. 38) suggests that Paul, perhaps at the beginning of the illness that would end his life, belittled his son and became a "shrunken, bitter man." Here is the unavailable father, present but not emotionally available and also discounted by the child. The discounting process is especially important as it removes the authority of the father and distorts his imago, making the personal father unable to mediate the archetype.

The interaction between an unavailable father and his son is subtle. A father who belittles his children, much like the Greek god Uranus, imprisons them in Gaia, the mother. It is not only the longing for the unavailable father that occurs but also the more intense immersion – perhaps imprisonment – in the primal forces of the mother archetype. In the case of Jung, he was immersed into his mother's pagan form, which perhaps accentuated his openness to numinosity.

Winnecott's (2016) review of *Memories, Dreams, Reflections*, in which he states that Jung had childhood schizophrenia and was psychotic, prompted replies from Jungians that penetrated more deeply into Jung's interaction with his mother. Feldman (1992, p. 256) argues that Jung was not schizophrenic but "needed to turn inward to find his own sources of healing, as the early interpersonal environment could not provide him with a sense of security which would engender trust." He attributes Jung's early eczema to "psychic catastrophe which Jung experienced on his separation from his mother" (ibid., p. 261).

Winnecott's (2016) idea of there being a "maternal failure" is accurate. How this is described diagnostically is beside the point, and schizophrenia is clearly a misdiagnosis (Morey, 2005, p. 340). What is not emphasised in these analyses of Jung is that the failure was magnified because it followed an entwinement in which Jung was brought deeply into his mother's emotional and psychic field in combination with a "paternal failure." These combined failures may be interpreted as yielding a need to heal, and this may have been an impetus for Jung's discoveries, creativity, and the presence of the numinous.

Interviewed mystics

Reducing Sri Aurobindo and C.G. Jung to a causal connection of related complexes may seem to discount extraordinary intelligence, unique creativity, and profound courage. There are, however, numerous other examples of mystics and mana personalities that follow the same developmental pattern. For instance, Teresa of Avila is known to have had a strict, cold father and an especially close relationship with her mother, who died when she was thirteen (Slade, 1995). Emily Brontë is another prime example (Wion, 1985).

The interviews with established mystics revealed the same pattern – an unavailable father and an entwining mother. There was no evidence of torment or a history of traumatic wounding. The cushioning by the positive aspect of the entwining may account for the resilience of the child to early trauma, although no conclusions may be drawn from the interviews. Most importantly, there was a *common thread* among most of the mystics that the mother had been especially connected in the very early years, as was the case with Sri Aurobindo and Jung, in a way that could be expected by an entwining mother; and, in almost all cases, this was accentuated by an unavailable father.

Of the twenty-nine mystics who were interviewed, twenty-one reported an unavailable father, defined widely as being cold and uncaring, incapable of engendering respect, or simply missing. None reported a father who was cruel or punishing. The realisation that the father was unavailable when he was physically present, between the ages of seven to thirteen, was usually accompanied by observing other fathers. Nineteen of the interviewees had a close relationship with their mother, and seventeen accepted that this may be classified as entwined. Seven refused to accept that their mother was entwining; however, of those, four acknowledged that they had become a confidant of their mother's personal revelations. Only twelve stated that they lost their mother before their teenage years, and some were still entwined after they became mystics. This last observation may mean that elimination of the entwining is less important than the entwining itself and a gradual separation as the child moves out of home in his or her later teenage years.

Although no claim is made as to the statistical significance of these findings, it was apparent that the unavailable father was the most common aspect of the mystics' upbringings and that entwining was present in most cases. Each of these configurations was, of course, different, and there was no common developmental pattern, such as separation at an early age or an alcoholic father. Indeed, only five of the interviewees mentioned the latter.

Chapter 9

Clinical exposition

In this chapter, three patients are discussed to put the theory into an analytical frame. The patients were all seen twice a week in analysis in New York between 2011 and 2016. Clinical vignettes are important because I interviewed each of the mystics in New York and India for no more than a few hours, which made it impossible to make an accurate assessment of other factors that may have led to their pursuit of the numinous. Most of them manifested the two complexes, but with subtle differences each time. For example, one German mystic who was living in Pushkar, India, was born in a shelter during the bombing of Hamburg in July 1943, and shortly thereafter her father disappeared without explanation. This may have created other variables in her development of longing and her pursuit of MEs. Meanwhile, although a Western Buddhist monk fitted the two complexes precisely, he pointed to the existence of other factors by repeatedly stating, "There is more to it."

At least once a year, one or more patients will report a ME, a powerful symbol of the Self in dreams, or a sense of communion with nature. However, only one or two have experiences that alter consciousness in a recognisable manner; in all other cases, the experiences are rejected as aberrant or irrelevant, or they fade over time.

The first vignette is of a patient who was receptive to the numinous; it is used to explore in detail the role of the parental complexes. The second is that of MH, who was cited earlier as an example of the rejection of a ME; it is used here to explore how this fits into a consideration of the combination of the two parental complexes. The third illustrates how the Epode mother complex may leave a trace of the void that limits the nature of a ME.

Vignette 1: Mel

At the time of writing, Melvyn ("Mel") was a sixty-four-year-old retired surgeon who had lost most of his savings in the Madoff scandal and was living off his remaining funds, minor royalty payments from two books on surgery, and occasional consultancy work. He and his family had made no attempt to alter their lifestyle, and their savings were rapidly diminishing as a result.

The significant trauma caused by the loss of the majority of his accumulated fortune, known as "Fraud Trauma Syndrome" (Glodstein, Glodstein, and Fornaro, 2010), which has been likened to physical trauma, culminated in his presenting problems of anxiety and panic attacks.

Mel was born to Eastern European Jews who had arrived with their parents from Poland in 1901, and he grew up in Queens. He married his first wife when he was eighteen and had been married to his second for twenty-five years. He has three adult, self-supporting children: two from the first marriage and one from the second.

Previous experiences

Mel has a forty-five-year interest in Theravada Buddhism and engages in twice-daily meditation. His practice consists of *Anapanasati* – awareness of breath – for thirty minutes, then scanning the bodily sensations (a *Vipassana* technique) for another fifteen minutes. Each year, without fail, he travels to Thailand, Myanmar, Vietnam, or India in search of enlightened teachers and their wisdom. On these trips, he avoids urban areas and travels to remote mountains or deserts that are not normally visited by Westerners. He goes alone and meditates in temples along the way. In Myanmar, he found his way into forest monasteries in forbidden areas, and he has lived as a monk for weeks at a time, and, in 2014, for a full month.

His experiences have ranged in intensity over the last forty years, but it was only recently that he had a ME with sufficient impact to alter his consciousness. His first encounter with a ME was when he was smoking marijuana in his early twenties. It amounted to a feeling that there may be something other than his normal, day-to-day consciousness. This led him to the practice of Buddhism. Research (Luke, 2012) is clear that psychotropic drugs may be part of an "incubation" stage for a ME as they act by "loosening" ordinary consciousness, although this does not result in long-term change (Batson, Schoenrade, and Ventis, 1993, p. 121). As Mel classified this experience as drug related, he discounted it as nothing more than a catalyst for a search for a different reality.

Thereafter, Mel had several non-drug experiences in which he felt an overwhelming sense of peace, had an insight that there was an interconnection between external objects, and experienced times in meditation when he was so absorbed that he felt he was connected to an inner light. None of these experiences fundamentally altered his consciousness and all appeared to be fleeting curiosities rather than profound revelations.

Mel's mystical experience

In 2014, three and a half years into analysis, Mel had a profound ME that defined his outlook:

> I was walking down a village road in northern India, on my way back to my hotel after a day of meditation in a temple. All of a sudden, everything around me turned white except for lines that distinguished where one object ended and another began. I realised it was not me looking at this scene; I was being used by a divine presence to examine its own creation. I was merely a witness to what it was seeing. This was not a momentary event that could have to do with dizziness or a meditative state; rather, it lasted for five or more minutes as I stood completely still, in awe of what I was experiencing. Then I felt it ending as if the divine presence was moving on to the next person for its own self-reflection.

As he explained it, through this experience Mel understood his relationship to the divine as a witness to its self-reflection. The experience altered his consciousness and, as described by Jung, was a numinous experience because it was also overwhelming.

The alteration of consciousness was observable in Mel's behaviour and outlook. In terms of behaviour, he became less guarded, more open to analytic interpretation, more concerned with affective experience, lost his fear of ageing, and had no interest in the pursuit of money and material success. Most importantly, he saw everything differently:

> I have this sense of divine presence at all times so I do not suffer, even when I am confronted by negativity. It is with me when I first wake and until I go to sleep and feels like I have reached some new or at least different level.

Inter-generational trauma

Mel is a descendant of Russian Jews who suffered in the *shtetlekh* of Poland in the late nineteenth century when Cossacks killed many of his grandparents' neighbours. Both pairs of grandparents escaped and arrived in New York with no money and settled first in the Lower East Side. As a child, his parents took him to the homes of Holocaust survivors, as they considered it their duty to listen to heart-breaking stories of horror and persecution. He remembered staring at the numbers on their arms when he was five, six, or seven and feeling ashamed that he was part of this group.

This inter-generational trauma was exacerbated by the suicide of his maternal grandmother just prior to his birth. She jumped off a building in Queens when she uncovered her husband's infidelity and he announced that he was going to leave her. This tragedy had a devastating effect on Mel's mother, although it was never discussed during his childhood. Indeed, Mel learned of it only a few years before starting analysis. He understood that it destroyed his mother, rendering her defenceless against the tragedy and horror of such a betrayal of life. Its power was magnified by the racial myth of suffering, vulnerability, and hopelessness.

The nature of the trauma could be seen openly and painfully in the life of Mel's sister, who was a constant reminder to him of the ultimate outcome of the guilt and tragedy that overcame his mother. She spent much of her life alone, lost in prescription drugs, unable to maintain relationships, before finally dying in 2013, unconscious of why she had chosen annihilation. It was only on the last day that she said, "I feel for the first time I am a separate person," revealing that she had never escaped the depression, fear, and anxiety of entwinement with her mother until that moment.

Shortly after Mel's birth, with the suicide a recent memory, his mother developed a painful stomach ulcer and entered a prolonged depression. Her emotional state reflected the degree of discomfort or pain. There were three states:

- If she felt well, she would be caring, although with little affect due to the underlying depression.
- If she experienced some discomfort, she would become anxious and upset and would leave Mel alone in the kitchen in his high chair with a loaf of bread and a mound of cheese.
- If there was severe pain, she would withdraw and neglect him, providing the bare minimum of care.

Although not diagnosed at the time, this pattern of behaviour is also consistent with post-partum depression (Cohn *et al.*, 1986). The consequence, especially as there was an underlying, persistent depression, was the development in Mel of an insecure attachment, perhaps to a greater degree than is seen in children who experience other forms of early maternal stress (Murray *et al.*, 1996).

His mother's depression and physical illness made her dependent on him. She would tell him constantly how bad she was feeling even when he was too young to understand; and later she forced him to run errands for her. She would insist that he must sit on the bed next to her and hold her hand for long periods of time, even when he told her he wanted to play with his friends. When he came home from school, she would immediately sit him down and explain her physical state, but then leave him abruptly if she became too ill to talk or relate.

Mel's father was a kind, gentle man who placed his duty to tend to his family above his own needs. He therefore worked two jobs and arrived home late each night, exhausted. He loved his son when he was home, keeping a diary of Mel's progress from birth. In this way, the usual symptoms of distress associated with insecure attachment were somewhat alleviated. However, Mel's father was unable to play a larger role as a substitute caretaker because he was rarely available on account of his long working hours and exhaustion when at home.

The manner in which Mel's father interacted with his wife's volatility created a complex for Mel in which he lost respect for the former. His father constantly tried to appease his wife's moods, for instance by writing her a love letter every day of his life and doing whatever she asked to dampen her overbearing and disruptive nature. As a result, he was unable or unwilling to protect his son from her behaviour.

Mel's earliest pre-verbal memories are of an undefined, intolerable panic. The possibility that his mother would love and care for him, which occurred on occasion by the close entwinement, was followed by harsh treatment or withdrawal because of her illness. This erratic behaviour caused Mel bewilderment and required him to separate from his mother. Winnecott (1958) refers to separation as the necessary consequence of "infringement": where the mother ignores the fact that the infant cannot accept frustration, and this pushes the infant to separate from the mother.

This imperative to separate from his mother because of her entwinement and ambivalent feelings created a premature or precocious self-awareness evidenced by Mel's memory of being in the crib at less than a year old, struggling to pull himself up, and feeling disconcerted when he realised that he was alone in the world. He remembered looking around the room and thinking he was a separate person as he stared through the bars of the crib and into the dark room. As the normal age for self-awareness is approximately two years old (Rochat, 2003), such premature feelings of separateness are signs of internalised shame. The need to develop a separate, grandiose self to overcome the early shame of being treated with ambivalence (Broucek, 1982) was triggered by this mother complex. Shame arose out of introjection of bewilderment, terror, disgust, and despair. Mel's grandiose persona was precipitated by a splitting off from this shame.

In addition to creating a compensatory, grandiose persona, Mel's ambivalent treatment – entwining followed by separation – generated a great, undefined *longing*. In his case, the first reason for this was that "nameless dread" naturally led to a search for something to assuage the suffering. When neglect alternates with moments of care, the memory of the possibility of solace remains. The second reason was that the longing became a motivating factor as it offered the possibility of the "good" – the search for solace – while the suffering remained the "bad." When there is a failure to have an unequivocally good experience with the mother, Britton (2004) suggests that there is an enshrinement of the "good" and a splitting off of the "bad" in order to avoid confusion within the infant. This enshrinement of the "good" is of the remnant experience of good aspects of the entwinement during positive caring and nurturing and a desire to seek out that remnant. In this critical way, the longing is associated with a return to the good and becomes the leitmotif for the search for containment. The third reason for the longing was that it arose from the desire to be protected from the bad by some organising principle or authority that could offer some stability, which was missing for Mel because of his non-protective father.

Developmental stages

As he was growing up and reaching puberty, Mel's mother became irration-
ally angry from time to time, due to her increasing discomfort. She would
slap Mel for the slightest perceived indiscretion, such as not finishing his
dinner. His father was aware that the punishment was unjust but continued
to support his wife and even occasionally added to the discipline by hitting
Mel with his belt. In analysis, Mel returned constantly to two themes resulting from this punishment. The first was that he could not predict what
behaviour would attract praise and what would attract punishment, and the
second was that he was always in a state of anxiety as he was not protected by
his father and was left to feel the shame of his mother's cruelty.

Mel managed these two themes in early adolescence by trying to appear
tough in junior high school and appearing aloof. He cultivated a persona that
he was mysterious and capable of striking verbally in order to minimise the
risk of attacks on him. In this manner, he developed a way to modulate
the uncertainty of others' responses and to avoid shame. However, over time,
the unnamed panic he felt as an infant intensified into conscious fears. During
later childhood, this manifested in sleeping with the covers over his head and
using magical thinking by touching the corners of furniture in his bedroom
to enable himself to fall sleep. The foreboding he experienced resulted in
several other strategies to ward off the panic. One of these was to be deceptive
by lying and another was to remove himself as much as possible from his
home. He left home for college at the age of just sixteen, having skipped a
grade in junior high school.

Most significantly, the split between the enshrinement of the good and the
retreat from the bad also led to Mel's attempt to evoke the good by pleasing
his mother. Hence, he tried to do better at school in order that, as his mother
required, "your father and I can be proud." This seemed to be one explanation
of his powerful desire to achieve success, as did his need for a separate, persona-based ego structure in order to yield self-esteem and self-efficacy. A
continuation of this pattern as he became a teenager was manifested in the
vigilance with which he approached his schoolwork to overcome his mother's
constant criticism that his achievements were inadequate.

His adolescence was characterised by risk taking. At sixteen, in his first
year of college, he borrowed a friend's car and drove it without a licence,
hitting a bus and damaging the car. The following year he bought a
motorcycle and, again without a licence, rode it at high speed. These were
attempts to define the boundaries of his ego, and they provided some
means to move closer to the pole of annihilation and become exceptional
by surviving the risk.

Ultimately, the risk taking resulted in several serious accidents in which
Mel injured his neck and smashed his coccyx. His damaged neck muscles
became a means by which he displayed affect as it caused those muscles to

tighten; when stressed, he would massage the back of his neck. This soma-tising of affect was also demonstrated by kidney stones, which he suffered when under extreme pressure at work.

Rytovaara (2014, p. 214) suggests that the split between the "good" and "bad" aspects of the mother manifests most fully in adolescence because that period witnesses activation of the alternative neurological brain functions of either seeking the good or panicking to avoid the bad. She continues (ibid.):

> A balance in the personality between the two systems is needed to moderate the risk taking aspect, so that the adolescent can venture out to explore and develop an appetite for the unknown and then return to the security of the safe base to enjoy his bounty.

Mel's academic success – in which he achieved the "good" – had the effect of legitimising the longing, while an appetite for the unknown perhaps balanced out the panic. He managed to please his parents, ward off the panic, and obtain some ego strength to venture further into the world.

The complex interaction of the longing, the need to find his ego boundaries, and the encapsulation of the good by achieving success formed a personality dominated by an overemphasis on achievement. The consequence was a grandiose, persona-based ego and consequent loss of affect. This created various splits in his psyche. He had an initial dream that illustrated the basic split:

> Alan, the most powerful surgeon in New York, was standing on a table, covered in medals, pontificating about surgery. There is a figure in beige pants and shirt lying inert on the floor directly in front of him at a forty-five-degree angle. Behind the chair a corrupt politician is crouching down and holding a gun.

This illustrates a split between the encapsulated "good" of achievement and the "bad" of annihilation. It is also a split between a persona-based ego and the dormant realisation of the Self and the triumph of rationality over affect. This split led to an endless pursuit of achievement to attain some security and to avoid the alternatives of nothingness and death, with the consequence of placing the vulnerable development of the Self in a distant place away from the ego (in Thailand, India, Myanmar, or Vietnam). The politician was explored as the means to protect this by deception and violence, if necessary.

Even though the split was a means of survival, it was Mel's longing that pushed him beyond rationality to a ME. His seeking in adult life became a longing for a merger with a secure feeling – the nurturing of the mother – and a safe return to the generative abyss. The Epode mother complex demanded this seeking as he had a taste of merger, which was then removed, increasing his longing. His absent father complex led him to find alternative religious structures.

In Mel's case, the longing was exaggerated by his innate sensitivity. Jung (1913, para. 399) considered that sensitivity can be innate: "A certain innate sensitiveness produces a special prehistory, a special way of experiencing infantile events, which in their turn are not without influence on the development of the child's view of the world." In Mel's adult life, he maintained a well-defined persona of a highly regarded professional, wealthy even after the financial problems, a nurturing father, and confident in his knowledge. This persona was needed to compensate for his insecure attachment. However, the initial dread stunted his ego formation and the emergence of the Self, making him, at his core, insecure and struggling for identity.

It was the longing for security that drove him to create the material world of money and accomplishment. As a consequence, he had great difficulty expressing his emotions. This alexithymia was the resistance he employed to protect himself from ambiguity and the "bad" feeling of annihilation. As the measure of the "good" was success, it was hard for him to surrender to the uncertainty of emotions. However, an enantiodromia occurred where the unconscious material could not be ignored, and as a result a breakthrough became necessary.

After losing money in the Madoff scandal, Mel appeared in court as a witness for the prosecution and was completely humiliated by Madoff's attorney. The implication was that he had been a willing participant in the fraud, and every one of his answers was attacked as a lie or a cover-up. He suffered terribly as his view of the "good" and the grandiose persona finally gave way to the experience of annihilation and shame that he had kept at bay for decades. However, this humiliation was a breakthrough and a gift as it allowed him to be that beige man who was lying on the ground, inert. The affect was released as the threat of financial ruin – he was at risk of being sued for fraud – was so unbearable that it provided the necessary element to understand that the apparent security of money was perhaps a longing for some deeper security.

Progress of the analysis

Mel began analysis with an intellectualising, inflated persona resulting from his early lack of containment. Somatisation of the unconscious and split off affect were evident through his frequent accidents and illnesses. There was also a notable split off of the Self as he had located the possible experience of that higher Self only in Asia.

The analysis, almost from the very start, facilitated a regression into the childhood, parental complexes. Over three years of sessions, regressions occurred in an almost continuous immersion in the components of these complexes. Initially, Mel became aware of his Epode mother complex as the "bad" because it was more evident than the harm caused by his loving father. He examined his mother's alternating entwining and withdrawal and the consequence of such an insecure attachment that had forced him to seek external structures of wealth and accomplishment.

When he was fully regressed into the Epode mother complex, he sought an explanation of his father's failure to protect him from the cruelty of his mother and the resulting shame. He then understood that he had abandoned hope of being protected by his father at an early age as he had perceived him as weak because of that lack of protection as well as his actual absence. He also understood that this unavailable father complex was the reason why he had abandoned Judaism and started the search for some other structure. His reliance on me increased as the constant return to the reality of the complexes created feelings of profound emptiness, anxiety, and loss of hope. Therefore, it could be said that he transferred the "good" – the positive parental object – to me as a chance for healing.

It was because of longing that he was willing and able to take the arduous journey to examine his unconscious ideations. It was longing that supplied the desire and also the curiosity to continue his almost unbearable descent into the complexes. If it can be maintained, curiosity has the power to keep enquiry alive and it may eventually lead to belief. Britton (2003) convincingly argues that the accumulation of belief allows experiences to become psychic objects. Mel's curiosity led to an examination of his MEs, abstract and complex as they had been, to yield a sense of truth and belief in the possibility of the Self.

Mel's receptivity to the numinous

Mel's ME of being an instrument of the divine, because of its depth, made the existence of a non-ego force apparent and undeniable. To Mel, the non-ego no longer needed to be approached by symbolic inference or conjecture; he understood it as the guiding force – his *spiritus rector*. His consciousness was altered by the emergence of a clear sense of wholeness buried in the psyche. His appreciation of the non-ego force had the effect of a more realistic interest in money simply as a tool of survival. This is not to say he could define the force or could speak about his wholeness; rather, he had the sense of being more grounded so that it was now always there, no matter what situations arose. His explanation was that he still reacted through his complexes when they were triggered, but his recovery time was more rapid, perhaps an hour or less, as opposed to a few days, and he was therefore restored quickly to a sense of equilibrium and peace.

He "attained" to the numinous, in Jung's terms, because he understood that the source of the experience was in his psyche, and it was to be respected, loved, and feared. He was gradually able to change his cadence to one who had come home to himself and was no longer subject to the agitation of overwhelming anxiety. The archetypal Pleromic forces came through with such force that he could no longer doubt their existence, and understood that his complexes were ultimately in the service of the Self.

The ME, to be understood, had to be placed *after the fact* into a psychological context. It was not enough that it had occurred; rather, it had to be understood clearly by the ego and grounded by contrasting his persona-based ego with the non-ego force that had looked through his eyes at its own creation. Mel's continued recitation of his significant ME, then tracing its possible origin to the longing experienced by the parental complexes, led to healing of the good–bad split and provided movement along the ego–Self axis.

The clinical importance of continuously bringing a ME into analysis and making it part of each session, where possible, is illustrated in Tony Wolff's and Jung's analysis of Tina Keller (Swan, 2006, p. 500), in which Jung amplified a ME by encouraging the patient to pray and write down her experiences. This made writing part of a significant, religious experience and an expansive subject matter in the analysis.

Mel was also able to understand through the analytical process that the "nameless dread" is indeed an early experience of the numinosum: nothingness, an empty void, death itself. He was able to see that dread had destroyed what appeared fixed, certain, and stable in his childhood – leaving only terror and doubt – and how that led to him compensating with his grandiose persona. He was able to re-envisage his complexes through an understanding that the numinous also created the opportunity for its realisation and provided the longing. Moreover, he became conscious that he had a precocious self-awareness at an early age to prevent complete psychic dissolution into the abyss. These insights raised his awareness of the complexes and reduced their hold on his psyche.

The efficacy of the hypothesis related to Mel

Mel's mother nurtured him at times and demanded his attention as a confidant, which highlighted the contrast when nurturance was withheld. No matter how this is described – as lack of secure attachment or the emergence of a complex – it brought about three elements that made Mel potentially receptive to numinosity: a hunger for the good; an awareness of the complete absence of good; and a discriminating facility that carried that awareness.

Mel was bound to move between good and bad and thus his whole being was directed at an understanding of the pathways he might travel to attain to the good. In his words, he needed to be a "good boy." The need to please his mother created a possible way to avoid the bad and he pursued this relentlessly, substituting academic success and money for the absent mother and lack of security. In this pursuit, he developed an ego that was honed for success and a devious streak to attain his goals.

The failure of his father to uphold the paternal archetype of authority led to a rejection of his Jewishness around the age of fifteen. As the need for authority is so great, in its absence, Mel's search within Eastern religions was intense and focused. As the father hunger never subsided, he needed an organising principle that might confer solace. As a result, he practised medi-tation diligently. The hunger for structure and the continued exploration of the parental complexes, combined with indelible contact with the void, appears to have made him ripe for the emergence of the Pleromic archetypes. The regression through introspection and reflection through meditation and analysis made the parental complexes the preconditions for his profound ME of being the agency of the divine witnessing its creation.

Vignette 2: MH

At the time of writing, MH was a forty-eight-year-old accountant. He is cited here as an example of how, if one part of the interconnection of complexes is absent, receptivity may not occur.

His presenting problem was twofold: fear of confrontation with his demanding employer; and an inability to decide whether to continue his relationship with a woman who needed to improve her immigration status. This indecision and his need for analysis appeared in his initial dream:

> I was on a subway platform and two trains were in the station, half in and half out, one uptown and one downtown, and I was not sure which one to go on. I saw a bird about to get crushed between a platform and the train but a hand reached down and saved the bird.

MH's mother was Catholic but then became an evangelical Christian when he was a boy. His father worked as a train conductor and was interested in and supportive of MH's progress as a sportsman in high school. His mother was over-involved with him as he grew up – coming into his room unannounced, interrupting him with her concerns, or getting him to kneel and pray. She remained, during the analysis, over-involved, phoning him daily, confiding in him, sending him constant aphorisms about God. He explained that she had "ridiculous love" and he was disdainful of her interference but felt guilty if he did not phone her back immediately. He visited her only on public holidays.

He reported that his father was interested in him only as a sportsman and was otherwise unavailable. When he was fourteen and rejected for the baseball team, his father lost interest. He described this as "the worst day of my life." When he was in his early twenties, his father admitted that he had fathered a child with another woman and MH's mother forced him out, then obtained a restraining order. The police came to the door and MH let them in, an inci-dent that the father never forgave. At the time of the analysis he was still refusing to speak with his son, despite MH's best efforts to re-establish con-tact over the course of the previous decade. MH was bewildered by what could have set his father's face against him to such an extent.

MH had the Marian ME that he attributed to a bad crabstick after months of analysis. During the session when he described the experience, he suggested that it could have been caused by his failure to act properly towards the woman who wanted to improve her immigration status or, indeed, his mother. He did not perceive any other possibility.

At the age of fourteen, around the time when he was rejected by his high-school baseball team, he occasionally visited the school's chapel. He reported that he experienced great peace there and felt an inexplicable presence. However, when asked to recall that feeling and bring it into the consulting room, he was unable to do so and explained that it was only available in the chapel.

The wounded spirit, symbolised by the bird in his initial dream, needed to be resurrected by the hand, which is a phallic symbol and the precursor to fire (Jung, 1912/1952d, para. 271), here representing MH's manhood and self-agency. This was a remnant of the unavailable father, leaving MH with a weakened spirit and an authority complex, illustrated in his fear of confronting his employer. His mother was – and remained – overbearing and therefore she possessed his libido. As Jung (1921/1952, para. 329) explains, "the son is unable to detach his libido from the mother-imago, he suffers from resistances because he is tied to the mother."

In this case, the unavailable father created MH's longing for authority as well as a hunger for his father. However, the longing for the return to the mother was absent, as the mother remained overbearing. Although the absent father may have been the basis for the emergence of the ME, the continued connection with the mother may explain why there was no apparent proclivity to embrace his ME or his earlier experience in the chapel.

Jung (ibid., para. 332) explains the longing for the mother as arising from incest, in the sense of "finding some way into the mother's body." The possible effect is to canalise the libido into new forms, because of the incest taboo. In this way, Jung maintains, the creative fantasies become inventive and the libido becomes "imperceptibly spiritualized." Accordingly, MH may have had a natural spirituality arising from his overbearing mother that led to the ME, but there was insufficient concentration of the libido for the autonomous complex to be sufficiently overwhelming to cause an alteration of consciousness, as the missing mother imago was not present.

Vignette 3: Fiona

At the start of analysis, Fiona was a thirty-two-year-old woman. She is examined here as a patient who had minor MEs that faded over time as they could not be held because of the predominance of the destructive aspect of the Epode mother complex.

The positive side of a ME is the fullness of the Pleroma. If this bursts through, the result is a diminution of the ego's supremacy and the realisation of the Self. Jung (1958, para. 735) explains that such experiences give meaning and "sate the soul's hunger."

The destructive aspect arises from the emergence of the negative side of the collective archetype that breaks through. In *The Seven Sermons to the Dead*, Jung (1998, p. 379) explains that "nothing and everything" are in the Pleroma. Accordingly, if the "nothing" of the collective archetype breaks through, it can be destructive by immersing the individual in the void. Otto (1923, p. 31) calls this the "Dionysian element in the numen" that is a "formless state in which the individual loses himself." Instead of being a new experience that informs by reflection, this aspect takes over the individual. In discussing Nietzsche, Jung (1988, p. 259) explains that the numinosum can become "identical with ourselves, how it is when we are the *numinosa*."

Fiona's affect was so dulled that she appeared lifeless in most sessions. This was not a feeling of the presence of depression, as she had high ego functioning and no inversion of mood. Instead, it was the presence of a void, so deep that it allowed for no understanding or structure. The pattern of analysis was that she would arrive, slump in the chair, and seem drained and exhausted. At some point in the session, a present issue would arise, and she would then engage with the images and leave with greater energy. The field, however, was one of profound emptiness, not offering any connection with the fulsome nature of the Self. The closest approximation in the psychoanalytic literature is perhaps the "dead mother" complex suggested by André Green (1986), in which the lack of the mother's emotional presence creates a core of emptiness and blackness. In the grip of this complex, his analysis is that the libido is wiped out by the dead mother imago (ibid., p. 159).

Fiona's mother was overbearing before she was eleven, imposing herself on Fiona and engaging her as a confidante about her troubles. As her marriage failed, the mother slipped into alcoholism, withdrew, and became unavailable. As the alcoholism progressed, she became more distant and eventually fell ill when Fiona was in her twenties. She died when Fiona was thirty – two years before Fiona entered analysis. Her father was never involved, even though he was present. She describes him as grumpy, irritable, and lethargic. Her parents divorced when she was fourteen and her father moved to an isolated farm in upstate New York.

Fiona fitted the two complexes well: there was an unavailable father complex and an Epode mother complex. These two complexes worked together, creating in her a great longing that she compared to "Jabba the Hutt" in *Star Wars*: a disgusting blob of desire that could never be satiated. Her relationships with men required them to "step up," but they were never able to do so, even though they tried.

Fiona meditated, was a prolific dreamer, was comfortable with fantasy thinking, and often had an insight that would break through and change her behaviour. MEs came to her frequently and initially caused minor alterations of consciousness, but then faded within a month or two. The insights were often small, but she processed them at the time. They appeared as guiding principles, and she seemed to change her behaviour and her outlook as she brought them into consciousness. Each experience seemed to buoy her up for several sessions, but eventually her outlook would return to a prior state, where there was a non-cognitive emptiness, a darkness in which she inhabited a void that appeared to overcome the positive side of the experiences.

Fiona had a dream that shows the negative, destructive result of her complexes:

> I am in a wooden house pouring gasoline on the floor and steps and the forest below. I felt naughty but expressive. I was about to light a match when my father appears and then I realise that I was doing something wrong. I am not sure if I lit the fire.

Examined on the level of numinosity, as there are many levels to this dream, this was an attempt to crystallise the void. The fire could destroy the newly formed aspects of the Self Fiona had acquired through her positive MEs. If destroyed, there could be no individuation and only ashes would remain. The longing was for a return to the void (a consequence of the negative aspect of the Epode mother complex) and some form of authority (a consequence of the unavailable father complex).

It was as if the negative side of the collective archetype had seeped through to overwhelm the positive side. A positive ME would then fade over time until it left no trace, as none of the insights nor the apparent change in outlook remained. The negative side of the Epode mother complex and the remaining effect when her mother died eventually obliterated the positive aspect of the MEs.

Conclusion

Despite the utter vastness and subtlety of the *opus mysticum*, the application of the theory of the effect of the combination of the two parental complexes to Mel affords valuable insights. There were two stages to Mel's analysis: before and after he became receptive to a ME. In the first stage, he experienced continued regression that provided the inward movement of libido that is a precondition for the emergence of the Pleromic archetypes, which occurred in the second stage. In that latter stage, he processed the ME, understood that it had arisen from within his unconscious and realised that it was the demonstration of a non-ego force as the central, guiding principle.

This suggests that the intensity of the longing, brought about by the intersection of the two parental complexes, which operate together, is an indicator of receptivity. In Rumi's terms, that intensity can be assessed by the "need" to reunite with the parental imagos and the primal archetypes. As with Mel, it appears that analysis is one effective vehicle for focusing the longing to manifest and for the libido to build. The benefit of analysis is that it filters or modulates the intense longing; for many patients, this may be a necessary step towards becoming and remaining receptive. The Chassidic mentor Rabbi Nachman of Breslov warns that it is dangerous for a person to seek more spirituality than he or she is prepared for: "A person's spirit [*ruach*] must be regulated in order for the heart to burn properly [for God]" (quoted in Kramer, 2014, p. 226). Thus, unlike deep immersion in meditation or other spiritual practices, analysis may be an effective means for modulating the intense longing brought about by deep-seated complexes through a careful process.

The clinical implication is that recognition of the two complexes, occurring together, may alert an analyst that this is a soul that may be capable of attaining to a ME. At this realisation, the steady exploration of the complexes is the *prima materia* for the breakthrough, even though the analysis must be undertaken without any agenda or orientation to elicit a ME. As James (1902/ 2008, p. 159) cautions: "When the new centre of personal energy has been subconsciously incubated so long as to be just ready to open into flower, 'hands off' is the only word for us, it must burst forth unaided!"

There is no clear method of analysis that is particularly effective for this purpose, as the French philosopher Henri Bergson has explained (Bergson and Mitchell, 1944). Analysis that breaks down parts of the unconscious process into known, clinical stages is only one method because, as Bergson reminds us, there is also "intuition," which operates as a mysterious process that is beyond any form of rational cognition (ibid., pp. 97–108). In the end, the mystery of numinosity overtakes any attempt to hypothesise or theorise, and suggests that the role of analysis cannot be known, merely postulated.

If the theory of combined personal complexes has any force, one cannot avoid the question of why Mel received these complexes that were the precursors to a profound ME. The answer may have its origins in developmental circumstances or inter-generational trauma, but the requirement of the *Deo Juvante* or alchemy's caelum cannot be avoided as providing the missing ingredient that put Mel on the road to transforming his consciousness. In *The Bezels of Wisdom*, Ibn 'Arabi (2004) reminds us that it is only God that makes the heart receptive to different levels of understanding. In his *Kernel of the Kernel* (Ibn 'Arabi, n.d., p. 23), he explains that when a person reaches the incarnation of human being, he has completed the first journey; when he becomes knowledgeable and of the intellect, he has completed the second journey; but the third journey "starts from Him." This does not deny the power of the unconscious in the evolution of that third journey, for, as Ibn 'Arabi states, "His interior universe is conjoined inseparably to God" (ibid.) – a statement that could well have been made by Jung.

This work is underpinned by the principle that the approach to the mystery in all mystical and religious traditions requires complete humility (Heft, Firestone, and Safi, 2011). The complexes may indeed be rivulets that come together in the vast confluence that is the unknown divine. Mel's theophany took the form of the divine using him for its own purposes to observe its creation, which suggests that the possible form and content of the experience will not permit any explanation, as the contents of the Pleroma – the source – cannot be understood. The Zohar, the sacred book of Kabbalah, explains that source as a "cluster of vapor forming in the formless" (Zohar 1:15a). Before that explanation, we all must bow.

References

Adler, G. (1978). A note on the analyst and the numinous. *Harvest: International Journal of Jungian Studies* 24: 1–4.

Aguillaume, R. (2008). Affects in psychoanalytic theory. *International Journal of Psychoanalysis* 17(3): 139–147.

Alho, P. (2009). The role of the feeling function in moral judgments. *Jung Journal: Culture and Psyche* 3(4): 48–58.

Anandamurti, Sri (1982). *Namah Shivaya Shántáya*. Howrah: Ananda Press.

Ancilli, E. (1984). La mistica: Alla ricerca di una definizione. In E. Ancilli and M. Paparozzi (eds) *La Mistica: Fenomelogia e Rifiessione Teologica*, Volume 1 (pp. 17–40). Rome: Citta Nuova.

Ashlag, Rabbi Y.L., and Cohen, Y. (2012). *Tapestry for the Soul: The Introduction to the Zohar by Rabbi Yehudah Lev Ashlag, Explained Using Excerpts Collated from His Other Writings Including Suggestions for Inner Work*. Israel: Nehora Press.

Ataria, Y. (2016). Traumatic and mystical experiences: The dark nights of the soul. *Journal of Humanistic Psychology* 56(4): 331–356.

Azari, N.P., Missimer, J., and Rudiger, J.S. (2009). Religious experience and emotion: Evidence for distinctive cognitive neural patterns. *International Journal for the Psychology of Religion* 15(4): 263–281.

Bair, D. (2003). *Jung: A Biography*. New York: Little, Brown.

Baird, M. (2009). Mysticism and the playful slippage of symbols. *Studies in Spirituality* 19: 183–197.

Batson, C.D., Schoenrade, P., and Ventis, W.L. (1993). *Religion and the Individual: A Social-Psychological Perspective*. New York: Oxford University Press.

Beebe, J., and Falzeder, E. (eds) (2012). *The Question of Psychological Types: The Correspondence of C.G. Jung and Hans Schmid-Guisan, 1915–1916*. Princeton, NJ: Princeton University Press.

Ben-Noun, L. (2003). What was the mental disease that afflicted King Saul? *Clinical Case Studies* 2(4): 270–282.

Bergson, H., and Mitchell, A. (1944). *Creative Evolution*. New York: Modern Library.

Bernard, Griffin, E., and Evans, G.R. (2005). *Bernard of Clairvaux: Selected Works*. San Francisco, CA: HarperSanFrancisco.

Bharati, A. (1976). *The Light at the Center: Context and Pretext in Modern Mysticism*. Delhi: Vikas Publishing.

Bharati, A. (1980). *The Ochre Robe: An Autobiography*. 2nd edn. Santa Barbara, CA: Ross-Erickson.

Bion, W.R. (1961/2014). Experiences in groups and other papers. In C. Mawson (ed.) *The Complete Works of W.R. Bion*, Volume 4 (pp. 99–245). London: Karnac.

Bion, W.R. (1962/2014). Learning from experience. In C. Mawson (ed.) *The Complete Works of W.R. Bion*, Volume 4 (pp. 259–365). London: Karnac.

Bion, W.R. (1963). *Elements of Psycho-analysis*. London: William Heinemann Medical Books.

Bion, W.R. (1965/2014). Memory and desire. In C. Mawson (ed.) *The Complete Works of W.R. Bion*, Volume 6 (pp. 1–43). London: Karnac.

Bion, W.R. (1965/2014a). *Transformations*. In C. Mawson (ed.) *The Complete Works of W.R. Bion*, Volume 5 (pp. 115–280). London: Karnac.

Bion, W.R. (1970). *Attention and Interpretation*. London: Karnac.

Bion, W.R. (1973/2014). Brazilian lectures: São Paulo. In C. Mawson (ed.) *The Complete Works of W.R. Bion*, Volume 7 (pp. 7–70). London: Karnac.

Bion, W.R. (1978/2014). Clinical seminars: São Paulo. In C. Mawson (ed.) *The Complete Works of W.R. Bion*, Volume 8 (pp. 135–230). London: Karnac.

Bion, W.R. (1994). *Cognitions*. London: Karnac.

Bishop, P. (2012). Jung's *Red Book* in relation to aspects of German idealism. *Journal of Analytical Psychology* 57(3): 335–363.

Bishop, P. (2014). *Carl Jung*. London: Reaktion Books.

Bjeragaard, C.H.A. (1913). *The Great Mother: The Gospel of the Eternally Feminine*. New York: Inner-Life.

Blanschot, M. (1986). *The Writing of the Disaster*. Lincoln: University of Nebraska Press.

Blass, R.B. (2004). Beyond illusion: Psychoanalysis and the question of religious truth. *International Journal of Psych-Analysis* 85: 615–634.

Block, N. (2011). Perceptual consciousness overflows cognitive access. *Trends in Cognitive Science* 15: 567–575.

Bob, P. and Laker, M. (2016). Traumatic stress, neural self and the spiritual mind. *Conscousness and Cognition* 44: 7–14.

Bollas, C. (1989). *Forces of Destiny: Psychoanalysis and Human Idiom*. London: Free Association Books.

Brainard, S.F. (1996). Defining "mystical experience". *Journal of the American Academy of Religion* 64: 359–393.

Branco, R. (2011). The Pistis Sophia. *Quest* 99(4): 144–151.

Bright, G. (1997). Synchronicity as a basis of analytic attitude. *Journal of Analytical Psychology* 42: 613–615.

Bright, G. (2014). Jung's concept of psychoid unconsciousness: A clinician's view. In A. Cavell, L. Hawkins, and M. Stevns (eds) *Transformation: Jung's Legacy and Clinical Works Today* (pp. 91–106). London: Karnac.

Britton, R. (2003). *Belief and Imagination: Explorations in Psychoanalysis*. London: Routledge.

Britton, R. (2004) Subjectivity, objectivity and triangular space. *Psychoanalytic Quarterly* 73: 47–61.

Broucek, F.J. (1982). Shame and its relationship to early narcissistic developments. *International Journal of Psychoanalysis* 63: 369–378.

Caruth, C. (1996). *Unclaimed Experience: Trauma, Narrative, and History*. Baltimore, MD: Johns Hopkins University Press.

Chandler, E. (2012). Religious and spiritual issues in DSM-5: Matters of mind and searching of the soul. *Issues in Mental Health Nursing* 33: 577–582.

Cicero (1923). *De Divinatione*. Boston, MA: Loeb Classic Library.

Clarke, I. (ed.) (2010). *Psychosis and Spirituality: Consolidating the New Paradigm*. 2nd edition. West Sussex: Wiley-Blackwell.

Cleary, T. (trans.) (2001). *Classics of Buddhism and Zen*. Volume 4. Boston, MA: Shambhala.

Cohn, J.F., Matias, R., Tronick, E.Z., Connell, D., and Lyons-Ruth, K. (1986). Face-to-face interactions of depressed mothers and their infants. *New Directions for Child and Adolescent Development* 34: 31–45.

Cole, S.L. (2010). *The Absent One: Mourning, Ritual, Tragedy, and the Performance of Ambivalence*. University Park, PA: Penn State University Press.

Corbett, L. (1996). *The Religious Function of the Psyche*. London: Routledge.

Corbett, L. (2006). Varieties of numinous experience: The experience of the sacred in the therapeutic process. In A. Casement and D. Tracey (eds) *The Idea of the Numinous: Contemporary and Psychoanalytic Perspectives* (pp. 53–67). East Sussex: Routledge.

Dalal, N. (2014). Contemplative grammers: Sankara's distinction of Upasana and Nididhyasana. *Journal of Indian Philosophy* 44: 179–206.

Dan, J. (1998). *Jewish Mysticism*, Volume 1: *Late Antiquity*. Northvale, NJ: Jason Aronson Inc.

Davidson, J., and Smith, R. (1990). Traumatic experiences in psychiatric outpatients. *Journal of Traumatic Stress Studies* 3: 459–475.

de Menezes Júnior, A., and Moreira-Almeida, A. (2009). Differential diagnosis between spiritual experiences and mental disorders of religious content. *Revista de psiquiatria clínica* 36(2). www.scielo.br/scielo.php?script=sci_arttext&pid=S0101-60832009000200006&lng=en&nrm=iso&tlng=en (last accessed 28 November 2017).

Decker, L.R. (1993). The role of trauma in spiritual development. *Journal of Humanistic Psychology* 33(4): 33–46.

Deikman, A. (1969). Deautomatization and the Mystic Experience. In G.T. Tart (ed.) *Altered States of Consciousness* (pp. 23–44). New York: Doubleday.

Deleuze, G. (2004). *Pure Immanence: Essays on a Life*. A. Boyman (trans.). New York: Zone Books.

Derrida, J. (1967). *Writing and Difference*. A. Bass (trans.). London: Routledge.

Dewey, J. (1969). The place of religious emotion. In J.A. Boydston and J.J. McDermott (eds) *John Dewey: The Early Works*, Volume 1: *1882–1898* (pp. 90–93). Carbondale: Southern Illinois University Press.

Dieckmann, H. (1985). Some aspects of the development of authority. In A. Samuels (ed.) *The Father: Contemporary Jungian Perspectives* (pp. 211–228). London: Free Association.

Dieckmann, H.. (1999). *Complexes: Diagnosis and Therapy in Analytical Psychology*. Williamette, IL: Chiron.

Dohe, C.B. (2016). *Jung's Wandering Archetype: Race and Religion in Analytical Psychology*. New York: Routledge.

Dolman, C., Jones, I., and Howard, L.M. (2013). Pre-conception to parenting: A systematic review and meta-synthesis of the qualitative literature on motherhood for women with severe mental illness. *Archives of Women's Mental Health: Official Journal of the Section on Women's Health of the World Psychiatric Association* 16: 173–196.

Donkin, W. (2000). *Meher Baba with the God-Intoxicated*. Myrtle Beach, SC: Sheriar Press.

Doucette, S., Horrocks, J., Grof, P., Keown-Stoneman, C., and Duffy, A. (2013). Attachment and temperament profiles among the offspring of a parent with bipolar disorder. *Journal of Affective Disorders* 150: 522–526.

Dourley, J.P. (1991). The Jung, Buber, White exchanges: Exercises in futility. *Studies in Religion/Sciences Religieuses* 20: 299–309.

Dourley, J. (2010). *On Behalf of the Mystical Fool: Jung on the Religious Situation*. New York: Routledge.

Dourley, J. (2018). Jung on the moment of identity and loss of history. *International Journal of Jungian Studies* 10(1): 34–47. Draper, P., and Harpending, H. (1982). Absence and reproductive strategy: An evolutionary perspective. *Journal of Anthropological Research* 38: 255–273.

Dreifuss, G. (2001). Experience of the Self in a lifetime. *Journal of Analytical Psychology* 46: 689–696.

Eckhart, M. (1981). *Meister Eckhart: The Essential Sermons, Commentaries, Treatises, and Defence*. New York: Paulist Press.

Edinger, E.F. (1972). *Ego and Archetype*. Boston, MA: Shambhala.

Edinger, E.F. (1996). *The New God-image: A Study of Jung's Key Letters Concerning the Evolution of the Western God-image*. Williamette, IL: Chiron Publications.

Eigen, M. (1998). *The Psychoanalytic Mystic*. London: Free Association Press.

Elkins, D.N., Hedstrom, L.J., Hughes, L.L., Leaf, J.A., and Saunders, C. (1988). Toward a Humanistic – Phenomenological Spirituality: Definition, Description and Measurement. *Journal of Humanistic Psychology* 28(4): 4–18.

Erlich, A. (1977). *Hamlet's Absent Father*. Princeton, NJ: Princeton University Press.

Fanous, S., and Gillespie, V. (2011). Preface. In S. Fanous and V. Gillespie (eds) *The Cambridge Companion to Medieval English Mysticism* (pp. ix–xiv). Cambridge: Cambridge University Press.

Feldman, B. (1992). Jung's infancy and childhood and its influence upon the development of analytical psychology. *Journal of Analytical Psychology* 37: 255–274.

Fink, B. (1995). *The Lacanian Subject: Between Language and Jouissance*. Princeton, NJ: Princeton University Press.

Fink, B. (1997). *A Clinical Introduction to Lacanian Psychoanalysis: Theory and Technique*. Cambridge, MA: Harvard University Press.

Finke, L.A. (1998). Mystical bodies and the dialogues of vision. In S. Smith and J. Watson (eds) *Women, Autobiography, Theory: A Reader* (pp. 403–414). Madison: University of Wisconsin Press.

Forman, R.C. (1990) Echkart, Gezücken, and the ground of the soul. In R.C. Forman (ed.) *The Problems of Pure Consciousness: Mysticism and Philosophy* (pp. 98–120). New York: Oxford University Press.

Forman, R.C. (1990a). Introduction: Mysticism, constructivism, and forgetting. In R.C. Forman (ed.) *The Problems of Pure Consciousness: Mysticism and Philosophy* (pp. 3–52). New York: Oxford University Press.

Forman, R.C. (1999). *Mysticism, Mind, Consciousness*. Albany: State University of New York Press.

Freud, A. (1981). The concept of development lines: Their diagnostic significance. *Psychoanalytic Study of the Child* 36: 129–136.

Freud, A. (1983). The past revisited. *Bulletin Hampstead Clinic* 6: 107–113.

Freud, S. (1900). *The Interpretation of Dreams*. In *SE* 4 (pp. 1–338).

Freud, S. (1912–1913). *Totem and Taboo*. In *SE* 13 (pp. 1–161).

Freud, S. (1915). Observations on transference love (further recommendations in the technique of psychoanalysis II). In *SE* 12 (pp. 157–171).

Freud, S. (1915a). The Unconscious. In *SE* 14 (pp. 159–216).

Freud, S. (1923) The ego and the id. In *SE* 19 (pp. 12–66).

Freud, S. (1927). The future of an illusion. In *SE* 21 (pp. 5–58).

Freud, S. (1930). Civilization and its discontents. In *SE* 21 (pp. 59–145).

Freud, S. (1938/1941). Findings, ideas, problems. In *SE* 23 (pp. 299–300).

Freud, S. (1953). *The Standard Edition of the Complete Psychological Works of Sigmund Freud*. J. Strachey (ed. and trans.). Twenty-four volumes. London: Hogarth Press. [*SE*].

Freud, S., and Riviere, J. (1949). *A General Introduction to Psycho-analysis: Authorized English translation of the Revised Edition by Joan Riviere, with a preface by Ernest Jones and G. Stanley Hall*. New York: Perma Giants.

Furlong, M. (1996). *Visions and Longings: Medieval Women Mystics*. Boston, MA: Shambhala.

Garb, J. (2004). Mystics' critiques of mystical experience. *Revue de l'historie des religions* 221: 293–325.

Garbarino, J., and Bedard, C. (1996). Spiritual challenges to children facing violent trauma. *Childhood* 3: 467–478.

Gellman, J. (2007). Mysticism and religious experience. In W.J. Wainwright (ed.) *The Oxford Handbook of Philosophy of Religion* (pp. 138–166). Oxford: Oxford University Press.

Gentilcore, D. (1992). *From Bishop to Witch: The System of the Sacred in Early Modern Terra D'Otranto*. Manchester: Manchester University Press.

Ghose, A. (1951). *Letters on Savitri*. K.D. Sethna (ed.). Pondicherry: Sri Aurobindo Ashram.

Ghose, A. (1970). *Letters on Yoga III*. Pondicherry: Sri Aurobindo Ashram.

Ghose, A. (1970a). *Savitri: Legend and a Symbol*. Pondicherry: Sri Aurobindo Ashram.

Ghose, A. (1972). *On Himself: Compiled from Notes and Lectures*. Pondicherry: Sri Aurobindo Ashram.

Ghose, A. (1973). *The Life Divine: Book One*. Pondicherry: Sri Aurobindo Ashram.

Ghose, A. (1973a). *The Life Divine: Book Two*. Pondicherry: Sri Aurobindo Ashram.

Ghose, A. (1973b). *The Synthesis of Yoga*. Pondicherry: Sri Aurobindo Ashram.

Ghose, A. (1988). *Letters on Yoga*. Pondicherry: Sri Aurobindo Ashram.

Ghose, A. (1996). *The Upanishads*. Twin Lakes, WI: Lotus Light Publications.

Ghose, A., and Purani, A.B. (1995). *Evening Talks with Sri Aurobindo*. Pondicherry: Sri Aurobindo Ashram.

Giller, P. (2000). *Reading the Zohar: A Sacred Text of Kabbalah*. Oxford: Oxford University Press.

Glodstein, D., Glodstein, S.L., and Fornaro, J. (2010). Fraud Trauma Syndrome: The victims of the Bernard Madoff scandal. *Journal of Forensic Studies in Accounting and Business* 2: 1–9.

Greeley, A. (1974). *Ectasy: A Way of Knowing*. New Jersey: Prentice-Hall.

Green, A. (1986). *On Private Madness*. K. Aubertin (trans.). London: Hogarth Press.

Greenberg, D., Witztum, E., and Buchbinder, J.T. (1992). Mysticism and psychosis: The fate of Ben Zoma. *British Journal of Medical Psychology*, 65: 223–235.

Grotstein, J.S. (2000). *Who is the Dreamer who Dreams the Dream? A Study of Psychic Presence*. Hillsdale, NJ: Analytic Press.

Grotstein, J.S. (2004). The seventh servant: The implication of a truth drive in Bion's theory of "O" . *International Journal of Psychoanalysis* 85: 1081–1102.

Gubitz, M.B. (1977). Amalek: The eternal adversary. *Psychological Perspectives* 8: 34–58.

Harding, E. (1973). *Psychic Energy: Its Source and its Transformation*. Princeton, NJ: Princeton University Press.

Hartranft, C. (2003). *The Yoga-Sutra of Patañjali: A New Translation and Commentary*. Boston, MA: Shambhala.

Haskell, E.D. (2012). *Suckling at my Mother's Breasts: The Image of a Nursing God in Jewish Mysticism*. Albany: State University of New York Press.

Hausheer, H. (1937). St Augustine's Conception of Time. *Philosophical Review* 46: 503–512.

Heehs, P. (1997). Genius, mysticism, and madness. *Psychohistory Review* 26: 45–75.

Heehs, P. (2008). *The Lives of Sri Aurobindo*. New York: Columbia University Press.

Heehs, P. (2017). Personal communication. 27 February.

Heft, J., Firestone, R., and Safi, O. (2011). *Learned Ignorance: Intellectual Humility among Jews, Christians, and Muslims*. New York: Oxford University Press.

Hellner-Eshed, M. (2009). *A River Flows from Eden: The Language of Mystical Experience in the Zohar*. Stanford, CA: Stanford University Press.

Herzog, J. (2001). *Father Hunger: Explorations with Adults and Children*. New York: Routledge.

Hood, R.W. (1977) Eliciting mystical states of consciousness with semistructured nature experiences. *Journal for the Scientific Study of Religion* 16: 155–163.

Hood, R.W., and Francis, L.J. (2013). Mystical experience: Conceptualizations, measurement, and correlates. In *APA Handbook of Psychology, Religion, and Spirituality*, Volume 1: *Context, Theory, and Research* (pp. 391–405). Washington, DC: American Psychological Association.

Hufford, D.J. (2005). Sleep paralysis as spiritual experience. *Transcultural Psychiatry* 42: 11–45.

Hunt, H.T. (2007). Dark nights of the soul: Phenomenology and neurocognition of spiritual suffering in mysticism and psychosis. *Review of General Psychology* 11: 209–234.

Huss, B. (2008). The mystification of the Kabbalah and the modern construction of Jewish mysticism. *Ben Gurion University Review*. http://in.bgu.ac.il/en/hekscerim/2008/Boaz-Huss.Pdf. (last accessed 30 January 2018).

Huxley, A. (2009). *Perennial Philosophy*. New York: HarperCollins.

Ibn 'Arabi. (2004). *The Ringstones of Wisdom*. C. Dagle (trans.). Chicago: Great Books of the Islamic World.

Ibn 'Arabi (n.d.). *Kernel of the Kernel: Issmail Hakki Bursevi's Translation*. Cheltenham: Beshara Publications.

Idel, M. (1988). *Kabbalah: New Perspectives*. New Haven, CT: Yale University Press.

Idel, M. (2005). *Kabbalah and Eros*. New Haven, CT: Yale University Press.

Jacobi, J. (1959). *Complex, Archetype, Symbol in the Psychology of C.G. Jung*. R. Manheim (trans.). Princeton, NJ: Princeton University Press.

Jacobson, E. (1964). *The Self and the Object World*. New York: International Universities Press.

Jacoby, M. (2006). *Longing for Paradise: Psychological Perspective on an Archetype*. Toronto: Inner City Books. Jaffe, A. (1959). *Complex Archetype Symbol in the Psychology of C.G. Jung*. Princeton, NJ: Princeton University Press.

Jaffe, A. (1989). *Was C.G. Jung a Mystic? And Other Essays*. Einseideln: Daimon Verlag.

James, W. (1902/2008). *Varieties of Religious Experience: A Study in Human Nature*. Rockville, MD: Arc Manor.

James, W. (1907/1995). *Pragmatism*. Philadelphia, PA: Courier Corporation.

James, W. (1909/1979). *A Pluralistic Universe: Hibbert Lectures to Manchester College on the Present Situation in Philosophy*. Norwood, PA: Norwood Editions.

Jhingran, S. (1981). Theory of types of religious experience: Some critical remarks. *Indian Philosophical Quarterly* 8: 283–292.

Jinpa, T. (trans.) (2008). *The Book of Kadam: The Core Texts*. Boston, MA: Wisdom Publications.

Johnson, L.T. (1998). *Religious Experience in Early Christianity: A Missing Dimension in New Testament Studies*. Minneapolis, MN: Augsburg Fortress.

Johnston, D.T. (2016). *Jung's Global Vision: Western Psyche Eastern Mind*. Victoria, BC: Agio Publishing.

Jones, R.H. (1996). *Mysticism Examined*. New York: State University of New York Press.

Jones, R.H. (2016). *Philosophy of Mysticism: Raids on the Ineffable*. New York: State University of New York Press.

Jung, C.G. (1904–1907/1910). The associations of normal subjects. In *Experimental Researches*. In *CW* 2.

Jung, C.G. (1907). The psychology of Dementia Paecox. In *The Psychogenesis of Mental Disease*. In *CW* 3.

Jung, C.G. (1909/1949). The father in the destiny of the individual. In *Freud and Psychoanalysis*. In *CW* 4.

Jung, C.G. (1910). The concept of ambivalence. In *The Symbolic Life*. In *CW* 18.

Jung, C.G. (1910/1946). Psychic conflicts in a child. In *The Development of Personality*. In *CW* 17.

Jung, C.G. (1912/1952). Symbols of the mother and of rebirth. In *Symbols of Transformation*. In *CW* 5.

Jung, C.G. (1912/1952a). The battle for deliverance from the mother. In *Symbols of Transformation*. In *CW* 5.

Jung, C.G. (1912/1952b). The concept of libido. In *Symbols of Transformation*. In *CW* 5.

Jung, C.G. (1912/1952c). The dual mother. In *Symbols of Transformation*. In *CW* 5.

Jung, C.G. (1912/1952d). The origin of the hero. In *Symbols of Transformation*. In *CW* 5.

Jung, C.G. (1912/1952e). The song of the moth. In *Symbols of Transformation*. In *CW* 5.

Jung, C.G. (1912/1952f). The transformation of libido. In *Symbols of Transformation*. In *CW* 5.

Jung, C.G. (1913). The theory of psychoanalysis. In *Freud and Psychoanalysis*. In *CW* 4.

Jung, C.G. (1916/1957). The transcendent function. In *The Structure and Dynamics of the Psyche*. In *CW* 8.

Jung, C.G. (1917/1926/1943). On the psychology of the unconscious. In *Two Essays on Analytical Psychology*. In *CW* 7.

Jung, C.G. (1919). Instinct and the unconscious. In *The Structure and Dynamics of the Psyche*. In *CW* 8.

Jung, C.G. (1920/1948). The psychological foundation of belief in spirits. In *The Structure and Dynamics of the Psyche*. In *CW* 8.

Jung, C.G. (1921). Definitions. In *Psychological Types*. In *CW* 6.

Jung, C.G. (1921a). Epilogue. In *Psychological Types*. In *CW* 6.

Jung, C.G. (1921b). General description of types. In *Psychological Types*. In *CW* 6.

Jung, C.G. (1921c). Schiller's ideas on the type problem. In *Psychological Types*. In *CW* 6.

Jung, C.G. (1921d). The type problem in aesthetics. In *Psychological Types*. In *CW* 6.

Jung, C.G. (1921e). The type problem in poetry. In *Psychological Types*. In *CW* 6.

Jung, C.G. (1927). Women in Europe. In *Civilization in Europe*. In *CW* 10.

Jung, C.G. (1927/1931). Introduction to Wickes's "Analyse der Kinderseele". In *The Development of Personality*. In *CW* 17.

Jung, C.G. (1927/1931a). Mind and earth. In *Civilization in Transition*. In *CW* 10.

Jung, C.G. (1927/1931b). The structure of the psyche. In *The Structure and Dynamics of the Psyche*. In *CW* 8.

Jung, C.G. (1928). Analytical psychology and "Weltanschauung". In *The Structure and Dynamics of the Psyche*. In *CW* 8.

Jung, C.G. (1928a). On psychic energy. In *The Structure and Dynamics of the Psyche*. In *CW* 8.

Jung, C.G. (1928b). The relations between the ego and the unconscious. In *Two Essays on Analytical Psychology*. In *CW* 7.

Jung, C.G. (1928c). The significance of the unconscious in individual education. In *Development of Personality*. In *CW* 17.

Jung, C.G. (1929). Commentary on *The Secret of the Golden Flower*. In *Alchemical Studies*. In *CW* 13.

Jung, C.G. (1931). A psychological theory of types. In *Psychological Types*. In *CW* 12.

Jung, C.G. (1934). A review of the complex theory. In *The Structure and Dynamics of the Psyche*. In *CW* 8.

Jung, C.G. (1934/1954). Conscious, unconscious, and individuation. In *The Archetypes and the Collective Unconscious*. In *CW* 9(1).

Jung, C.G. (1935). Principles of practical psychotherapy. In *The Practice of Psychotherapy*. In *CW* 16.

Jung, C.G. (1935a). The Tavistock Lectures. In *The Symbolic Life*. In *CW* 18.

Jung, C.G. (1935b). What is psychotherapy? In *The Practice of Psychotherapy*. In *CW* 16.

Jung, C.G. (1935/1953). On "The Tibetan Book of the Great Liberation". In *Psychology and Religion: West and East*. In *CW* 11.

Jung, C.G. (1936). Individual dream symbolism in relation to alchemy. In *Psychology and Alchemy*. In *CW* 12.

Jung, C.G. (1936a). Psychology and national problems. In *The Symbolic Life*. In *CW* 18.

Jung, C.G. (1936b). The concept of the unconscious. In *The Archetypes and the Collective Unconscious*. In *CW* 9(1).

Jung, C.G. (1936c). Yoga and the West. In *Psychology and Religion: East and West*. In *CW* 11.

Jung, C.G. (1937). Religious ideas in alchemy. In *Psychology and Alchemy*. In *CW* 12.

Jung, C.G. (1938/1940). Psychology and religion (the Terry Lectures). In *Psychology and Religion West and East*. In *CW* 11.

Jung, C.G. (1938/1954). Psychological aspects of the mother archetype. In *The Archetypes and the Collective Unconscious*. In *CW* 9(1).

Jung, C.G. (1938/1954a). The visions of Zosimos. In *Alchemical Studies*. In *CW* 13.

Jung, C.G. (1939). Conscious, unconscious, and individuation. In *The Archetypes and the Collective Unconscious*. In *CW* 9(1).

Jung, C.G. (1939a). Foreword to Suzuki's "Introduction to Zen Buddhism". In *Psychology and Religion: East and West*. In *CW* 11.

Jung, C.G. (1939b). On the psychogenesis of schizophrenia. In *The Psychogenesis of Mental Disease*. In *CW* 3.

Jung, C.G. (1939c). What India can teach us. In *Civilization in Transition*. In *CW* 10.

Jung, C.G. (1942/1948). A psychological approach to the Trinity. In *Psychology and Religion West and East*. In *CW* 11.

Jung, C.G. (1942/1954). Transformation symbolism in the Mass. In *Psychology and Religion West and East*. In *CW* 11.

Jung, C.G. (1943). The psychology of Eastern meditation. In *Psychology and Religion West and East*. In *CW* 11.

Jung, C.G. (1943/1948). The spirit Mercurius. In *Alchemical Studies*. In *CW* 13.

Jung, C.G. (1944). Introduction to the religious and psychological problems of alchemy. In *Psychology and Alchemy*. In *CW* 12.

Jung, C.G. (1944a). The holy men of India: Introduction to Zimmer's "Der Weg zum Selbst". In *CW* 11.

Jung, C.G. (1945). After the catastrophe. In *Civilization in Transition*. In *CW* 10.

Jung, C.G. (1945/1948). The phenomenology of the spirit in fairytales. In *The Archetypes and the Collective Unconscious*. In *CW* 9(1).

Jung, C.G. (1945/1954). The philosophical tree. In *Alchemical Studies*. In *CW* 13.

Jung, C.G. (1946). Psychology of the transference. In *The Practice of Psychotherapy*. In *CW* 16.

Jung, C.G. (1947/1954). On the nature of the psyche. In *The Structure and Dynamics of the Psyche*. In *CW* 8.

Jung, C.G. (1951). *Aion: Research into the Phenomenology of the Self*. In *CW* 9(2).

Jung, C.G. (1952). Answer to Job. In *Psychology and Religion West and East*. In *CW* 11.

Jung, C.G. (1952a). Foreword to White's "God and the Unconscious" and Werblowsky's "Lucifer and Prometheus". In *Psychology and Religion West and East*. In *CW* 11.

Jung, C.G. (1952b). Synchronicity: An acausal connecting principle. In *The Structure and Dynamics of the Psyche*. In *CW* 8.

Jung, C.G. (1953). *C.G. Jung Letters*. G. Adler and A. Jaffe (eds). Princeton, NJ: Princeton University Press.

Jung, C.G. (1953–1983). *The Collected Works of C.G. Jung*. H. Read, M. Fordham, G. Adler, and W. McGuire (eds), R.F.C. Hull (trans). Twenty volumes. Princeton, NJ: Princeton University Press. [*CW*].

Jung, C.G. (1955–1956). Rex and Regina. In *Mysterium Coniunctionis*. In *CW* 14.

Jung, C.G. (1955–1956a). The components of the conjunctio. In *Mysterium Coniunctionis*. In *CW* 14.

Jung, C.G. (1955–1956b). The conjunction. In *Mysterium Coniunctionis*. In *CW* 14.

Jung, C.G. (1958). Flying saucers: A modern myth. In *Civilization in Transition*. In *CW* 10.

Jung, C.G. (1958a). Schizophrenia. In *The Psychogenesis of Mental Disease*. In *CW* 3.

Jung, C.G. (1959). Foreword. In J. Jacobi, *Complex, Archetype, Symbol in the Psychology of C.G. Jung* (pp. ix–xi). R. Manheim (trans.). Princeton, NJ: Princeton University Press.

Jung, C.G. (1959a). Good and evil in analytical psychology. In *Civilization in Transition*. In *CW* 10.

Jung, C.G. (1961). Symbols and interpretation of dreams. In *The Symbolic Life: Miscellaneous Writings*. In *CW* 18.

Jung, C.G. (1972). Foreword. In SriRamanaMaharshi, *Spiritual Teachings of Ramana Maharshi* (pp. x–xiii). Boston, MA: Shambhala.

Jung, C.G. (1988). *Nietzsche's Zarathustra: Notes of the Seminar Given in 1934–1939*. J.L. Jarrett (ed.). Princeton, NJ: Princeton University Press.

Jung, C.G. (1989). *Analytical Psychology: Notes of the Seminar Given in 1925*. W. McGuire (ed.). Princeton, NJ: Princeton University Press.

Jung, C.G. (1998). *Memories, Dreams, Reflections*. A. Jaffe (ed.). London: Collins/Routeledge and Kegan Paul.

Jung, C.G. (2009). *The Red Book: Liber Novus*. S. Shamdasani (ed.). New York: W.W. Norton.

Kakar, S. (1991). *The Analyst and the Mystic: Psychoanalytic Reflections and Mysticism*. Chicago: University of Chicago Press.

Kalsched, D. (2013). *Trauma and the Soul: A Psycho-Spiritual Approach to Human Development and its Interruption*. New York: Routledge.

Katz, S.T. (1978). Language, epistemology, and mysticism. In S.T. Katz (ed.) *Mysticism and Philosophical Analysis* (pp. 22–74). New York: Oxford University Press.

Kelley, C.F. (2009). *Meister Eckhart on Divine Knowledge*. Cobb, CA: DharmaCafe Books.

Kemp, D. (2000). A Platonic delusion: the identification of psychosis and mysticism. *Mental Health, Religion and Culture* 3: 157–172.

Kernberg, O.F. (1985). *Borderline Conditions and Pathological Narcissism*. Northhvale, NJ: Jason Aronson.

Kierkegaard, S. (1957). *The Concept of Dread*. W. Lowrie (trans.). Princeton, NJ: Princeton University Press.

Kikuchi, S. (2014). *From Eckhart to Ruusbroec: A Critical Inheritance of Mystical Themes in the Fourteenth Century*. Leuven: Leuven University Press.

Kim, E., Garrett, A., Boucher, S., Park, M.H., Howe, M., Sanders, E., Kelley, R.G., and Singh, M.K. (2016). Inhibited temperament and hippocampal volume in offspring of parents with bipolar disorder. *Journal of Child and Adolescent Psychopharmacology* 27: 258–265.

Klein, A.C. (2012). *Knowledge and Liberation: Tibetan Buddhist Epistemology in Support of Transformative Religious Experience*. Boston, MA: Snow Lion Publications.

Ko, C. (2007). Subliminal consciousness. *Review of English Studies* 59(242): 740–765.

Komarovski, T. (2015). *Tibetan Buddhism and Mystical Experience*. Oxford: Oxford University Press.

Kramer, C. (1998). *Anatomy of the Soul: Rebbe Nachman of Breslov*. Jerusalem: Breslov Research Institute.

Krinksy, S. (2017). *Readings in Sri Aurobindo's The Synthesis of Yoga*. Volume 2. Twin Lakes, WI: Lotus Press.

Krippner, S. (ed.) (1972). The plateau experience: A.H. Maslow and others. *Journal of Transpersonal Psychology* 4: 107–120.

Kristeva, J. (2009). *The Incredible Need to Believe*. B.B. Brahic (trans.). New York: Columbia Uniervsity Press.

Kuijpers, H.J.H., van der Heijden, F., Turner, S., and Verhoeven, W. (2007). Meditation-induced psychosis. *Psychopathology* 40: 461–464.

Kukla, A. (2005). *Ineffability and Philosophy*. New York: Routledge.

Kuras, M. (2006). Numinosity/femininity in the idea of the numinous. In A. Casement and D. Tracey (eds) *The Idea of the Numinous: Contemporary and Psychoanalytic Perspectives* (pp. 68–83). East Sussex: Routledge.

Lacan, J. (1979). *The Four Fundamental Concepts of Psych-analysis*. A. Sheridan (trans.). London: Penguin.

Lacan, J. (1988). Introduction to the commentaries on Freud's papers on technique 1953–1954. J. Forrester (trans.). In J.A. Miller (ed.) *The Seminar of Jacques Lacan: Book I* (pp. 7–18). New York: Norton.

Lacan, J. (1992). The moral goals of psychoanalysis 1959–1960. D. Porter (trans.). In J.A. Miller (ed.) *The Seminar of Jacques Lacan: Book VII* (pp. 302–310). New York: Norton.

LacanJ. (1996). *Ecrits: A Selection*. D. Fink (trans.). New York: W.W. Norton.

Lacan, J. (2014). Anxiety: Signal of the Real. In J.A. Miller (ed.) *The Seminar of Jacques Lacan: Book X* (pp. 157–169). Cambridge: Polity Press.

Larue, O., and Juvina, I. (2016). A call for unification of dual – and single – process accounts in cognitive models of intuition. *Journal of Applied Research in Memory and Cognition* 5: 338–340.

Leuba, J.H. (1925). *The Psychology of Religious Mysticism*. New York: Harcourt Brace.

Lehtsaar, T. (2002). The relationships between religious experiences and the rest of life experience: An autobiographical study. *Tramos* 6: 79–84.

Levin, J., and Steele, L. (2005). The transcendent experience: Conceptual, theoretical, and epidemiologic perspectives. *Explore* 1: 89–101.

Lochrie, K. (1991). The language of transgression: Body, flesh and word in mystical doctrine. In A. Frantzen (ed.) *Speaking Two Languages: Traditional Disciplines and Contemporary Theory in Medieval Studies* (pp. 115–140). Albany: State University of New York Press.

Luke, D. (2012). Psychoactive substances and paranormal phenomena: A comprehensive analysis. *International Journal of Transpersonal Studies* 31(1): 98–156.

Lukoff, D. (1985). The diagnosis of mystical experiences with psychotic features. *Journal of Transpersonal Psychology* 17: 155–181.

Lukoff, D., Lu, F., and Turner, R. (1992). Toward a more culturally sensitive DSM-IV: Psychoreligous and psychospiritual problems. *Journal of Nervous and Mental Disease* 180: 673–682.

Lutz, A., Dunne, J.D., and Davidson, R.J. 2012. Meditation and the neuroscience of consciousness: An introduction. In P.D. Zelazo, M. Moscovitch, and E. Thompson (eds) *The Cambridge Handbook of Consciousness* (pp. 499–554). Cambridge: Cambridge University Press.

Maclean, K.A., Leoutsakos, J.M., Johnson, M.W., and Griffiths, R.R. (2012). Factor analysis of the Mystical Experience Questionnaire: A study of experiences occasioned by the hallucinogen Psilocybin. *Journal of the Scientific Study of Religion* 5: 721–737.

Magid, B. (2002). *Ordinary Mind: Exploring the Common Ground of Zen and Psychoanalysis*. Boston, MA: Wisdom Publications.

Main, R. (2008). Secularisation and the "holistic milieu": Social and psychological perspectives. *Religion Compass* 2: 365–384.

Marshall, W. (1954). *The Gospel-Mystery of Sanctification*. Grand Rapids, MI: Zondervan Publishing House.

Maslow, A.H. (1964). *Religions, Values, and Peak-experiences*. Columbus: Ohio State University Press.

Maslow, A.H. (1970). New introduction: Religious, values, and peak-experiences (new edition). *Journal of Transpersonal Psychology* 2: 83.

Matt, D.C. (2006). *The Zohar: Pritzker Edition*. Stanford, CA: Stanford University Press.

Mead, G.R.S. (1921). *Pistis Sophia: A Gnostic Miscellany*. London: Watkins.

Meier, C.A. (ed.) (2001). *Atom and Archetype: The Pauli/Jung Letters 1932–1958*. Princeton, NJ: Princeton University Press.

Merkur, D. (1999). *Mystical Moments and Unitive Thinking*. Albany: State University of New York Press.

Merkur, D. (2006). Interpreting numinous experiences. *Social Analysis: The International Journal of Social and Cultural Practice* 50: 204–223.

Merkur, D. (2010). *Explorations of the Psychoanalytic Mystics*. New York: Rodopi.

Mezei, B.M. (2017). The mystical after Auschwitz. In M. Vassány, A. Daróczi, and E. Sepsi (eds) *The Immediacy of Mystical Experience in the European Tradition* (pp. 215–229). Switzerland: Springer.

Mitra, S. (1976). *Sri Aurobindo: Towards Victory of the Light Supreme*. Delhi: Orient.

Molino, A. (1998). Zen, Lacan, and the alien ego. In A. Molino (ed.) *The Couch and the Tree: Dialogues in Psychoanalysis and Buddhism* (pp. 290–306). New York: North Point Press.

Montgomery, P., Tompkins, C., Forchuk, C., and French, S. (2006). Keeping close: Mothering with serious mental illness. *Journal of Advanced Nursing* 54: 20–28.

Moreira-Almeida, A. (2012). Assessing clinical importance of spiritual experiences. *Asian Journal of Psychiatry* 5: 344–346.

Morey, J.R. (2005). Winnicott's splitting headache: Considering the gap between Jungian and object relations concepts. *Journal of Analytical Psychology* 50(3): 333–350.

Morrison, A.P. (2006). Psychological factors in people at ultra-high risk of psychosis: Comparisons with non-patients and associations with symptoms. *Psychological Medicine* 36: 1395–1404.

Murray, L., Fiori-Cowley, A., Hooper, R., and Cooper, P. (1996). The impact of postnatal depression and associated adversity on early mother-infant interactions and later infant outcome. *Child Development* 67: 2512–2526.

Neumann, E. (1948/1969). Mystical man. In J. Campbell (ed.) *The Mystic Vision: Papers from the Eranos Conference* (pp. 375–414). London: Routledge & Kegan Paul.

Neumann, E. (1972). *The Great Mother: An Analysis of an Archetype*. R. Manheim (trans.). Princeton, NJ: Princeton University Press.

Neumann, E. (2014). *The Origin and History of Consciousness*. Princeton, NJ. Princeton University Press.

Nietzsche, F. (1960). On truth and lies in the nonmoral sense. In W. Kaufmann (trans.) *The Portable Nietzsche* (pp. 42–46). New York: Viking Press.

Nisargadatta, Sri (2004). *Sri Nisargadatta Maharaj's Discourses on the Eternal*. R. Powell (ed.). Delhi: Motilal Banarsidass.

Noh, J.J. (1977). *Do You See What I See?* Wheaton, IL: Quest.

Noyes, R., and Kletti, R. (1976). Depersonalization in the face of life-threatening danger: A description. *Psychiatry* 39: 19–27.

Oates, T. (1736). *The Witch of Endor: or, a plea for the divine administration by the agency of good and evil spirits*. London: John Millan.

Odajnyk, W.V. (2011). *Gathering the Light: A Jungian View of Meditation*. Carmel, CA: Fisherking.

Odier, D. (2005). *Yoga: Spandakarika: The Secret Texts at the Origins of Tantra*. C. Frock (trans.). Rochester, VT: Inner Traditions.

Otto, R. (1923). *Idea of the Holy, an Inquiry into the Non-rational Factor in the Idea of the Divine and its Relation to the Rational*. London: Oxford University Press.

Paloutzian, R.F., Richardson, J.T., and Rambo, L.R. (1999). Religious conversion and personality change. *Journal of Personality* 67: 1047–1079.

Parsons, W.B. (1999). *The Enigma of the Oceanic Feeling: Revisioning the Psychoanalytic Theory of Mysticism*. New York: Oxford University Press.

Peck, R.C. (1968). Psychological developments in the second half of life. In B.L. Neugarten (ed.) *Middle Age and Aging* (pp. 88–92). Chicago: University of Chicago Press.

Perry, J.W. (1991). *Lord of the Four Quarters: The Mythology of Kingship*. Mahwah, NJ: Paulist Press.

Pilard, N. (2015). *Jung and Intuition: On the Centrality and Variety of Forms and Intuition in Juan and Post Jungians*. London: Karnac.

Plaut, A. (1966). Reflections about not being able to imagine. *Journal of Analytical Psychology* 11: 113–134.

Plutarch (1961). The Eleusinian mysteries. In G.E. Mylonas (trans.) *Eleusis and the Eleusinian Mysteries* (pp. 224–286). Princeton, NJ: Princeton University Press.

Poulain, A. (1996). *The Graces of Interior Prayer: A Treatise on Mystical Theology*. Kila, MT: Kessinger.

Pratyagatmananda, Swami (2002). *Studies on the Tantras*. Kolkata: Ramakhrisna Mission.

Progoff, I. (1966). The man who transforms consciousness: The inner myths of Martin Buber, Paul Tillich, and C.G. Jung. *Eranos Jahrbücher* 35: 99–144.

Pruyser, O. (1983). *The Play of Imagination: Toward a Psychoanalysis of Culture*. New York: International University Press.

Puech, H.-C. (1968). The concept of Redemption in Manichaesim. In J. Campbell (ed.) *The Mystic Vision: Papers from the Eranos Yearbooks* (pp. 217–314). Princeton, NJ: Princeton University Press.

Pulver, M. (1985). The experience of light in the Gospel of St John, in the "Corpus hermeticum," in Gnosticism and in the Eastern Church. In J. Campbell (ed.) *Spiritual Disciplines: Papers from the Eranos Yearbooks* (pp. 239–266). Princeton, NJ: Princeton University Press.

Purani, A.B. (1959/1982). *Evening Talks with Sri Aurobindo*. Pondicherry: Sri Aurobindo Ashram Trust.

Radhakrishnan, S., and Moore, C.A. (eds) (1957). *A Source Book in Indian Philosophy*. Princeton, NJ: Princeton University Press.

Ramakrishna, Sri (1974). *The Gospel of Sri Ramakrishna*. Madras: Sri Ramakrishna Math.

Rambo, L.R. (1993). *Understanding Religious Conversion*. New Haven, CT: Yale University Press.

Reiner, A. (2012). *Bion and Being: Passion and the Creative Mind*. London: Karnac.

Reis, P.T. (1997). Eating the blood: Saul and the Witch of Endor. *Journal for the Study of the Old Testament* 22(73): 3–23.

Rizzuto, A. (2001). Metaphors of a bodily mind. *Journal of the American Psychoanalytic Association* 49(2): 535–568.

Rochat, P. (2003). Five levels of self-awareness as they unfold early in life. *Consciousness and Cognition* 12: 717–731.

Ross, C.F.J. (1992). The intuitive function and religious orientation. *Journal of Analytical Psychology* 37: 83–103.

Roth, H.D. (2000). Bimodal mystical experience in the "Qiwulun" chapter of Zhuangzi. *Journal of Chinese Religion* 28: 31–50.

Roy, D.K. (1968). *Sri Aurobindo Came to Me (Reminiscences)*. 3rd edition. Bombay: Jaico.

Russ, S.L., and Elliott, M.S. (2017). Antecedents of mystical experience and dread in intensive meditation. *Psychology of Consciousness: Theory, Research and Practice* 4: 38–53.

Rytovaara, M. (2014). The great mother and the terrible mother: Mimesis, alterity, and attachment in adolescence. *Journal of Analytical Psychology* 59: 211–228.

Sadhguru, J.V. (2010). *Enlightenment: Life the Way it is*. Coimbatore: Isha Foundation.

Samuels, A. (1985). The development of personality: Jung's contribution to developmental psychology: Post Jungian views on early development. In A. Samuels, *Jung and the Post Jungians* (pp. 148–161). London: Routledge & Kegan Paul.

Sandford, A. (1985). *King Saul, the Tragic Hero: A Study in Individuation*. Mahwah, NJ: Paulist Press.

Sannella, L. (1992). *The Kundalini Experience: Psychosis or Transcendence?* Lower Lake, CA: Integral Publishing.

Sarbacker, S.R. (2005). *Samādhi: The Numinous and Cessative in Indo-Tibetan Yoga*. Albany: State University of New York Press.

Schaeffer, K.R., Kapstein, M., and Tuttle, G. (eds) (2013). *Sources of Tibetan Tradition*. New York: Columbia University Press.

Scharf, R. (1998). Experience. In M. Taylor (ed.) *Critical Terms for Religious Studies* (pp. 94–116). Chicago: University of Chicago Press.

Schjoedt, U. (2009). The religious brain: A general introduction to the experimental neuroscience of religion. *Method and Theory in the Study of Religion* 21: 310–339.

Schlamm, L. (1991). Rudolf Otto and mystical experience. *Religious Studies* 27: 389–398.

Schlamm, L. (1992). Numinous experience and religious language. *Religious Studies* 28: 533–551.

Schlamm, L. (2000). C.G. Jung, mystical experience and inflation. *Transpersonal Psychology Review* 4(4): 50–61.

Schlamm, L. (2006). C.G. Jung's visionary mysticism. *Harvest: International Journal of Jungian Studies* 52: 7–37.

Scholem, G. (1941). *Major Trends in Jewish Mysticism*. 3rd edition. New York: Schocken Books.

Seligman, E. (1985). The half-alive ones. In A. Samuels (ed.) *The Father: Contemporary Jungian Perspectives* (pp. 69–94). London: Free Association Books.

Sells, M.A. (1994). *Mystical Languages of Unsaying*. Chicago: University of Chicago Press.

Seybold, K.S. (2010). Biology of spirituality. *Perspectives on Science and Christian Faith* 62(2): 89–98.

Shah, I. (1997). *Tales of the Dervishes: Teaching-stories of the Sufi Masters over the Past Thousand Years*. London: Octogon Press.

Shamdasani, S. (2003). *Jung and the Making of Modern Psychology: The Dream of a Science*. Cambridge: Cambridge University Press.

Sherry, J. (2012). *Carl Gustav Jung: Avant-garde Conservative.* New York: Palgrave Macmillan.

Sivananda, Swami (1954). *Mind: Its Mysteries and Control.* Rishikesh: Yoga-Vedanta Forest University.

Shoemaker, S. (2003). *Identity, Cause and Mind: Philosophical Essays.* Oxford: Oxford University Press.

Singh, S.P. (1986). *Sri Aurobindo and Jung: A Comparative Study in Yoga and Depth Psychology.* Aligarh: Madhucchandas Publications.

Slade, C. (1995). *St Teresa of Avila: Author of a Heroic Life.* Los Angeles: University of California Press.

Slote, M. (2016). *From Enlightenment to Receptivity: Rethinking our Values.* New York: Oxford University Press.

Smart, N. (1964). *Doctrine and Argument in Indian Philosophy.* London: Allen & Unwin.

Smart, N. (1970). *Philosophy of Religion.* Oxford: Oxford University Press.

Smart, N. (1974). *The Religious Experience of Mankind.* London: Collins.

Smith, A. (2014). *Thinking about Religion: Extending the Cognitive Science of Religion.* Houndsmills: Palgrave Macmillan.

Sopa, GesheL. (2008). *Steps on the Path to Enlightenment: A Commentary on Tsongkhapa's Lamrin Chenmo.* Boston, MA: Wisdom Publications.

Spielrein, S. (1994). Destruction as the cause of coming into being. *Journal of Analytical Psychology* 39: 155–186.

Spilka, B., Brown, G.A., and Cassidy, S.A. (1992). The structure of religious mystical experience in relation to pre- and post-experience lifestyles. *International Journal for the Psychology of Religion* 2: 241–257.

Stace, W.T. (1960). *Mysticism and Philosophy.* Philadelphia: J.P. Lippin-cott.

Stearns, C. (trans.) (2006). *Taking the Result as the Path: Core Teachings of the Sakya Lamdré Tradition.* Somerville, MA: Wisdom.

Stein, G. (2011). The case of King Saul: Did he have recurrent unipolar depression or bipolar affective disorder? *British Journal of Psychiatry* 198(3): 212.

Stein, L.A. (2012). *Becoming Whole: Jung's Equation for Realizing God.* New York: Helios Press.

Stein, L.A. (2013). Jung and Tantra. *Spring Journal of Archetype and Culture* 90: 179–203.

Stein, L.A. (2015). Jung and divine self-revelation. *Jung Journal* 5: 18–30.

Stein, M. (2006). On the importance of numinous experience in the alchemy of individuation. In A. Casement and D. Tracey (eds) *The Idea of the Numinous: Contemporary and Psychoanalytic Perspectives* (pp. 34–42). East Sussex: Routledge.

Stein, M. (2017). Where East meets West: in the house of individuation. *Journal of Analytical Psychology* 62: 67–87.

Stendahl, K. (1963). The Apostle Paul and the introspective conscience of the West. *Harvard Theological Review* 56: 199–215.

Stephenson, C.E. (2017). *Possession: Jung's Comparative Anatomy of the Psyche.* Revised edition. New York: Routledge.

Suzuki, D.T. (2014). *Selected Works of D.T. Suzuki,* Volume 1: *Zen.* Los Angeles: University of California Press.

Swan, W. (2006). Tina Keller's analyses with C.G. Jung and Toni Wolff, 1915–1928. *Journal of Analytical Psychology* 51: 493–511.

Teresa of Avila, St (1987). *The Collected Works of St Teresa of Avila*. Volume 1. 2nd edition. K. Kavanaugh and O. Rodriguez (trans.). Washington, DC: ICS Publications.

Tobin, F. (1986). *Meister Eckhart: Thought and Language*. Philadelphia: University of Pennsylvania Press.

Trungpa, C. (1973). *Cutting through Spiritual Materialism*. Boulder, CO: Shambhala.

Tyler, P.M. (2011). *The Return to the Mystical: Ludwig Wittgenstein, Teresa of Avila and the Christian Mystical Tradition*. London: Continuum.

Ullman, C. (2013). *The Transformed Self: The Psychology of Religious Conversion*. New York: Springer.

Ulrich, E.T. (2010). Poetic influences on the development of Aurobindo's spiritual and nationalistic convictions. *International Journal of Hindu Studies* 14: 121–146.

Underhill, E. (1920). The essentials of mysticism. In E. Underhill, *The Essentials of Mysticism and Other Essays* (pp. 1–24). New York: E.P. Dutton.

Underhill, E. (1990). *Mysticism: The Preeminent Study in the Nature and Development of Spiritual Consciousness*. New York: Doubleday.

Voegelin, E. (1990). The beginning and the beyond: A meditation on truth. In T.A. Hollweck and P. Caringella (eds) *The Collected Works of Eric Voegelin*, Volume 28: *What is History? and Other Late Unpublished Writings* (pp. 173–232). Baton Rouge: Louisiana State University Press.

van Elk, M., and Aleman, A. (2017). Brain mechanisms in religion and spirituality: An intergrative predictive processing framework. *Neuroscience and Biobehavioral Reviews* 73: 359–378.

von Franz, M.L. (1979). *Alchemical Active Imagination*. Boston, MA: Shambhala Publications.

von Franz, M.L. (1980). *Alchemy: An Introduction to the Symbolism and the Psychology*. Toronto: Inner City Books.

von Franz, M.L. (1995). *Creation Myths*. Boston, MA: Shambhala Publications.

von Gontard, A. (2017). *Buddhist Understanding of Childhood Spirituality: The Buddha's Children*. London: Jessica Kingsley.

Walther, G. (1955). *Phänomenologie der Mystik*. 2nd edition. Otten: Walter Verlag.

Ware, O. (2007). Rudolph Otto's idea of the holy: A reappraisal. *Heythrop Journal* 48: 48–60.

Washburn, M. (1995). *The Ego and the Dynamic Ground: A Transpersonal Theory of Hum Dev*. 2nd edition. Albany: State University of New York Press.

Werblowsky, R. (1966). On the mystical rejection of mystical illuminations: A note on St John of the Cross. *Religious Studies* 1: 177–184.

Wiesel, E. (1981). *Five Biblical Portraits*. Notre Dame, IN: Notre Dame University Press.

Winnecott, D.W. (1958). *Collected Papers: Through Pediatrics to Psych-analysis*. New York: Basic Books.

Winnecott, D.W. (2016). Review: *Memories, Dreams, Reflections* by C.G. Jung. In L. Cardwell and H.T. Robinson (eds) *The Collected Works of D.W. Winnecott*, Volume 7: *1964–1966*. New York: Oxford University Press.

Wion, P.K. (1985). The absent mother in Emily Brontë's "Wuthering Heights". *American Imago* 42: 143–164.

Woodroffe, J. (1974). *The Serpent Power*. Madras: Ganesh & Co.

Wuff, D. (2000). Mystical experience. In E. Cardeña, S. J. Lynn, and S. Krippner (eds) *Varieties of Anomalous Experience: Examining the Scientific Evidence* (pp. 396–440). Washington, DC: American Psychological Association.

Yaden, D.B., Eichstaedt, J.C., Kern, M.L., Le Nguyen, K.D., Wintering, N.A., Newberg, A.B., Hood, R.W., and Schwartz, A. (2015). The language of ineffability: Linguistic analysis of mystical experiences. *Psychology of Religion and Spirituality* 8: 244–252.

Yandell, J. (2009). Graven images: Idol and icon. *Psychological Perspectives* 52: 413–435.

Yao, Z. (2007). Four-dimensional time in Dzogchen and Heidegger. *Philosophy East and West* 57: 512–532.

Yearley, L. (1983). The perfected person in the radical Chuang-tzu. In V. Mair (ed.) *Experimental Essays on the Chuang Tzu* (pp. 125–139.) Honolulu: University of Hawaii Press.

Young-Eisendrath, P. (1997). *Gender and Desire: Uncursing Pandora.* Texas: Texas A&M Press.

Zepf, S. (2010). Libido and psychic energy: Freud's concepts reconsidered. *International Forum of Psychoanalysis* 19: 3–14.

Zimmer, H. (1969). *Philosophies of India.* J. Campbell (ed). Princeton, NJ: Princeton University Press.

Žižek, S. (1989). *The Subline Object of Ideology.* London: Verso.

Zola, L. (2001). *The Father: Historical, Psychological and Cultural Perspectives.* H. Martin (trans.). East Sussex: Brunner-Routledge.

Index

For Product Safety Concerns and Information please contact our EU
representative GPSR@taylorandfrancis.com
Taylor & Francis Verlag GmbH, Kaufingerstraße 24, 80331 München, Germany

www.ingramcontent.com/pod-product-compliance
Lightning Source LLC
Chambersburg PA
CBHW070322270326
41926CB00017B/3729